ECONOMIC DEVELOPMENT

ECONOMIC DEVELOPMENT

Theory and Policy Applications

Fidelis Ezeala-Harrison

PRAEGER

Westport, Connecticut
London

Library of Congress Cataloging-in-Publication Data

Ezeala-Harrison, Fidelis.
    Economic development : theory and policy applications / Fidelis
Ezeala-Harrison.
      p. cm.
    Includes bibliographical references and index.
    ISBN 0–275–95479–X (alk. paper)
    1. Economic development. I. Title.
HD82.E95   1996
338.9—dc20   96–904

British Library Cataloguing in Publication Data is available.

Library of Congress Catalog Card Number: 96–904
ISBN: 0–275–95479–X

First published in 1996

Praeger Publishers, 88 Post Road West, Westport, CT 06881
An imprint of Greenwood Publishing Group, Inc.

Printed in the United States of America

The paper used in this book complies with the
Permanent Paper Standard issued by the National
Information Standards Organization (Z39.48–1984).

10 9 8 7 6 5 4 3 2 1

To the memory of
Ihuoma Lora Ezeala-Harrison,
for lives that we *only briefly* shared together.

Contents

Tables and Figures   *ix*

Preface   *xi*

Acknowledgments   *xiii*

PART I: DEFINITION OF ECONOMIC DEVELOPMENT

1. Economic Growth and Development: Concepts and
   Measurement   3

2. A Global Profile of Development and Underdevelopment   21

3. History of Economic Development and Underdevelopment   33

PART II: THEORIES OF ECONOMIC GROWTH AND DEVELOPMENT

4. The Classical Theories of Economic Growth and
   Development   61

5. The Neoclassical Theories of Economic Growth and
   Development   85

6. The Structuralist Theories of Economic Development   101

PART III: THE PROCESS OF ECONOMIC DEVELOPMENT: THE INTERNAL DIMENSIONS

7. Capital Accumulation and the Process of Development   129

8. Population and Human Resources in Development   141

9. Agriculture in the Process of Economic Development   169

10. Industrialization in the Process of Economic Development   185

11. Environmental Issues in the Process of Economic
    Development   195

12. Development Planning and Policy Issues   215

PART IV: THE PROCESS OF ECONOMIC DEVELOPMENT: THE
        EXTERNAL DIMENSIONS

13. International Trade and Economic Development   235

14. Role of Free Trade and Regional Integrationism   247

15. International Finance and Economic Development   253

Selected Bibliography   259

Index   271

Tables and Figures

TABLES

2.1 Structural Diversities in World Regional Economies, 1992 23

2.2 Relative Population and Income Growth by Continent, 1992 27

2.3 World Regional Trends in Per Capita GDP, 1950-1990 27

2.4 World Regional Resource and Productivity Growths 1950-1990 29

2.5 Human Development Index for Selected Countries, 1990 30

2.6 Economic Performance of Selected LDCs, 1992 31

9.1 World Labor Force Distribution by Regional Classification, 1988 170

11.1 Pollution Levels (Averages) and Costs (Expenditures) in DCs 197

12.1 Hypothetical Input-Output Table 225

FIGURES

1.1 The Lorenz Curve of Income Distribution 16

4.1 Determination of Rent   65

4.2 Theory of Rent   68

4.3 The Socially Optimal Labor in Marxian Theory   74

6.1 Economic Growth in the Lewis Two-Sector Model   119

8.1 The Model of Optimum Population   144

8.2 Education as a Merit Good   154

9.1 The Inelasticity Better-Harvest Poorer-Farmer Syndrome   180

11.1 Trade-off Between Level of Economic Development and
     Environmental Quality   199

Preface

Often researchers and practitioners in the field of economic development fail to find a single source of adequate material that provides exhaustive coverage of both the key theoretical constructs on economic development, and the major strands in the process(es) of sustained economic growth and development of nations. As a result, while the bulk of the existing sources may be effective, there is still a noticeable gap that demands to be filled. This gap is felt because while the theoretical models, on their own, do not realistically address themselves to the real-world structural problems of development and underdevelopment, the structuralist case-oriented approaches also prove inadequate in scope and exposition for policy applications. There is a need to provide a synthesis in the above regard.

This book addresses the dual challenges of providing comprehensive and complete coverage of the theories of economic development, and offering exhaustive treatment of the issues involved in the process of sustained economic growth and development of nations. Economic development is an evolving subdiscipline that may have been the most misunderstood in the wide body of studies that is economics. As the problems of poverty, income inequality, and economic stagnation continue to beset many countries in Asia and Latin America, and most countries of sub-Saharan Africa, economists are increasingly looked upon to provide explanations and prescribe policy solutions.

The study of economic development must provide answers for not only how, but also why, these problems arise, whether or not they can be prevented, and how to effectively address them. Practitioners and students of economic development must have a ready source of explanations and expositions of the issues surrounding underdevelopment, in some analytical depth, within a single volume. This is the essence of the present volume, which is a compilation of the mix of research in development theory and policy issues. This work is geared toward meeting the need for a more complete source of guidance and explanation on the issues of economic underdevelopment of societies. Specifically, it seeks to provide a more complete source of both theoretical and empirical expositions, analyses, modeling, simulations, and structural paradigms on the nature and process(es) of economic development and underdevelopment.

This book is intended primarily to provide solid undergraduate training in economic development, but it also meets the needs of graduate students, college and university teachers, researchers, and practising economists. It is written in a mix of technical and nontechnical language, and only a course in intermediate economic theory (or even a very good one in principles of economics) would be required in using this book. In addition, only a background equivalent to first-year university mathematics is needed. Those who lack these prerequisites but are determined to explore new ground toward understanding and the pertinent issues involved in the "development question," are also welcome to the use of this text. These in particular can avail themselves of the book's step-by-step approach in studying development from its basic rudiments to more advanced levels.

This volume will also be highly beneficial to other practitioners in the field, such as economic planners and regional development planners; to policy strategists in international development agencies such as the World Bank, the International Monetary Fund (IMF), the U.S. Agency for International Development (USAID), and the Canadian International Development Agency (CIDA); and to all people interested in the economic development of less developed countries. For all practitioners this book can serve as an important guide in formulating desired economic changes in the developing regions of the world.

Acknowledgments

The immense help of many has been invaluable in the production of this book. To these, I owe much gratitude. For her enduring patience, understanding, and immeasurable supportive work, first mention is due to my dear wife, Chichi Ezeala-Harrison. I also thank my very helpful children: Adanna, Kelechi, Ebere, Nnedi, and Emezie, not only for their understanding when this work kept us from spending time together, but also for close cooperation in diverse ways.

Dr. M. Kabir of the University of New Brunswick, Saint John, provided much appreciated encouragement, moral support, and warm friendship. Thanks are due to my other faculty colleagues at the Department of Economics, University of New Brunswick in Saint John: Dr. Rod Hill, Dr. Neil Ridler, Dr. Rob Moir, and to Department of Economics Secretary Mrs. Kari Bourque. The hard work of Wilfred Morris of the Research Services Department, University of New Brunswick in Saint John, is gratefully appreciated.

I extend many thanks to two anonymous reviewers, one of who painstakingly evaluated the various chapters, and also my research assistant for great proofreading skills. Finally, I thank the staff at Greenwood Publishing Group.

Part I

DEFINITION OF ECONOMIC DEVELOPMENT

1

Economic Growth and Development: Concepts and Measurement

Often the terms *economic growth* and *economic development* are used interchangeably as if they were synonymous, but there is a big distinction between them. Economic growth refers to the increase in an economy's real gross domestic product (GDP) and income over time. Real GDP is the economy's total output of goods and services, usually measured over a period of one year. The amount of achievable economic growth would depend on the human resource acquisition of the economy, technological improvement, amount of capital investment, natural resource endowment and degree of its exploitation, and the managerial know-how existing in the economy.

Economic development, however, must be preceded and prompted by economic growth. To reflect economic development, economic growth is defined in terms of increases in per capita real output or per capita income. Development encompasses the *process* through which societies, or nations, or regions, raise their per capita output and income by improvements and increases in productivity, and how these translate into per capita economic well-being in the society.[1] Economic development involves economic growth accompanied by *structural transformation*, that is, economic growth plus (positive) structural changes in the economy. Thus, economic growth may be seen as *necessary*, but not *sufficient,* for economic development. Structural transformation provides the sufficiency condition for economic development. We now examine in turn, these two conditions of economic growth and structural change, to enable us to provide a complete and precise understanding of *economic development*.

THEORETICAL FORMULATION OF ECONOMIC GROWTH

Economic growth may be regarded as a steady increase in national income and per capita income of the society over time. Before we move to consider practical quantifications and measurement of economic growth, it will be helpful to present an in-depth theoretical analysis of what growth is, and how it can be interpreted. No matter how it is looked at, that economic growth implies increase in output and income has been consistently maintained by all aspects of the definition. We would assume that the economy's national income is a close proxy for its national output, and let the level of national income (GDP) be given by Y. Then, economic growth at any time may be depicted as

$$g_t = \Delta Y/Y_t > 0 \qquad (1.1)$$

where

$$g = \text{growth}$$
$$\Delta Y = Y_t - Y_{t-1}$$
$$Y_t = \text{GDP at time } t$$

This indicates that economic growth occurs when relative income changes are positive over time.

To achieve any level of growth at all, an economy must put its resources to use. National income is created out of the use of these resources, according to the following implicit production function:

$$Y = Y(N, L, K, \Omega) \qquad (1.2)$$

where the symbols are

$$N = \text{natural resources}$$
$$L = \text{labor force and human resources}$$
$$K = \text{capital resources}$$
$$\Omega = \text{entrepreneurial and technological know-how}$$

This function states that national output depends on the amount of natural resource endowment of the society (N), the labor force and human resource endowment, capital resources, and the entrepreneurial and technological state of the art in the economy. We can easily use this production function to derive a formulation of *economic growth*. A total differential of the production function (Equation 1.2) gives:

$$dY = \partial Y/\partial N.dN + \partial Y/\partial L.dL + \partial Y/\partial K.dK + \partial Y/\partial \Omega.d\Omega$$

Dividing this through by Y gives us

$$dY/Y = \partial Y/\partial N.dN/Y + \partial Y/\partial L.dL/Y + \partial Y/\partial K.dK/Y + \partial Y/\partial \Omega.d\Omega/Y$$

and multiplying each of the terms of the right-hand side by a form of 1, that is by, N/N, L/L, K/K, Ω/Ω, respectively, we obtain:

$$dY/Y = \partial Y/\partial N.N/Y.dN/N + \partial Y/\partial L.L/Y.dL/L + \partial Y/\partial K.K/Y.dK/K$$
$$+ \partial Y/\partial \Omega. \Omega/Y.d\Omega/\Omega \qquad (1.3)$$

Upon close examination of Equation (1.3) we see that its right-hand side is simply the sum of the products of the input-elasticities of output and the growth rates of the various inputs.[2] That is, defining:

$\xi_N = \partial Y/\partial N.N/Y$ = natural resources-elasticity of output
$\xi_L = \partial Y/\partial L.L/Y$ = human resource-elasticity of output
$\xi_K = \partial Y/\partial K.K/Y$ = capital-elasticity of output
$\xi_\Omega = \partial Y/\partial \Omega. \Omega/Y$ = organizational know-how-elasticity of output

and

$g_N = dN/N$ = growth rate of natural resources
$g_L = dL/L$ = growth rate of labour and human resources
$g_K = dK/K$ = growth rate of capital resources
$g_\Omega = d\Omega/\Omega$ = growth rate of organizational know-how

we can then express this relationship as

$$g = \xi_N g_N + \xi_L g_L + \xi_K g_K + \xi_\Omega g_\Omega \qquad (1.4)$$

Equation (1.4) gives the expression of the growth rate of the economy's GDP, that is, *economic growth*. It implies that the GDP growth rate is given by the sum of the products of input-elasticities of output and the inputs' growth rates. Furthermore, we see that this stipulates that growth is made up of the total contribution of each resource weighted by its growth rate. Total contribution means the resource's (factor) share in total output. Each input-elasticity is, in fact, made up of the product of the marginal productivity of the input and the relative size of the value of the input in national output. For example, labor's elasticity of national output (labor's factor share or relative contribution in national output), ξ_L, is made up of the product of $\partial Y/\partial L$, the marginal productivity of labor, and L/Y, the relative size of the value of labor in national output.

This derivation of the definition of economic growth from the fundamental basis of what the term *growth* actually defines, offers a clear understanding of what economic growth involves and what it does not involve. Explained in this way, economic growth will be expected to occur in an economy if resource-elasticities of output are positive and if resource exploration and exploitation are positive. The former condition would further require that the resources have positive marginal productivities in the economy.

Resource exploration and exploitation would involve the extent of discovery and effectual tapping of all aspects of the economy's natural, human, capital, and entrepreneurial resources. Natural resources would include mineral deposits and aquatic livestock. Human resource development would include education, training, and technical development. Capital resources development would include investment in physical equipment, construction of infrastructure and financial capital resources, whereas entrepreneurial development would involve managerial, organizational, and technological skills.

While some resources may have positive marginal productivities, others may have zero or negative marginal productivities. Using Equation (1.4), we can visualize that the net effect of such a situation in the economy will depend on whether the productive or the unproductive resources will be dominating economic activity. Thus, it is easy to understand how and why an economy might still forge on with positive growth despite evidence of misallocation and uneconomical use of some of its resources. For example, in many LDCs today the human resource acquisitions are not effectively utilized (owing to such problems as the "brain drain" and political repression), yet their economies are able to achieve some low to moderate levels of economic growth.

Having given a firm theoretical concept of economic growth, we now focus on how growth can be measured. Here we recall the definitions of economic growth we examined earlier. But the measurement of economic growth can open up differences about the domestic and international application of the concept. This is because, economic growth, for domestic purposes, serves to indicate the economy's performance in relation to its population and resource endowment. Outside the economy's borders, however, the question of inter-country comparison of economic welfare (or well-being) arises, for the most internationally accepted single index (indicator) of economic well-being is national income per head. We now examine how economic growth may be measured, both as an internal index and as an international economic indicator.

MEASUREMENT OF ECONOMIC GROWTH

As a practical means of determining the overall economic well-being of a country's population, an index of economic growth must be clearly measurable. Traditionally, the GDP, as well as its per capita level, are used. The GDP is an appropriate index of internal measurement of an economy's economic performance, namely, economic growth. The per capita income is used as the index of international comparison of economic well-being, and therefore, measures much more than mere economic growth. We now examine these measurements individually in greater detail.

Internal Measurement

Growth in an economy reflects increases in the productive capacity (expansion of GDP) and changes in the rate of utilization of this capacity (percentage increase). Letting the GDP be Y, and regarding the productive capacity as the potential national (output) income, Y_p, the rate of utilization (denoted in percentage form) is given as Y/Y_p. Capacity utilization is different from increases in the total capacity itself.

It is important to avoid a great deal of confusion by specifying whether the rate of capacity utilization (short-term growth rate) is being measured, involving the calculation of the growth trends of Y, or whether the growth rate of the economy's productive capacity (long-term growth rate) is meant, involving the calculation of the growth rate of Y_p. The former, measuring the GDP and its growth rate, appears to be easier in terms of practical measurement.

The national income of a country provides the basis for measuring the total volume of (output) goods and services in that country. The GDP measures the total output of final goods and services produced by the residents of the country over a given period of one year. The GDP (Y) may be defined in terms of the annual gross national expenditure of the economy. The economy's total gross national expenditure is made up of its total domestic expenditure and its net foreign (balance of trade) transactions. The total domestic sector expenditure comprises the individual and household private-sector expenditure (consumption, C), the total business-sector expenditure (Investment, I) and the total public-sector expenditure (government spending, G). The net foreign trade transactions is the total volume of exports (X) minus total volume of imports (M). The GDP is then expressed as

$$Y = C + I + G + X - M \tag{1.5}$$

Economic growth would occur in accord with growth in each of the sectors indicated in Equation (1.5). The combined growth effects of all sectors would show in GDP growth rate over time.

Limitations of GDP as a Measure of Economic Growth

Although GDP is a most appropriate measure of economic growth, at least for short-term purposes, it suffers a number of shortcomings in this regard. One of the most important problems it presents concerns the unreliability that arises because of its components. That is, the GDP tends to suffer from instability. To demonstrate this, we consider the definition of GDP:

$$Y = P.Q \tag{1.6}$$

where P = the Consumer Price Index and Q = the volume of total physical output.

The GDP is potentially unstable because of problems associated with changes in the Consumer Price Index, P. This parameter is sensitive to changes in several economic factors ranging from the volume of the money supply to the nature of demand and cyclical fluctuations. The rate of change of P itself defines the rate of inflation in the economy, and the rate of inflation in the economy would thus affect the stability of the GDP. GDP could, however, be *deflated* to obtain *real GDP* and thus nullify the inflationary effect on it. But barring the process of continuously deflating it, the GDP would not be a reliable index for measuring growth.

The volume of physical output, Q, could also be subject to instability as it follows *business cycle* trends. In such a case, the GDP would give an erroneous indication of economic growth because the business cycle output level does not incorporate the true indicators of growth. It merely shows the level of output during that particular point of the trend, and does not reflect the key growth indicators such as actual productivities, resource utilization, technological progress, and relative resource shares.

Another shortcoming of the GDP as an index of growth measurement stems from its inadequacy as the true representation of total output produced in the economy. The output of goods and services in (GDP) national income computations refers to "market" goods and services only, to the exclusion of "nonmarket" production. The GDP often fails to incorporate the unreported output and earnings of the so-called *underground economy*. Earnings in most productive but illegal activities in the economy, such as smuggling, prostitution, gambling, and tax evasion, are not included in GDP calculations, nor are services-in-kind included.

The output of *informal sector* economic activities would also not be included in GDP measurements because of the impracticality of calculating informal sector output. In economies with high informal sectors and high underground economy components, and most LDCs would be included in this category, the growth rate of the GDP would simply be, at best, a partial indication of economic growth. There is no question that major portions of production in LDCs take place within the individual household and never enter the "market." Such would include productions in subsistence agriculture, handicraft activities, and local services. One therefore doubts that the growth rate of the GDP would provide an adequate index for measuring a country's economic growth, especially if that country is an LDC.

External Measurement

For purposes of international comparisons of economic performance, a growth index that takes into account a nation's ability to expand its output relative to (or, rather, at a rate faster than) the growth rate of its population is often used. In this connection, levels and rates of growth of "real" per capita GDP are normally used to measure the population's overall economic state of being. The term *real* indicates the nominal or monetary value minus the rate of inflation. This index suggests how much of real goods and services would be available to the nation's average citizen. By using this index, it is easy to carry out a straightforward comparison of economic "well-being" or "welfare" across nations, a parameter that gives a quantitative measure of standards of living.[3] The per capita income (PCI) is given as

$$PCI = GDP/population \tag{1.7}$$

Limitations of PCI as a Measure of Economic Performance

The limitations of the PCI as a measure of international economic performance go beyond the purely technical problems that we noted about the use of the GDP growth as an indicator of economic growth. Several factors beset the PCI as a measure of economic "well-being" and as a parameter that is used for international welfare comparison. These range from concerns of how welfare should be defined to problems of externalities that affect economic well-being across nations.

Calculations of PCI figures do not take account of external costs (negative externalities) and external benefits (positive externalities), factors that, to a very large extent, affect the social and economic well-being of a country's citizens. Modern economic activities, especially industrial production and mass consumption, are necessarily accompanied by these externalities. Examples of external costs (negative externalities) include environmental pollution of the atmosphere, rivers, and land surface, giving rise to acid rain, smog, and disruption or destruction of aquatic life. They also include traffic congestion, crime waves, and disruptions in family life. To the extent that the PCI does not address how these externalities bring to bear on standards of living, it cannot be a reliable index of welfare measure.

Problems surround the definition of welfare for any given society. Cultures differ across countries, and accordingly, what may constitute well-being in one culture or across a culturally uniform region or subregion of the world may, in fact, be regarded negatively within another culture or across another culturally uniform region or subregion of the world. For example, most economically developed societies would tend to define well-being in terms of purely economic parameters to the exclusion of social factors. The economic indicator would most ostensibly include material consumption levels of goods (e.g., number of cars per person or volume of caloric intake per person) and services (e.g., number of medical doctors per 1000 persons or kilowatts of electricity per household per year).

Most LDCs, on the other hand, would assess well-being in terms of a broad array of social indicators. In these societies, such economic indicators as cited above may be seen rather as secondary indicators of well-being. Social indicators such as degree of social harmony (correlated with the level of crime wave), number of successful marriages per 1000 households (indicated by the divorce rate in the society), number of children born out of wedlock (termed the illegitimacy rate), and family size of the individual would be regarded as crucial parameters indicating the well-being of a person.

Another social index could be the "level of morality" of the society (indicated by the degree to which moral decadence is tolerated in the given society), and the purity of religion (in a fundamentalist religious society). The problem then is that whereas the PCI would capture the economic indicators considered important in measuring well-being in most developed countries, it would not reflect the social factors considered important in most LDCs. In this respect, the PCI is seriously deficient as an index of well-being, and more so if it is used for international comparisons.[4]

The PCI also suffers from the technical problems associated with the use of the GDP that we discussed in the preceding section. But the most important technical shortcoming of the PCI concerns the pattern of income distribution in the country. Since the PCI is an average measure, it does not reflect the manner in which incomes or wealth may or may not be concentrated in a few people among the population. Should there be a situation of gross income inequities in the country, the growth rate of the PCI would hardly imply individual economic improvement. Although it may show positive growth, the true picture would be an economic growth that barely affected the generality of the population. Unequal income distribution would severely diminish economic well-being: increasing social and political tension would arise if a small number of people or group are perceived as more affluent to the detriment of a large number of people who live in deep poverty. Low standards of nutrition and health would threaten the entire society with epidemic and disease outbreaks.

Thus, we are not to attribute too much significance to the use of the PCI as a welfare measure and international comparison. Caution is needed in interpreting the PCI altogether. Nonetheless, it remains a very useful index with which we can quantify growth and economic performance. But that should be that—an index. The PCI should only be used as a *rough* indicator of economic performance, and not a measure of it *per se*. We now consider the concept and measurement of economic development as a whole.

DEFINITION AND MEASUREMENT OF ECONOMIC DEVELOPMENT

Having exhausted the meaning, definition, and measurement of the concept of economic growth, we now turn to the concept of economic development. It is important not to confuse these two closely related but nevertheless distinct concepts. To recap from the definition given for economic development at the beginning of the chapter, economic development must be preceded and prompted by economic growth. Economic development involves the *process* through which a country or region achieves economic growth in addition to *structural transformation* of its economy. Economic development reflects the underlying qualitative, structural, and institutional changes that are needed to expand a nation's potentials and capabilities in the utilization of scarce economic resources. Whereas economic growth represents the *necessary* condition, structural transformation provides the *sufficiency* condition for economic development.

First, we consider what is meant in qualifying economic development as a *process*. Ordinarily, a process refers to a series of interconnected or linked chain of actions, reactions, and interactions of activities—that is, various chain reactions that affect and are affected by each other toward some ultimate end or final state. For the process to be complete and to succeed in achieving the end state, there should be no breaks or permanent or semipermanent stoppages in the chain of events. Nor could the end state be successfully reached if there are "jumps" that avoid or bypass any stage(s) of the process. Such would only delay, or even abort, the entire due process and prevent the achievement of the end state. Such is economic development. Having presented the "growth" part of this process, we now deal with the structural transformation aspect of economic development.

The Structural Transformation Aspect of Economic Development

To fully grasp the concept of structural transformation, we consider what an economic structure really is. The structure of the economy constitutes the fundamentals of the economy's makeup: the nature and constituents of its production, employment, distribution, and consumption, as well as its geography, environment, and resource acquisition. We now provide a detailed study of what is meant by the economic structure of a country.

Economic Structure

In studying the structure of an economy, an important factor to consider is the nature and degree of industrialization, or otherwise, of that economy. Also considered are the proportion of the country's GDP that is made up of agricultural (primary) production relative to industrial (secondary) and services (tertiary) production; the degree of mechanization relative to the degree of labor intensity involved in production activities.

The economic structure also involves the occupational and geographical distributions of the labor force: the proportion of the population that depends on *primary sector* occupation relative to *secondary- and tertiary-sector* occupations for their livelihood, and the proportion that lives and works in the rural areas relative to urban sectors. The primary sector of the economy constitutes the agricultural activities of farming, fishing, hunting, handicraft, and petty trade and local commerce; the secondary sector is made up of manufacturing and processing industrialization; and the tertiary includes the services sector (including distribution) and infrastructural utilities (including communication, banking and finance, education, health services, and entertainment).

The structure of the economy would also encompass the degree of foreign trade dependence and "openness" of the economy, as well as the composition of the country's items of trade (imports and exports). Whether or not the country is monocultural (depending on a single commodity export for much of its foreign exchange earnings), or whether or not the country's economy is susceptible to external trade and international market shocks is considered.

Structural transformation, therefore, implies positive changes in the above respects. The items specified must change with a view toward self-sustenance. The process of this transformation is long term and fundamental. But from what state would the economy be transforming? It is important to examine the nature of *underdevelopment* (or an underdeveloped economy) to help us appreciate what is being transformed. For in the absence of structural transformation, the economy would be in a state of underdevelopment even if a substantial level of *economic growth* were achieved. There could be "growth without development," as we have witnessed in many contemporary LDCs (although there could not be "development without growth").

The Phenomenon of Economic Underdevelopment

Underdevelopment can be defined simply as a state of inadequate pace of the process of economic development. A more resolute definition is that it represents a state of economic deprivation, dependence, and a vicious circle of long-term poverty. Absolute poverty pervades economic underdevelopment: a significant part of the society's population remains below a minimally acceptable level (standard) of living, while the prospects of the economy's ability to raise incomes and to effect desired structural changes remain bleak. To fully understand the meaning of underdevelopment, we outline the major common characteristics of underdeveloped countries.[5]

Characteristics of Underdevelopment

It is tempting to view all LDCs in the same light. Apparently, since they are all underdeveloped or "developing," they could all be seen as almost always having low incomes per capita and smaller proportions of their population employed in modern industry, and so they all could be said to be alike. Far from it: tremendous diversities exist among LDCs. Some are sparsely populated, while others are densely populated. Some have very huge geographical land mass, while others occupy only a meagre expanse of land. Some possess very large natural resources, while others are very poor and may be landlocked. Most LDCs were colonized at one time or another by one or a few European countries, while some were never colonies. Most LDCs have authoritarian or military regimes, while others maintain political democracies or quasi-democracies. Furthermore, LDCs are diverse in their social and cultural mixes.

Despite the disparities noted above, a wide range of basic economic characteristics are common to all LDCs. These characteristics may, indeed, be considered as the common *indices* of underdevelopment. They permit us to view LDCs in a similar light, and to study and analyze their circumstances with the application of similar paradigms and model framework. We discuss six of the most widely accepted characteristics:

1. Underdevelopment is consistent with a situation of low GDP levels. Specifically, an underdeveloped nation's GDP would be lower than one-quarter of the GDP of the United States of America. In this connection, the per capita income would also be quite low, even for those LDCs with relatively low population levels.

2. The economy of an underdeveloped country would tend to be *agrarian*; that is, the GDP and overall production activities are dominated by the agricultural sector. Not only is the greatest proportion of the GDP made up of agricultural output, but also agriculture would be the largest single employer of the labor force. The greatest proportion of the population would rely on the primary-sector activities for their income and livelihood.

3. An underdeveloped economy would tend to have a substantial rate of population growth, notably in excess of 2 percent per year. Its population growth rate would also tend to be greater than the rate of growth of GDP.

4. Foreign trade dependence is another common characteristic of an underdeveloped economy. Usually, the LDC is able to massively produce one or two agricultural or mineral products that it exports to earn needed foreign exchange with which it imports capital resources and manufactured consumer goods from the rest of the world. The *monocultural* nature of the LDCs exports not only make it vulnerable to world market vagaries, but it also makes it wholly dependent on the world demand of its produce, on the one hand, and on foreign sources of required capital needs for development, on the other. The LDC fails to diversify its economy. Related to this is the LDC's tendency toward incessant balance-of-payments adversities and external indebtedness.

5. An underdeveloped economy is characterized by the vicious circle of poverty (VCP) syndrome. The VCP can be illustrated from the supply side and the demand side. On the supply side, the VCP occurs in the following manner: low income (poverty) leads to low savings rate, low savings rate results in low investment and capital formation, low investment and capital formation results in low output, and low output means low income, and hence low savings, and the circular enclave of poverty continues. From the demand side, the VCP involves the low level of income that means low level of effective demand to warrant industrialization and expanded productive capacity. Low level of market demand weakens business and entrepreneurial innovation, and this would mean low level of investment and employment, which would result in low income. Again, a circular poverty enclave continues. It is generally supposed that the LDC must break the VCP from either the demand side or the supply side, or

both. In either case, it would then reverse the course of the enclave of poverty to a course of the enclave of prosperity.

6. The most general characteristic of underdevelopment is the existence of *economic dualism* within an LDC. Economic dualism refers to the coexistence of two interrelated and interdependent sectors, the *traditional* sector and the *modern* sector, within the same economy. This coexistence is chronic rather than merely transitional. The traditional sector (also often referred to as the subsistence sector) is the rural and informal sectors, including subsistence production, and is largely agrarian. It is dominated by low-level and unskilled-labor-oriented production activities. The traditional sector is also relatively less monetized and less market oriented. The modern sector of the dualistic economy is the industrialized and economically highly developed sector, with application of modern technology and capitalistic modes of production. The modern sector is analogous to the economies of the economically developed countries.[6]

The most peculiar aspect of the dualism of an LDC is that the traditional sector is significantly larger than the modern sector, both in geographical expanse and in the range of economic activities. There are glaring structural distinctions between the two sectors: the coexistence of modern cities with advanced technology and highly educated, skilled, and wealthy elites with large masses of poor, uneducated, and malnourished people living in rural and peasant settings. Economic dualism is doubtlessly the most striking attribute of underdevelopment, and single-handedly sets the LDC apart from a developed economy.[7]

The Measurement of Economic Development

When we adhere to the true and complete definition of economic development, it becomes clear that it would not be easy to actually quantify it at any point in time. There seems to be no universally accepted standard for measuring economic development, as the term itself encompasses a significant amount of value judgments. Only a proxy consensus seems to be possible if we must be able to assess the pace of development within a nation or across nations.

For purposes of measurement, we would offer the following version of the definition of economic development: the process through which, over time, sustained increases occur in the nation's per capita real income (output), accompanied by significant structural changes that allow for elevated income distribution and large increases in individual economic well-being. This implies that economic development must be associated with the general masses of the country's population benefiting from the changes it brings, rather than just a small portion of the population being the beneficiaries. The rise in income must be evident through such changes in basic living conditions as improved nutrition and high nutritional and clothing standards, improved (modern) housing, improved health and health care, low infant mortality rates, higher literacy rates, and a general environmental face-lift from a predominantly rural to an increased metropolitan flavor.[8]

This opens up a quality aspect in the definition and measurement of development. How development or lack of development affects the "quality of life" has come to be regarded as crucial in determining of whether or not progress is made in economic development. In this vein, the yardstick for assessing development is now termed the human development index (HDI) and the physical quality of life index (QLI). Here we outline the key parameters that are used in the applications of the HDI and QLI, and discuss how they are used.

Equity in Income Distribution

The foremost economic indicator in the measurement of economic development is the pattern of the *distribution* of output and income: the shares of total income received by high-income, middle-income, and low-income families. This indicator is referred to as the size distribution of income and is used as a direct measure of economic well-being. It is calculated from average income levels of families covering several years. The data are ranked in order of magnitude, corresponding to the cumulative percentage of the recipients.

A *Lorenz Curve* is constructed by plotting the graph of these data with the cumulative percentage of the recipients (population), %*P*, on the horizontal axis and the cumulative percentage of income (GDP), %*Y*, on the vertical axis.[9] A Lorenz Curve is depicted in Figure 1.1, showing the percentage of total GDP received by any given cumulative percentage of the country's population.

The shape of the Lorenz Curve offers an immediate perusal of the degree of income inequality in society. For instance, should the Lorenz Curve be the 45°-line, it indicates perfect equity of complete egalitarianism, whereby, say, 10 percent of the population receives 10 percent of the GDP, or 30 percent of the population receives 30 percent of the GDP, or 75 percent of the population receives 75 percent of the GDP, or 92 percent of the population receives 92 percent of the GDP, and so on.

The actual Lorenz Curve of a country, however, tends to correspond more closely to the bulging curve, *LC*, shown in Figure 1.1, indicating the actual pattern of a country's income distribution. It shows that income is not distributed equally across the population; that is, the poorest 40 percent of the population, say, might be receiving only about 10 percent of the income. The closer the *LC* gets to the 45° line, the greater is the degree of equity, and the more the *LC* curves away from the 45° line, the greater is the degree of income inequality. The area, *A*, between the *LC* and the 45° line, relative to the entire area of the right-angled triangle, *A+B*, is used to measure the degree of inequality. The statistic:

$$G = A/(A+B), \text{ where } 0 \le G \le 1$$

Figure 1.1
The Lorenz Curve of Income Distribution

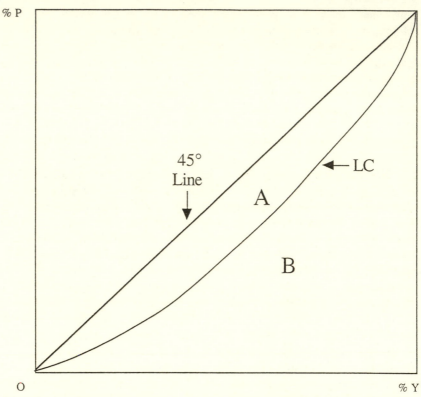

termed the *Gini Coefficient*, is used to measure the degree of inequity.[10] *G* has a theoretical range of between 0 (perfect equality) and 1 (absolute inequality). The larger the area between the 45° line and the *LC*, the higher the value of the *Gini Coefficient*. Economically developed countries generally have lower income inequality compared to LDCs which generally have higher income inequality.

The Consumption Index

The quality of life can be measured by the average level of consumption of goods and services in the country. This includes the consumption of durable goods such as housing (average number of persons per room), clothing, transportation facilities (number of vehicles per capita or cars per household or number of cars per 1000 households or number of households that have cars), or, say, number of radios per capita; and nondurable goods such as quantity and quality of food (caloric or fiber) intake per capita. Also considered are the consumption of services, such as communication services (number of telephones per capita, newspaper circulation per capita), and per capita energy consumption. At the national level, the quality of life can often be assessed using the level of consumption of basic industrial products—for example, quantity of steel consumption or quantity of cement consumption.

The Level of Literacy

The literacy rate is also used as a measure of development. This measure would be correlated with the level of educational achievement. School enrollment in primary, secondary, postsecondary, and vocational and trade school levels could be used as a proxy for literary achievement. This index also lends itself to comparison with other countries and is relatively easy to measure.

Nutrition and Health

Included in this index are such *physical quality of life* components as the number of physicians per capita, life expectancy at birth, death rate, and, say, level of protein consumption per capita.[11] Based on the percentage of literacy, infant mortality, and life expectancy, the physical quality of life index (PQLI) is calculated. Scores ranging from 1 to 100 are assigned in each category of the parameters, and an average PQLI is calculated for each country. The main advantage of the PQLI is that it permits easy comparison across countries.

Industrialization and Occupational Patterns

Levels of development can also be measured by considering the occupational distribution of the country's labor force, such as the percentage of the economically active population engaged in agricultural employment as against the nonagricultural sectors. In addition, the level of wage and salary workers as a percentage of the entire labor force is considered. Other related indices are the manufacturing share in total GDP, or the percentage of the population that lives and works in the urban sector relative to the rural sector.

This chapter has offered a detailed study of the concept and measurement of economic development. Stress has been placed on the underlying distinctions between the concept of economic growth and the broader notion of economic development. As this chapter makes clear, the measurement of economic development is potentially fraught with difficulties.

Although one can clearly maintain a sharp distinction between economic growth and economic development by adhering strictly to their respective definitions, the measurement of these two concepts must involve some degree of value judgment. No doubt, the GDP and its per capita level represent the best quantitative measures of growth, and therefore a significant yardstick for development. It is inconceivable to imagine any significant long-term development without significant rises in per capita GDP.

Overall economic development, however, cannot be judged without the important qualitative criteria, namely, equity in income distribution, unemployment, and the other elements of the quality of life index. For if these qualitative indicators are declining or worsening, then even a very high growth level of the GDP and per capita GDP cannot really be seen as economic development.

NOTES

1. Although economic development is generally associated with higher output and rising levels of income, the association may not always be necessary. Rising productivity might lead people to prefer increased leisure rather than increased income; in that case a doubling of productivity, say, may result in people cutting their daily or weekly hours of work by half. This would then represent a case of economic development being achieved while not accompanied by growth (no increasing real income).

2. The input-elasticity of output measures the degree to which a proportional change in the level of the input would affect the level of total output. It simply measures the input's relative contribution to total output and is equal to the input's share (or factor share) in total output.

3. A measure of growth in productive capacity per capita (output per man-hour, or average output per man-hour employed) is generally referred to as *productivity*. However, the most widely used measure of economic growth is output (GDP) per capita. This approach focuses on the growth of material living standards rather than on the growth of productivity.

4. Where a common social indicator of well-being could be used, the problem of "clash of cultures" surrounding its use could arise. An example is in using a country's political situation to assess individual well-being. In Western economically developed countries, political democracy and the functioning of democratic institutions are highly rated as indicators of well-being. Many LDCs would not consider political democracy and the functioning of democratic institutions as necessarily indicative of their citizens well-being.

5. The term *underdevelopment* must not be viewed in the sense that a country is "undeveloped." Underdevelopment has a sense of being "imposed," rather than a situation where a country merely fails to achieve development (see Frank, 1969). To see this point clearly, it is imperative to understand that whereas the present-day economically developed countries of Europe, North America, and Australasia were never *under*developed, they were certainly *undeveloped* at one time prior to their achieving economic takeoff into development. Contrarily, the present-day "developing" countries of Africa, Asia, and Latin America have not only been *undeveloped*, but they have also been *subjected to* and kept *under*developed. Thus, underdevelopment is imposed on a country, either by external or by internal means (Ezeala-Harrison, 1995a).

6. For a more detailed analysis of economic dualism, including its implications for rural-urban migration and the unemployment problem, see Lewis (1954, 1979), Singer (1970), and Harris and Todaro (1970).

7. The term dualism must always be used with caution. As we have postulated it so far, economic dualism within an economy should be understood as internal dualism. This is because there is also the existence of "global dualism," which refers to the existence and persistence of increasing economic divergence between rich (developed) nations and

poor (underdeveloped) nations. Nor could the global dualism be rectified in time, given the ever widening productivity and income gap between people in the developed and underdeveloped societies. See Frank (1967, 1969).

8. Some economists would even include the effectiveness and reliability of social institutions, political freedom, efficiency of governments, and government (officials') accountability to the public as crucial factors in assessing the level of economic development. For an elaborate study of these, see Sen (1987) or Dreze and Sen (1990).

9. The curve is named after the American statistician, C. Lorenz, who invented its use in 1905. For an extended survey and further studies on the application of the Lorenz Curve, see Cline (1975) or Fields (1980).

10. The term derives from the name of the Italian statistician who developed it in 1912.

11. The United Nations Development Program supports the use of the *Human Development Index (HDI)* which combines the *quality of life* components with adjusted GDP figures. This HDI uses the three crucial parameters: GDP per capita, life expectancy, and literacy to generate and assign values ranging between zero (for the lowest HDI) and one (for the highest HDI). Using this index, Japan received the highest score of 0.996 in 1990, while Niger Republic (West Africa) received the lowest score of 0.116. In 1992, Canada received the highest HDI score.

2

A Global Profile of Development and Underdevelopment

Economic development encompasses how economic circumstances of nations and societies change over time. It also envisions how they can be made to change positively. In this regard, one would not need to look far to observe that the past two decades have been difficult for less developed countries (LDCs). Most of the regions of Africa, Asia, and Latin America suffered severe declines in per capita incomes, and this situation only worsened as the 1990s brought a global recession coupled with the heavy burden of accumulated debt.

The momentous inroads into the world economy made by the former socialist economies of Eastern Europe and Soviet Union tended to shift world attention slightly away from the dire economic circumstances in LDCs. The "new world (economic) order" seemed to be one that poor nations might not find very hospitable. The end of the cold war meant redirection of emphasis and investment resources and aid away from many LDCs toward the emerging democracies of the East.

This chapter provides a broad overview of the existing economic development situation in the world. It examines the challenges, opportunities, risks, and obstacles of effecting development in the LDCs. Of central concern in the profile of world development and underdevelopment are the vexing problems of widespread poverty, rising gross disparities in the distributions of income and wealth, rapid population growth, urban congestion, rural desertification and neglect, and increasing environmental degradation. Of equal concern are the severe imbalances in the global economy, especially between developed and underdeveloped countries. We examine these disparities in greater detail with a view toward shedding light on what the fundamental problems are, and what pertinent policies might be adopted to better address them.

THE GLOBAL ECONOMIC HEMISPHERES

The world economic order clearly demarcates between two hemispheres: the

Northern Hemisphere and the Southern Hemisphere. The terms *North* and *South* are quick reference groupings of countries (and continents) with quite different structural characteristics (see Chapter 1). This incidentally corresponds with a neat classification of continents of the world. The Northern Hemisphere comprises of the economically developed countries of Western Europe, North America, and Australasia (a specially framed reference to the group of countries made up of Australia, New Zealand, Japan, and the newly industrializing countries [NICs] of Asia, namely, Hong Kong, South Korea, Taiwan, Thailand, Singapore, and Malaysia).

The Southern economic hemisphere is made up of the nations found in the underdeveloped continents of the world: Africa, Asia, and Latin America and the Caribbean.[1] These nations are often referred to as the *Third World*, primarily to distinguish them from the industrialized and economically advanced free market economies of the (North) First World. There is then, presumably, the Second World: China, particularly, and the former socialist and industrializing command economies of Eastern Europe and the Soviet Union. Some of these may, however, more correctly be classified in the Third World. The Second World clearly forms part of the South.

It is estimated that the Southern Hemisphere comprises about the poorest two-thirds of the world's population, clearly the vast majority but not all of the LDCs' population. The problem is that this majority has very low incomes, inadequate nutrition, inadequate housing, poor health, and poor educational levels; and live in countries whose economies do not have bright prospects of growth and development. Current estimates indicate that the average income level in the two North American countries (United States and Canada) ranks in the richest 10 percent of the world's population.[2]

The World Bank follows a classification of the world into *low income countries* (LICs), *middle income countries* (MICs), and *high income countries* (HICs). The LICs are those with per capita income of about US$580 or less; the MICs are those with per capita income of between US$580 and US$6000; and the HICs are those with per capita incomes above US$6000. Again, these correspond to the classifications of First, Second, and Third worlds discussed above.

Table 2.1 reveals key structural differences that largely demarcate the regions of the globe and create the present world economic (dis)order. It highlights the population (and its geographical compositions), the proportion of the labor force engaged in primary economic activities for their livelihood, and the share of agricultural production in GDP in the world's regions and subregions.

There is a striking difference between the proportionate size of, say, Africa's agricultural population (75 percent) and South Asia's (63 percent), on the one hand, and North America's agricultural population (5 percent) and Europe's (9 percent), on the other. However, whereas Europe's agriculture is highly productive, North America's productivity is relatively quite low.

Table 2.1
Structural Diversities in World Regional Economies, 1992

Region	Population (millions)	% Urban population	% Rural population	% Agric Labor	% Agric in GDP
World	5420	43	57	45	
LDCs					
South Asia	1682	28	72	63	33
East Asia	1386	34	66	51	21
Africa	654	30	70	75	32
S. America*	453	70	30	32	10
All LDCs	4196	34	66	62	17
DCs					
Former USSR	284	66	34	20	—
Europe	511	75	25	9	7
Japan	124	177	23	11	3
North America	283	75	25	5	2
All OECD	18.2	89.4	3.1		

* Including Central America and Caribbean.
Source: (1) World Bank: *World Development Report*, 1992, (2) *World Population Data Sheet*, Washington, D.C., 1992.

The structural differences shown in Table 2.1 are indicative of the factors that have helped shape the present rich-poor division in the world economic situation. The poor regions have the highest populations, and a great majority of the population dwell in the rural sector and are employed in the agricultural sectors. The rich regions of the world have smaller populations, most of whom live in the urban sectors and are employed in nonagricultural activities with high productivities. Following the inequality inherent in this structural diversities, significant imbalances have emerged between the world's North-South economic hemispheres.

The North-South Economic Imbalance

Any serious study of issues in global economic development must assess the economic relations between the two distinct groups of the world's inhabitants: the North and the South. The present world economic picture is one of severe imbalance in the acquisition, flow, production, and consumption of economic resources between the North and the South. This represents a continued transfer of real resources, the outcomes of which include the debt overhang and the gross inequity in the economic situations of the two hemispheres.

Here we shall examine some key components of the world economic activity, namely, the flow of trade, aid, capital and resource movements, and human resources in order to ascertain their North-South trends. It is generally agreed that activities in these components have placed the North in a more favorable position, and the imbalance seems to be permanent. The South has continued to face relative terms-of-trade adversities in the world markets of agricultural and mineral raw materials, while the North has control of producing and marketing industrial manufactures and high-tech products. We survey the data on two major indices of North-South economic links in order to obtain a clearer picture of the global profile of economic development and underdevelopment.

North-South Trade Imbalance

The famous "trade as engine of growth" caption that has captivated economic development studies and research since the early times of classical economic thinking seems to have doubtlessly lost its appeal, simply because it is no longer tenable for present-day LDCs. One recalls the great potentials of international trade that accrued to countries such as Japan (trading silk to achieve takeoff into development in the mid-nineteenth century), Britain (trading wool and cotton over the period of the Industrial Revolution), the United States (trading grain and corn), Canada (trading wheat), and Russia (trading cereal). Apparently, international trade has lost its "engine of growth" for contemporary LDCs.

Even crude petroleum production and exportation by many countries in the South have not had a significant impact in closing the North-South imbalance. World trade data from the International Monetary Fund (IMF) *International Financial Statistics (IFS)* for 1955 to 1992 indicate that the volume of total Southern exports to the North over this period was a mere fraction of the volume of total Northern exports to the South. Some studies have provided theoretical explanations of how and why this massive imbalance has occurred: the works of Bhagwati (1985, 1987), Sapir (1985), and Schumacher (1988) are a few important ones.

North-South Aid Versus South-North Resource Flows

The granting of economic aid and assistance has traditionally been a way by which the North had provided support to the South. The flow of aid had always been understood to be a one-way movement: from the Northern rich to the Southern poor. This North-South flow that occurred during the 1950s to 1970s, many of it in the form of loans, created a huge debt load, leading to the South's debt crisis of the 1980s. As the aid loans came to maturity, resources flowed from South to North to meet the servicing and other debt-management obligations. It is now wondered whether, in fact, the net resource flow has not been rather from the South to the North.

As the debt crisis threw their economies under severe strain, most LDCs adopted structural economic reforms aimed at revamping their devastated and debt-ridden economies. Southern experiences during the 1980s indicate that their economic reforms are increasingly frustrated by, among other factors, a hostile international economic environment, of which the conduct of foreign aid is an important part.

North-South aid has been used as an integral part of the donors' diplomatic and foreign policy, which seek to further narrow national self-interests especially on matters of defense, commercial linkage, political ties, and ideological spheres. In many instances erstwhile (Northern) colonial powers sought and succeeded in maintaining their spheres of influence by giving foreign "aid" to the (Southern) ex-colonies. It has been argued that the superpowers fought their cold war with foreign aid to the South.

In examining the possible "reverse effect" of foreign aid, Maizels and Nissanke (1984) studied the degree of correlation between such things as the donors' share in total imports of the recipient, colonial association, base rights, arms sales, and the like, and the volume of aid. They discovered that North-South aid was motivated largely by donor interests according to these criteria, rather than by the recipients' economic needs. North-South aid has always fallen far short of what is required for any meaningful development impact to be made in the South; it has also created a situation where there is now a net overall resource transfer to the North from the needy South. There is growing evidence of net capital transfer to the North from the South (Boltho, 1988).

THE GLOBAL ECONOMIC DIVIDE

Today, there nearly to 180 nations in the world. The 1990 *World Development Report* offers the following classification of these countries: least developed (the forty-two LDCs whose per capita GDP was below US$580; middle-income (the seventy LDCs whose per capita GDP was between US$580 and US$6000); and oil-producing or manufacturing but still undeveloped (the eleven middle-income countries whose per capita GDP was above US$6000; and developed (the nineteen industrially advanced countries).[3] The world is clearly divided economically. On the one side is the cluster of rich and well-to-do countries, and on the other side is the collection of poor and economically deprived countries, largely overcome by poverty. In between are a mix of societies that are not so well-to-do and not really overcome by poverty.

Central and Eastern European countries (including Russia and the newly independent states of the former Soviet Union) are presently regarded as economies in transition, because they have not yet achieved a full-fledged market-based orientation. Together with China, these economies are distinct from the Western developed economies, on the one hand, and the (Third World) less developed countries, on the other. The main differences among these groups, however, lie is various economic characteristics.

The LDCs are characterized by low incomes among the population (who are almost always employed mainly in the primary sector agricultural and low productive activities rather than modern industry. They tend to have large pools of unemployed (or underemployed) labor, with most of these existing as open involuntary unemployment in the cities. They tend to be export-dependent, and their exports consist mainly of primary-product raw materials, while they depend on imports for much of their capital resources and food needs. Their trade transactions are mainly with the developed countries and not with each other.

The LDCs also differ from each other in various respects ranging from their political arrangements to resource acquisition. While some possess huge crude-oil resources and are members of the Organization of Petroleum Exporting Countries (OPEC), others are leading exporters of certain important primary produce in world markets. And while some maintain and operate political democracies, others are under the rule of authoritarian or military regimes; some may have stable and honest governments, while others may be under the rule of corrupt dictatorships. These countries also vary in their economic and political organizations. The operational structures of some of these organizations lean heavily on socialist central planning, while others are purely free-enterprise market-based economic structures. Others also operate a mixture of free-enterprise and regulated economies. These important diversities mean that it is not very easy to devise single and universal solutions to the LDCs as an entity. Measures that may work for, say, Central America may not be very applicable to Central Africa, say. A close grasp of the diversities among LDCs is an important requirement for a development economist.

The developed countries (DCs), on the other hand, generally have very close similarities and little diversities other than general structural differences such as population, market sizes, geography, culture. Almost all the DCs operate free-enterprise market-based economies and political democracies.

The DCs of the world are joined together by the economic association known as the Organization for Economic Cooperation and Development (OECD).[4] The OECD's policy objectives are: (1) to promote and achieve the highest sustainable economic growth, employment, and living standards in member countries, while maintaining financial stability, and thereby contribute to the development of the world economy at large; (2) to contribute to sound economic expansion in member countries; and (3) to contribute to the expansion of multilateral world trade. Most of the *OECD* countries are industrialized and economically developed. The newly-industrializing countries (NICs) of Asia (Hong Kong, Taiwan, South Korea, Singapore, Thailand) are rapidly progressing toward developed country status, and may soon join the OECD.

The *global economic divide* is highlighted and illustrated by the data in Table 2.2. It shows the relative shares of the world's population and income across the various continents (or world regional groupings). Whereas over 80 percent of the world's population live in the LDCs, and have only about 10 percent of the world's income, the DCs have only about 18 percent of the world's population but earn almost 90 percent of the world's income. Although the growth rates of GDP look promising for LDCs together, huge disparities and disappointing differences in growth performance exist among the subregions.

The 1993 *World Development Report* data indicate that the East Asia subregion (China, Hong Kong, Indonesia, Malaysia, Thailand, Singapore, South Korea, and Taiwan) achieved high growth records, averaging 5.2 percent over the 1972-1992 period. It shows that the Middle East and North Africa performed at about the LDCs' average recorded in Table 2.2, while Latin America and the

Table 2.2
Relative Population and Income Growth by Continent, 1992

Region	% of World Population	% of World Income	Average % GDP Growth 1972-1992
LDCs			
Asia	59.2	5.2	6.7
Africa	13.0	1.7	2.2
South America*	9.5	3.7	2.5
All LDCs	81.7	10.6	3.6
DCs			
USA	5.7	23.0	
All OECD	18.2	89.4	3.1

    * Including Central America and Caribbean.
Source: Calculated from (1) World Bank: *World
        Development Report*, 1991, (2) IMF: *World Economic
        Outlook*, 1993.

Caribbean achieved an average of 2 percent growth. South Asia (including India, Pakistan, and Burma), growing at about 1.8 percent, and the Sub-Saharan Africa subregion, growing at 0.2 percent, performed very poorly, a fact that is hidden by the averages calculated in Table 2.2.

While there is a great deal of optimism about the long-term development prospects of some LDCs, others present a pessimistic picture. There has been a growing sense of general progress, and the gap between rich and poor countries has narrowed especially if we include the data on the Eastern European countries.

Table 2.3 shows per capita GDP levels by region and subregion, and average annual growth rates for the period 1950-1990. The Asian countries show the highest growth rates in per capita GDP between 1950 and 1990, with an annual average of 3.6 percent. All LDCs achieved an average annual growth rate of 2.7 percent. These growth rates exceeded those of the high-income OECD countries, which averaged 2.3 percent per year over this period, and were only slightly higher than the 2 percent growth rate achieved by the Eastern European economies.

Table 2.3
World Regional Trends in Per Capita GDP, 1950-1990

Region	Per Capita GDP 1950	1973	1990	Average % Growth
Asia	487	1215	2812	3.6
Sub-Saharan Africa	348	558	513	0.8
South America*	1729	2969	3164	1.2
All LDCs	839	1599	2796	2.7
Eastern Europe	2128	4658	5618	2.0
Europe, Middle East and North Africa	940	2017	2576	2.0
All OECD	3298	7396	10104	2.3

    * Including Central America and Caribbean.
Source: Calculated from (1) World Bank: *World
        Development Report*, 1991.

The major disappointments occurred in Sub-Saharan Africa, which averaged under a 1 percentage growth rate during this twenty-year period and where there were absolute declines in per capita income between 1973 and 1990. A 1990 study by the Worldwatch Institute reported a much more pessimistic situation about the *world economic divide.*[5] Based on per capita GDP data (adjusted for real purchasing power) for 130 countries, the world is classified in four categories. The rich are those with per capita income of US$6000 U.S or more, middle income countries are those with US$2500 to US$6000, poor (low-income) countries are those with $1000 to $2500, and poorest (or least income) countries are those with less than $1000 per capita income.

The study also shows that since 1950 the high-income countries have nearly tripled their income, while the least income countries have only managed to increase theirs minimally. Therefore, the gap between rich and poor has actually widened considerably.

The Problem of Uneven Development

Economic growth and development in a society depends largely on the combined use of the resources and atmosphere provided by the political, social, cultural, and environmental circumstances of that society. By resources are meant the natural, physical, and human resources at the disposal of the society (see Chapter 1). Therefore, under a given state of *minimally conducive* sociopolitical conditions (that is, provided a minimal state of political, social, cultural, and environmental conditions exist), a country's development will depend on the degree of utilization of these resources.

If a country effectively utilizes its human resources (labor force and organizational and managerial know-how), natural resources (available in its land and waters), and material resources (capital stock and equipment), relative economic development is apt to be achieved. If these resources are not effectively utilized, development may not occur. The combined effects of human and material resources in creating productivity is the principal factor underlying uneven economic development among the different regions of the world. A measure of the combined effects of all resource inputs together in creation of output, total factor productivity (TFP), is used by economists. The TFP measure captures the efficiency with which all resource inputs are used in the production process and to a very large extent affects (and even mainly determines) the productivities of individual resource inputs.[6]

Table 2.4 highlights how uneven development could be explained by differences in degrees of resource utilization among the various regions of the world. It gives the growth rates of GDP, resource inputs, and TFPs in both DCs and LDCs over the period 1960-1990. While Sub-Saharan Africa and South America show zero annual increase in TFP, East Asia and Europe record relatively high levels of TFP growth.

Table 2.4
World Regional Resource and Productivity Growths, 1950-1990

Region	Average Annual % Growth			
	GDP	Labour	Capital	TFP
East Asia	6.8	2.6	10.2	1.9
South Asia	4.4	2.1	7.7	0.6
Sub-Saharan Africa	3.3	2.2	6.3	0.0
South America*	3.6	2.6	6.3	0.0
All LDCs	4.2	2.3	7.2	0.6
Europe, Middle East and North Africa	5.0	1.7	7.6	1.4
France	3.9	-0.2	4.8	1.7
West Germany	3.1	-0.6	4.2	1.4
United Kingdom	2.4	-0.2	3.1	1.2
United States	3.0	1.8	3.4	0.5
All OECD	3.2	1.6	4.4	1.8

* Including Central America and Caribbean.
Source: Calculated from (1) World Bank: *World Development Report*, 1991.

We also see the differences in capital utilization. Clearly, there is a high correlation between the TFP, capital use, and GDP growth. The poorest regions of the world, Sub-Saharan Africa, South Asia, and South America, consistently show low TFP growth and relatively lower GDP growth. Uneven development must largely be explained by differences in the efficiency of resource utilization as measured by the TFP of various countries and regions of the world.

The differences in development across the various regions and subregions of the world can also be explained in terms of the differing sociocultural and political differences that exist among these regions. The influence of culture and religion on economic development cannot be overlooked. It has been argued, for example, that regions of Europe and North America where religion and culture are based on the Protestant ethic have acieved more rapid economic growth and development relative to other regions. This has been viewed as due to the so-called *Protestant work ethic* which is conducive to free-enterprise, disciplined work effort, and the use of well-functioning social institutions to foster economic activities.

Whether or not this thinking is correct, experiences in various parts of the globe seem to indicate strongly that cultural and religious norms and values do have significant effects on achievement or lack of achievement of economic development in societies. Some cultures and religions tend to place greater emphasis on material achievement than others, and this would undoubtedly shape the amount of stress placed on individual economic aspirations, desires, plans, and goals. Moreover, observance of certain cultural norms and values tend to shape and influence the attitudes and approaches to work as well as the acquisition and maintenance of property in a society. The pace of production and accumulation of wealth between different societies would therefore vary according to their sociocultural differences.

Nor can we overlook the roles of geographical and climatic differences across different world regions and subregions in explaining uneven development. There is no doubt that the harshness and unconducive climate of Sub-Saharan Africa constrains development in that region. Without doubt, too, extreme heat negatively affects development in Asian countries.

The evidence of uneven development across the various regions of the world is depicted in Table 2.5. It shows the 1990 *Human Development Index* (HDI) for selected countries ranked as high income (developed), low income (less developed), and least income (least developed).[7] These countries are drawn from the various continents. Canada (North America), Japan (Australasia), the United States (North America), the United Kingdom (Europe), and South Korea (East Asia) rank first, second, third, fourth, and fifth, respectively, in terms of having the highest HDI. Guinea (Africa), Chad (Africa), Bangladesh (South Asia), Cameroon (Africa), and Vietnam (South Asia), respectively, rank as the countries with the lowest HDI. Overall, it is seen that while poverty pervades the regions of Africa, South America, and South Asia, the regions of Europe, North America, East Asia, and Australasia continue to experience relative economic growth and development. This is the present situation in the world's profile of development and underdevelopment.

Current *World Tables* from the suggest that only about 0.2 percent of the population of the developed countries live in poverty, while nearly 39 percent of the population of all LDCs together live in poverty. A further breakdown among the LDCs indicates that the percentages living in poverty are as follows: 51 in Sub-Saharan Africa, 47 in South Asia (59 in Southeast Asia), 27 in China, 18 in Middle East, 14 in South America, and 7 in East Asia.

Table 2.5
Human Development Index for Selected Countries, 1990

Country	HDI	Relative World Ranking	Real GDP per Capita (1980=100)
High Income Countries			
Canada	0.982	1	5051
Japan	0.982	2	5018
United States	0.976	6	5074
United Kingdom	0.962	10	5016
South Korea	0.871	34	4901
Low Income Countries			
United Arab Emirates	0.740	57	5079
Brazil	0.739	59	4851
Cuba	0.732	61	2500
Saudi Arabia	0.687	67	4944
Sri Lanka	0.651	76	2253
Oman	0.598	82	4997
Algeria	0.582	95	3088
Least Income Countries			
Vietnam	0.464	102	1000
Cameroon	0.313	118	1699
Tanzania	0.268	126	557
Bangladesh	0.185	135	820
Chad	0.088	150	582
Guinea	0.050	160	602

Source: UNDP: *Human Development Report* 1992. New York: Oxford University Press, 1992.

About 50 percent of the world's poor are in South Asia, about 17 percent live in Sub-Saharan Africa, another 17 percent or so in East and Southeast Asia, and about 15 percent in Latin America and the Caribbean, and the Middle East. Most of the poor in all regions live in rural areas and urban slums, mostly under crowded conditions.

While occupations among the rural poor are mainly in sharecropping (Asia), landless tenancy (Asia), peasant-level agriculture (Africa), and small-scale land ownership (Africa, Asia, Latin America), most of the urban poor are irregularly employed or unemployed in the *informal sector*, or engage in menial jobs, artisanship, and petty trading and hawking, or shopkeeping. A relatively small percentage are employed wage earners. The majority of the self-employed are small-scale farmers, vendors, artisans, or hired workers who work very long hours.

The LDCs collectively have continued to fare poorly in terms of overall economic performance relative to the developed countries for a considerable length of time now. Table 2.6 gives a list of selected LDCs and shows their performance in the areas of three major economic indicators, namely, per capita income, rate of growth of GDP, and levels of (external) debt overhang (external debt expressed as a percentage of GDP). The figures are dismal. As they are, most of these LDCs do not show promising signs of reversing the trends shown.

Since no single factor is responsible for promoting or retarding economic development, no single policy direction or redirection can be effected to foster the complex processes of development in LDCs. A wide variety of approaches are necessary, both from internal and external sources.

Table 2.6
Economic Performance of Selected LDCs, 1992

Country	Pop. (1991) million	PCI (1991$)	Annual Growth 1965-90	External Debt (% of 1990 GDP)
Argentina	32.7	2790	-0.3	61.7
Brazil	151.4	2940	3.3	22.8
Cameroon	11.9	850	3.0	56.8
Chile	13.4	1940	0.4	73.6
Colombia	32.8	1260	2.3	44.3
Costa Rica	3.1	1850	1.4	69.2
Ivory Coast	2.4	690	0.5	203.9
India	866.5	330	1.9	25.0
Indonesia	181.3	610	4.5	66.4
Kenya	25.0	340	1.9	81.2
Mexico	83.3	3030	2.8	42.1
Morocco	25.7	1030	2.3	97.1
Nigeria	99.0	340	0.1	117.9
Pakistan	115.8	400	2.5	52.1
Sri Lanka	17.2	500	2.9	73.2
Thailand	57.2	1420	4.4	32.6
Turkey	57.3	1780	2.6	46.3

Source: (1) World Bank: *World Development Report*, 1992, (2) *World Population Data Sheet*, Washington D.C., 1992.

Economic development involves people and their human resources components, physical resources of capital and natural resource inputs, technological change and institutional transformation, and the degree of global and international interaction. The following chapters of this book address these issues in various respects.

NOTES

1. Just as the NICs of Asia belong in the North, South Africa, because of the advanced nature of its economy, is considered as belonging in the North as well. However, one may find a few countries in the North that more closely resemble LDCs; Portugal, Turkey, and Albania in Europe are good examples. Although Mexico may geographically be regarded as part of North America, it is not considered as belonging to the Northern economic hemisphere.

2. Although poverty and low incomes are pervasive in the Southern countries, there are also rich and high-income people, even much richer than many in the Northern countries. In the same vein, there are many low-income and poor people in Northern countries. The most appropriate way to view the situation is to reckon that in Northern countries, the majority of the population would be high-income people, while in the South, the majority would be low income. One must avoid the common stereotype about Third World countries: agrarian, peasant, and poor societies; this is generally a false premise.

3. These data exclude many of the Eastern European countries and the former Soviet Union. The World Bank's research data have not started to include these countries yet, but as the pace of reform toward free-market economies quickens, these countries may soon be included in the study of world development data.

4. The OECD was originally formed under a 1960 Paris Convention by the Western European countries of Austria, Belgium, Denmark, France, Germany, Greece, Ireland, Italy, Luxembourg, the Netherlands, Norway, Portugal, Spain, Sweden, Switzerland, Turkey, and the United Kingdom; the North American countries of the United States of America and Canada; and Iceland. Japan joined in 1964; Finland in 1969; Australia in 1971; New Zealand in 1973; and Mexico in 1994.

5. Summers and Heston (1990).

6. TFP may be defined as the difference between the growth in total factor input and the growth in output. For example, assuming real GDP increases of 5 percent due to a total resource input increase of 3.5 percent, then subtracting the 3.5 percent increase in total resource input from the 5 percent increase in real GDP yields 1.5 percent growth attributable to TFP. In other words, of the 5 percent increase in real GDP, 3.5 percent is attributable to increases in resources, and 1.5 percent is the result of factor productivity: a measure of the *efficiency* of resource utilization.

7. The HDI gives a broad perspective on a country's overall state of development, especially the effects of the pace of development on the population's general *quality of life*. See Chapter 1 for an explanation of the meaning, interpretation, and use of the HDI measurement.

3

History of Economic Development and Underdevelopment

This chapter deals with the major practical issues surrounding economic development and underdevelopment in the less developed countries (LDCs): Africa, Asia, and Latin America and the Caribbean. The relatively slow momentum of economic development in LDCs over the past fifty years has remained a source of concern to development economists and international development experts. Much of the concern has focused on why the development efforts and initiatives in most LDCs have not seemed to yield the expected fruits. As seen in Chapter 2, the LDCs have continued to perform poorly in terms of most development indices. GDP per capita in most LDCs fell between 3 percent (for Latin America) and 15 percent (for Sub-Saharan Africa) between 1970 and 1990. In particular, the 1980s witnessed a period of economic decline during which the combination of external factors, domestic economic policy inefficiencies, and political instabilities resulted in protracted cycles of economic underdevelopment in LDCs.

It is important that we clearly understand the historical situation of modern LDCs in order to avoid the unfortunate error of assuming that their past (and indeed their present) might be similar to the experiences of the DCs during their developmental stages. We must realize that present DCs were never *underdeveloped*, although they may have been *undeveloped* (see Chapter 1). Any assumptions to the contrary can only lead to very serious misconceptions and confusion surrounding the entire subject of development versus underdevelopment. Furthermore, such faulty assumptions may mean that we forget that economic development in one region of the globe must necessarily mean (and lead to) economic underdevelopment in another region. That is to say, economic underdevelopment is a necessary byproduct of economic development.

While the process and failure of economic development in LDCs has been the subject of extensive research and documentation, the major natural, physical, environmental, and socioeconomic and cultural factors that have contributed to perpetuate underdevelopment in LDCs have been copiously and elaborately documented.[1] Most of these diagnoses have been illuminating and insightful, promoting a clearer understanding of the extent and complexity of underdevelopment. However, the fact remains that most LDCs, especially those of Sub-Saharan Africa and South Asia, have continued to face "a crisis of exceptional proportions and persistence" in the search for sustainable economic development (Adedeji, 1989a).

Despite the existence of several common features among LDCs, there are great diversities in their national circumstances and experiences. This is also true of the DCs. Before the Industrial Revolution, for example, there were great differences between societies. England had a free labor environment in which laborers were free to change jobs and migrate to various areas and regions of the country. Banking and commerce developed significantly, and the free market mechanism had grown to a remarkable level of sophistication. By contrast, mid-nineteenth-century Russia was a feudal society. Most serfs and peasants were tied to their lords, and commerce, industry, transportation, and other infrastructure were still undeveloped.

In the regions of Africa, Asia, and Latin America, sociocultural and political experiences were much more diverse than those of Europe. Thriving nation-states had flourished in many parts of Sub-Saharan Africa, while other parts had remained autonomous entities with lively economic structures. In Asia, powerful self-governing empires had been established in China and Japan for more than a hundred years. These had functioned as single, unified political entities rather than collections of ethnically distinct tribal regions. Latin America's history took a somewhat different course. Indigenous peoples were subjected to foreign rule, and the type and pace of immigration into the region became the principal factors that shaped the region's development future.

Beginning with an account of the historical background, this chapter deals with the development effort in LDCs with a view to highlighting the peculiar circumstances that may have contributed to their states of underdevelopment. It gives a detailed economic analysis of the issues that impinge on the perpetual dormancy of the LDCs' economic development, and analyzes the various factors and circumstances surrounding the prospects for developmental achievements in the LDCs in the coming decades.

HISTORY OF ECONOMIC DEVELOPMENT OF DEVELOPED COUNTRIES

The presently developed countries of Europe, North America, and Australasia achieved economic development by following the course of the classical paradigm of comparative (cost) advantage and "trade as the engine of growth." International trade made tremendous contributions to the development of the DCs in the nineteenth and twentieth centuries. Trade facilitated the international division of labor, which enabled countries to specialize and to export those products that it had comparative advantage in producing (cheaply) in exchange for the relatively cheaper produce of others. In this way, output expanded, productivities increased, and incomes rose; and the greater the volume of output, the greater was the rate of growth of income and of economic growth. Savings and investment expanded, and the potential for growth rose even further. This process gave rise to the "takeoff" into self-sustained growth and development.

The development efforts in the present DCs during the eighteen and nineteenth centuries were basically fostered by the direct benefits and the indirect, dynamic, and potential benefits of international trade. A few examples can be enumerated. International trade readily provided nineteenth- and early twentieth-century "developing" countries with the material means (financial capital, machinery and equipment, semi-finished goods, and raw materials) indispensable for economic development. It also served as a vehicle for disseminating technological and managerial know-how, ideas, skills, and entrepreneurship. Above all, international trade created a condition of healthy competition that was needed to maintain an efficiently performing industrial productive network.

The Industrial Revolution was ongoing in Britain in the eighteenth century. The development of the steam engine, the exploration and effective exploitation of coal, coupled with the eruption of a booming textile industry that made effective use of wool and cotton, had all combined to propel Britain onto the route to massive industrialization. Flourishing trade in manufactures and complementary industrial establishments in continental Europe (Germany, Italy, France, and the Scandinavian region) heralded the advent of the take off into self-sustained economic growth and development in Europe.

Studies by O'Brien (1982) indicate that the economic development of Europe, particularly Britain (as the pioneer of the economic revolution) was greatly aided by the exploitation of resources from (colonial) Africa, Asia, and the West Indies.[2] For Europe in general, the cheaper production opportunities afforded by the colonial region, which depended on African slave labor, resulted in massive surpluses for European entrepreneurs, and ensured and sustained a higher rate of economic growth than would have prevailed otherwise. Sheridan (1973) found that the colonial export economies in the West Indies played a major role in Britain's economic growth and development. Moreover, the British growth process specifically involved the diversion of capital and labor from domestic agriculture (an activity that was subject to diminishing returns) and conspicuous consumption, into the Atlantic empire trade where they yielded massive increasing returns.

Inikori (1989) states that the slave trade and the slave plantation system made enormous contributions to Europe's economic development. Darity (1990) stresses that the development of the cotton textile industry in eighteenth-century England, a development that is so closely identified with the Industrial Revolution, was fueled by the export trade that provided fabrics to purchase slaves on the African coast and clothing for the slaves on the plantations. In the seventeenth century, English manufacturers already were shipping brass, amber, blankets, bells, beads, cloth, carpets, pistols, gunpowder, silk, hats, knives, beef, bread, butter, sugar, medicines, and liquor to Africa, to be exchanged for African produce. However, as slavery intensified, woollen textiles came heavily into play in exchange for slaves (Darity, 1992).

The growth of Manchester, which was England's first great manufacturing center, was intimately linked to Liverpool slavers' requirements for exports to Africa to obtain slaves. Williams (1966) emphasizes that Manchester, to the extent that it not only made cotton textiles for export to the slave coast and to the plantations, but also imported raw cotton from the Americas, received a "double stimulus" in propelling economic development. The West Indies in this "double stimulus" served as an important outlet for English manufacturers, especially for English iron mongers who produced and supplied not only the tools and implements for the plantation farms but also the chains used in the slave trade (Inikori, 1989).

Bristol, the second largest slave port in Britain, was also the site of a major shipbuilding industry whose development also depended on the trade to Africa. Kea (1971) suggests that the growth of Birmingham is also closely linked to the slave trade to the extent that Birmingham's firearms featured strongly among the array of goods traded for African slaves.[3] Metcalf's (1987) study indicates that guns and gunpowder constituted 10 to 30 percent of the value of cargoes exchanged for slaves. Between 1.6 million and 2 million firearms were shipped to West Africa around the period 1796-1805 alone.

Japan, after the restoration of the Meiji dynasty, became the classic case of industrialization and economic development within a capitalist world system. It has often been wondered why a resource-deficient island-country such as Japan was able to industrialize so quickly by the end of the nineteenth century, while other resource-rich countries such as those of Latin America, or Russia, were not able to do so. The answer is that Japan effectively utilized and highly benefited from the potentials of international trade as an "engine of economic growth." Under the Tokugawa and Meiji dynasties, the country was never conquered, nor was it colonized, or turned into a *satellite* enclave of some *metropolis or center* power. Therefore, Japan's development was not structurally hampered and limited as was that of, say, Latin America. Japan freely and forcefully exported raw silk and relied on its agricultural sector (led by silk) to achieve self-sustained growth and development.

The discovery and development of the so-called new world of North America represented a classic success of trade as a vehicle for the transmission of capital as well as for the transmission and application of technological know-how. The United States of America utilized the potentials provided by locomotive transportation, grain and cereal, as well as plantation agriculture under massive exploitation of slave labor. Canada relied on wheat, grain, forestry products, and mineral resources. International transfer of capital and technology from Europe was greatly put to great advantage in these cases. Thus, Europe and North America complemented each other, and their respective developments were fostered. Australia, New Zealand, South Africa, Israel, and Cyprus, in the course of their respective developments all followed and benefited from this trend.

But the development potential and the development trends that international trade possessed and so generously spread across the then "developing" world were to evaporate greatly by the turn of the twentieth century. By this time colonialism and expansionism had accelerated among the countries of continental Europe. International trade was being transformed from an "engine of growth" for any society into a "weapon of exploitation" against some societies.

The Industrial Revolution transformed England's economy by the late eighteenth , whereas other nations in Europe and North America caught on by the middle of the nineteenth century. Toward the end of the nineteenth century, Japan, the first non-European population to achieve massive economic advancement, had begun to industrialize rapidly. The two world wars and the Great Depression only interrupted and rather delayed the spread of economic development from the pioneers to the other parts of the world.

HISTORY OF ECONOMIC DEVELOPMENT IN LESS DEVELOPED COUNTRIES

Economic development essentially comprises some degree of continuous evolutionary changes in the economic, social, political, and institutional fabric of societies. To the extent that this definition is applicable, it can be said that most LDCs in Africa, Asia, and Latin America have not really experienced economic development.

Taking lessons from history, we can examine the processes of development in the Western DCs between the seventeenth and twentieth centuries. Western development was faced with the need for change in the social structure in order to accommodate the progress-oriented middle class, who were the leaders of society. In many instances this change often involved violent struggles for supremacy between the old socioeconomic order and the emerging new one. The English Revolution of 1640 that ended with the Supremacy of Parliament Act in 1688 replaced the feudal lords with the landed gentry and the urban middle class as the dominant classes in England, thereby preparing the way for the later economic changes that ushered in Industrial Revolution. Similarly, the French Revolution of 1789 replaced the old aristocracy with the new middle class.

Today's LDCs lack the type of changes that precondition economic development. Their historical circumstances account for this lack. Stagnation brought about by a mix of external and internal forces has kept LDCs from sufficiently preparing the ground for economic development. This stagnation may have been largely generated by the same historical processes that launched the DCs onto their development threshholds. The evidence indicates that the forcible incorporation of African and Latin American countries into the world capitalist order has resulted in pervasive underdevelopment for these societies. That is, the hierarchical relations between the First World (DCs) and the Third World (LDCs) prevented the effective possibility of sustained capitalist development for the Third World. And as can be seen, it is not surprising that the most underdeveloped societies today are those that had the strongest ties in the past with one or more DCs (notably, Africa and Latin America), while the strongest *developing* regions today are those that had looser or no ties with the DCs (China and east Asia).

In the seventeenth century, Asia and Africa were not significantly less developed than Europe. But between this period and the mid-twentieth century, during which European countries colonized Africa and the Indian subcontinent, the ratio between European per capita income, on the one hand, and the African and Asian per capita incomes, on the other, increased immensely as indicated in the studies of Darity (1982, 1990), Dutt (1992), Rodney (1972), and Williams (1966). The relative stagnation of these underdeveloped regions is largely attributable to colonialism, for India and other continental Asia, and to slavery and colonial domination, for Africa.[4]

History of Economic Development in Latin America

The economic history of Latin America is unique in some sense. Political independence in most of the countries of the region was achieved in the early nineteenth century, unlike the countries of Africa and Asia where independence were post-World War II experiences. Upon the arrival of the European colonizers, the local populations of the region were suppressed and enslaved. As the colonial plantations and industries grew and required more labor, the voluntary immigration of more Europeans was encouraged, complemented by the forced immigration of African slaves. Spanish and Portuguese immigrants, who were from areas that were still the most economically backward parts of Europe, dominated and ruled the various countries of the region until the late 1880s. They apparently transplanted the feudal value structures that existed in their parts of Europe to the new world of South America. The indigenous native population was ignored and bypassed, but they continued to survive in varying concentrations across the continent. For example, Peru, Bolivia, and Mexico maintained large indigenous populations, but the native peoples of Argentina almost disappeared in the surge of the largely European immigrant onslaught.

Most Latin American and Caribbean countries who suffer from underdevelopment have economic and social histories that gave rise to their present status as LDCs. Spanish and Portuguese colonizers overran these regions and established a center-periphery colonial relationship. In his expansive case studies of the economic and social histories of the region, Frank (1967, 1969) shows that Latin America's present underdevelopment is the result of the region's centuries-long exploitative participation in world capitalist development.

Frank argues that the conquest and colonization of Chile, for example, not only incorporated the country fully into expansion and development of the world mercantile and industrial capitalist system, but also introduced the monopolistic center-periphery structure into the Chilean domestic economy and society itself. This has only resulted in increased polarization of the country's domestic economy.

For Brazil, the result has been a clearer and more devastating case of national and regional *development of underdevelopment*. The expansion of the world economy since the sixteenth century successively converted the Northeast, the Minas Gerais interior, the North, and the Center-South (Rio de Janeiro, Sao Paulo, and Parana triangle) into exclusively export economies. Despite what may have appeared to be economic development during these regions' transitory booming period, what really occurred was a spate of what Frank termed *satellite development*, which was neither self-generating nor self-perpetuating. As the markets and productivity of these regions declined (following any major recessions in the center), foreign and domestic economic interests in them declined as well, and they were left to *develop the underdevelopment* they are in today.

By the time of the First World War and through the Great Depression, Brazil began to industrialize Sao Paulo into the largest Latin American industrial enclave that it still is at present. However, this industrial development has not been able to break Brazil's cycle of (satellite) underdevelopment. Rather, the regional industrialization seemed to have only converted the other regions of Brazil into internal colonies, decapitalizing them further and deepening their underdevelopment.

One of the strongest hypotheses on the underdevelopment of Latin America is that the traces of relative economic development that have occurred in Latin America appear to have taken place when the ties between the countries in the region and the Western DCs were weakest. Latin America's periods of temporary isolation from the Western DCs appear to have been the only times when the region achieved appreciable economic growth. Five such instances were the European (especially Spanish) Depression of the seventeenth century, the Napoleonic Wars, the First World War, the 1930s Depression, and the Second World War. Historical studies reveal that during Europe's seventeenth-century Depression, manufacturing grew strongly in the Latin American countries, and several of them (such as Chile) became exporters of manufactured goods, while the period of the Napoleonic Wars gave rise to independence movements in Latin America.

The most important recent industrial development of Argentina, Brazil, Mexico, and Chile took place precisely during the periods of the two World Wars and the Depression. During these periods, a consequent loosening of trade and investment ties took place, and the satellite regions could then initiate requisite autonomous industrialization and growth. Moreover, it was the geographic and economic isolation of regions, which at one time were relatively poorly integrated and weakly tied to the Western system, that initiated the most promising self-generating economic development. Examples include Tucuman and Asuncion in Chile, as well as Mendoza and Rosario in Argentina and Paraguay during the late eighteenth and early nineteenth centuries. Antioquia in Colombia, and Puebla and Queretaro in Mexico are other examples. All of these regions became manufacturing centers and exporters of textiles.

History of Economic Development in Asia

Asia's marked diversities in cultural and political settings provide ample reasons why the countries in the region experienced vastly different development histories. As mentioned earlier, powerful self-governing empires had been established in China and Japan for more than a century, and functioned as single, unified political entities rather than collections of ethnically distinct tribal regions. Furthermore, China and Japan also had developed high levels of urbanization and commerce. They shared Confucian values which emphasized the importance of self-discipline, selfless service, and education.

Decades of comparative social stability had contributed to massive population increases in the region, resulting in severe shortages of arable land relative to the population. This problem still exists in most parts of Asia today. In East Asia, however, because of the relatively high level of development, especially in commerce, foreign (European and American) merchants were never able to break into the economic activities of this region.

South Asia's development history is sharply different from East Asia's. The British had colonized the Indian subcontinent by the turn of the century, ruling a vastly populated area that included the present-day countries of India, Pakistan, and Bangladesh. The British were compelled to train large numbers of Indians for entrepreneurship and industry. At the time of its 1948 political independence from Britain, Indians were in charge of running much of their own economic and political affairs. The experience was different in Indonesia, which experienced more economic and political devastation from colonial domination. All parts of South Asia have continued to remain underdeveloped, a situation that is in marked contrast to neighboring East Asia.

The Asian experience is perhaps one of the striking examples of the crucial roles of social and political stability in promoting economic development. A stable social and political climate is necessary for the establishment of economic enterprises. Civil wars, guerrilla warfares, insurrections, invasions or threats of invasions by hostile forces, and social unrests not only deter domestic entrepreneurships and investment, but they also jeopardize the inflow of foreign investment while encouraging the flight of capital from the country. It is widely believed that it was the prolonged instability arising from civil wars and foreign invasion that inhibited China's attainment of takeoff into economic development until the early 1950s. Vietnam and Cambodia have also been severely devastated by raging civil wars and domestic insecurity. Furthermore, the Japanese invasion and colonization of Korea is believed to have retarded development there.

History of Economic Development in Africa

Precolonial Africa achieved and maintained its own level of "development" (relatively speaking) by the turn of the seventeenth 17th century. Their economies were based on primary production activities (such as agriculture -- farming, fishing, hunting, and animal husbandry -- and handicraft). Surpluses were produced as markets developed for the exchange of food crops, livestock, farm equipment, and precious metals (Oliver and Fage, 1988). Trade also developed over great distances, for not only were gold and ivory from Western Africa traded internationally as early as the eighth century, but also spices and tropical products were traded between Eastern Africa and the Middle East during the Middle Ages (Neumark, 1977). During this time, gold, salt, and slaves were exclusively the items of trade along the trans-Saharan caravan routes connecting Sub-Saharan Africa (especially Western Africa) with Northern Africa. Clearly, Sub-Saharan African economies were interdependent and operated long-distance lucrative trade long before the intrusion of European adventurism in the fifteenth century.

Foreign technological transfers and exchanges occurred through associations with Muslim scholars who were employed in the courts of such emperors as Mansa Musa of Mali and Askia Mohammed of Songhai (Oliver and Fage, 1988). Precolonial contacts with the international economy beyond the continental borders of Africa had already developed in Eastern Africa through trade along the perimeter of the Indian Ocean with Asia and the Middle East. Austen (1987) reports that some of the earliest occurrence of this trade had taken place as early as A.D. 150, in commodities such as ivory, iron, gold, and mangrove tree poles for house construction.

Although precolonial industrial development in Africa may not be at the same level as today's, historical studies indicate that such major civilizations as the Kingdoms of Ghana (fifteenth century), Mali (sixteenth century), and Songhai (seventeenth century), were contemporaneous with the pre- and post-Norman conquest of Britain. Clearly, as has been forcefully argued by Darity (1992), the main factor that constrained Africa's development was colonization and its associated act of slave trade. European countries' need for industrial raw materials, markets, prestige, and prevention of domestic social unrest presented by the unemployment of their growing populations, combined to produce a calculated and carefully executed series of plans and events which culminated in the forcible acquisition and colonization of Africa. Increasing need for industrial raw materials and the need for cheap labor led to the slave trade, which was executed and defended militarily. By the sixteenth and seventeenth centuries, the gold trade with the Portuguese, Dutch, British, and Danish, along the West African coastline, had reached its peak. It declined only because of the increase in the demand for slaves, which expanded with the development of European-owned sugar plantations (in the new world) later in the 1800s.

When the slave trade could no longer be profitably continued owing to its immoral nature, and was abolished, the more expanded commodity trade that succeeded it led to even more expeditious explorations of the African hinterland. Both governmental and religious organizations vigorously engaged in these activities, *albeit* their fundamental objectives was to prolong the economic and political exploitation of the region. By the early sixteenth century, the Portuguese tried to gain control of the Indian Ocean trade along the coasts of East Africa. By the nineteenth century, manufactured goods from Britain, France, and the United States were being traded as far south as Mozambique through Zanzibar in exchange for ivory, resins, cloves, and other "legitimate" products.

The partition of Africa among European countries occurred during the late 1800s. Thus, the economic development policy of colonial Africa was one of commercialization. European currencies became the media of exchange. To obtain these currencies for the purchase of cheap manufactured goods that flooded the African market, Africans had to engage in economic activities that would give them the necessary medium of exchange, namely, produce agricultural and industrial raw materials (see Ezeala-Harrison, 1995d).

Colonization was more of an economic than a political undertaking.[5] It was intended simply to oversee the continuous and uninhibited massive transfer of resources (raw materials and profits) from the African colony (the periphery) to the European metropolis (the center). As a result, at the time of independence, African economies had become strongly dependent, producing what they neither ate nor processed (cash crops, such as coffee, cocoa, tea, cotton, peanuts, and rubber for export) and consuming what they could not produce (industrial manufactured goods). The cultivation of these export crops rendered many Africans exclusively dependent on the cash economy, thereby prematurely alienating them from their self-sufficient peasant modes of living. They remained smallholder land croppers or low-wage earning employees of plantation farms.

The colonizers also became settlers in parts of the continent where the climate and environmental conditions were favorable. They selected the best, most fertile land, particularly in Eastern, Central, and Southern parts of Africa, and established their own farms and plantations. They also explored the mines of these areas. These enterprises utilized cheap African labor. Young men migrated from their enclaves to supply labor to these enterprises at very low wages. Rhodesia and South Africa immediately come to mind in this regard. Forced labor was not uncommon, for it was often demanded by colonial governments to build roads, railroads, and bridges to connect the interiors in order to facilitate the movement of produce. In these circumstances, there could be no possibility for savings and investment for long-term development of the local economies.

The most injurious economic effects of the slave trade were the loss of an enormous source of productive human labor and its adverse population redistribution in the continent. It also caused civil disruption and social and economic upheaval. The mass destruction of human and animal lives during the *slave-raids* seriously affected agriculture. The devastation was so great that when the Industrial Revolution in Europe ushered in a new era of opportunity for Africans to benefit from the "legitimate" trade in raw materials needed for European industry, Africa was ill-prepared to cash in on the "boom."

Colonialism negatively affected production, distribution, consumption, and savings and investment aspirations in Africa. Colonies provided "captive consumers"; many of the resulting center-periphery trade arrangements and special trade preferences still remain strong today. African workers entered the cash economy and "got hooked" on imported (European) consumer luxuries. Distribution suffered because transportation was merely developed to cater for the movement of produce to the seaports for export to Europe; the countries of the continent were not at all connected and integrated. Again this is a pattern that persists today and continues to constrain African countries from implementing smooth regional economic integration.

According to the colonial administration system, the home government at the center made the colonial administrators responsible for their own budget financing in each colony. This meant that colonial administrations had to find sources of revenue, and so it was that various forms of taxation were exacted on Africans, the surplus budgets of which were often repatriated to the metropolis (Rodney, 1972).

According to Inikori's (1992) estimates, Africa lost about 300 years of economic growth and development as a direct result of slavery and colonization. The export slave trade deprived it of a general industrial stimulus. These wanton acts of impoverishment perpetrated and imposed on Africa by its current external mentors led to the continent's disposition to comparative economic backwardness. Darity (1992) terms this the "original sin" which began the partition between the rich and the poor regions of the world.

Africa did receive some benefits from colonization, nonetheless, *albeit* at a very high price. Some development did take place, but it was mainly peripheral to Europe's growth and development. For only as it became apparent that the colonies would fight for independence did the colonizers begin to guide some of them toward developing their own local economies. In so doing, a few domestic industries were established.[6] However, the African economies still in concentrated on the production of primary produce for export. By the 1960s, most colonial administrations were being rapidly dismantled across Africa, although many economic (and in many cases political) ties to the former colonial powers remained strong -- hence, the continuation, to-date, of the *satellite* nature of African economies.

Postindependence Economic Development in Africa

One key postcolonial economic legacy was the formulation of long-term development plans for most African countries which covered time spans of three to seven years, and the practise is rife today. The objectives were to promote rapid economic growth and development through industrialization and agricultural development. The rallying cry was that once independence was achieved and the colonial powers left the countries, rapid prosperity would be imminent.

Most African countries followed the achievement of independence with elaborate and ambitious plans for rapid economic development (Green, 1967; Waterston, 1965). National Development Plans were formulated and implemented in Nigeria, Ghana, Kenya, Tanzania, Ethiopia, Zambia, and Uganda; some of these plans had target growth rates of 9 to 10 percent every year in real terms and a 6 percent annual per capita income growth. The days following independence were full of optimism that the plans would succeed.

In order to promote greater equity in income distribution as well as quicken the pace of economic growth, most African countries resorted to central planning in the belief that greater government intervention and control were necessary for the pursuit and closer supervision of the national development strategies. Moreover, it was thought that central planning had yielded appreciable results in the Soviet Union. China's model of socialist planning was also attractive. Most African countries therefore established regulatory controls and institutionalized monopolies. The political elite in Africa at the time, with little or no vested interest yet in supporting large-scale capitalist enterprises, emphasized the role of the state rather than corporate business in the economy.

Marketing Boards (statutory monopolies that buy cash crops from domestic producers for export) were established and used as mechanisms whereby governments could effectively tax agricultural producers. State-owned industrial projects were established under tariff protection. Foreign investment was discouraged and subjected to controls in bids to "indigenize" the economy, as many foreign-owned enterprises were nationalized. Many African countries introduced market price controls and fixed exchange rate regimes for their national currencies.

Many of these initial development efforts, however, failed to bring about the desired results. For one, Africa lacked the infrastructure and capital resources; any physical infrastructure left from the colonial era was minimal and was designed mainly to produce and export primary commodities to Europe and to support the colonial administration. Thus, the newly independent country had to build new road systems, water supply, electricity, post and telecommunication networks, and the like.

Appropriate educational and training systems had to be designed to develop the human resources in a society with not only a very low literacy level but also where the existing educational system was irrelevant to the peculiar needs of the economy. Besides the lack of an educated, skilled labor force, few indigenous

Africans had been trained in management and public administration as well as in practical aspects of running a government or a large-scale business enterprise.

The economic structures of most African countries have always been unique. On achievement of independence, most African economies were largely agrarian. This characteristic has continued, and more recent data indicate that not only are about 70 percent of the African population rurally based, but also over 65 percent of the African labor force engage in rural agriculture for livelihood, compared with under 7 percent in developed countries.

African development policymakers of the time, however, strongly believed that industrialization was the best strategy to achieve economic development. Agricultural development was seen rather as a complement to industrialization, and thus the agricultural sector was not given as much attention and was not emphasized in many development plans.

The first attempts were to set up import-substitution industries to produce previously imported manufactured goods. The economic benefits of these industries were obviously enormous: the creation of jobs, a domestic ready-market demand for locally produced raw materials, and the saving of foreign exchange. Unfortunately, there were significant bottlenecks. Most countries ended up spending huge foreign exchange to import the necessary capital equipment for these industries, many of which came to be dependent on imported raw materials as domestic sources proved inadequate. Moreover, the market demand for the industries' produce was limited in the face of the low-income character of the general population. Consequently, the industrialization effort proved disappointing as the countries came to be saddled with balance-of-payments problems and broken-down, fragmented industrial base.

The main economic damage that was brought upon African countries as a result of the apparently misguided industrial pursuit was the failure of the agricultural sectors. The industrialization drive stimulated rural-urban migration in search of urban industrial jobs, many of which were low-paying and usually insufficient to absorb the migrants. The agricultural sector therefore suffered severe manpower losses, food production declined, and the African food crisis began.

As African countries came to realize their mistakes and make amends in their second and third phases of development plans (1970s and 1980s), attempts were rife to recognize the problems in the agricultural sector and invest heavily in it. However, by this time the African economies had become "dependent" economies: they were still tied to their former colonial powers through as preferential trade agreements, foreign investment, bilateral aid, educational and technological transfers, and military aid. This dependency ensured that African exports would continue to be primary produce, while both the import and export trade would still be largely (if not exclusively) with the former colonial powers.[7]

By the late 1980s, most African economies were still monocultural. That is, their economies relied mainly on a single commodity production to generate national revenue and foreign exchange. *World Development Report* data indicate that by 1986 Nigeria depended on crude petroleum for 90 percent of export revenues; Zambia, 88 percent on copper; Congo, 89 percent on crude petroleum; Ghana, 66 percent on cocoa; Chad, 70 percent on cotton; Uganda, 95 percent on coffee; Burundi, 84 percent on coffee; and Guinea, 91 percent on ores. This situation rendered Sub-Saharan African economies vulnerable to capricious events in the international commodity markets. As the prices of these unprocessed materials fluctuated (and mostly declined over time in a highly industrialized external world), African countries found that they had to export more to receive the same or lesser revenues to maintain needed imports.

Simply put, economic underdevelopment in Africa has been labeled "overstretched" in reference to its quasi-permanent feature (Ezeala-Harrison, 1995). Prospects for the future are bleak. Controversy surrounds the direction that renewed development efforts should take.

In a bid to reverse the cycle of economic decline, many African countries have undertaken structural adjustment economic reform programs since the mid-1980s as a necessary step in search of sustainable poverty-reducing growth. Self-reliant development has been the favorite theme of African leaders. However, despite a few signs of improvement in some countries, economic performance for the region as a whole has remained dismal and disappointing. In fact, many countries have continued to suffer economic declines.

THE STALLED TAKEOFF INTO ECONOMIC DEVELOPMENT IN LDCs

Economic development failure in LDCs has continued to be widely studied and documented. Any credible efforts made to achieve economic takeoff in most LDCs can only be said to, at best, have been stalled. Sustained development must imply a development process whereby real per capita income is rising over time without being interrupted by periods of incessant or prolonged adversities such as high unemployment, inflation, balance-of-payments crisis, or huge external indebtedness. No LDC can be said to have, in the least, achieved this necessary growth aspect of economic development.

The deterioration in the LDCs' economic performance in recent years can be traced to two fronts: external versus internal factors. The external factors that are identified include the colonial legacy of poor skill and educational preparation of the population, the impact of the international energy crises of the 1970s, the effect of natural disasters such as droughts and famines, and the ever present declining terms-of-trade that primary product exporters face. The domestic factors are notably the poor domestic economic policies, political ineptitude and instability, and *human factor* depravity (Ezeala-Harrison, 1995d).

In this section, we explore the key sectoral indicators with a view to examining how they were developed in the course of the bid to achieve economic growth and development in LDCs. The sectoral indicators discussed here are those that are generally recognized as most crucial in the LDCs' development.

Human Resources and Rural Development

For most LDCs, the colonial legacies in education have been very dismal indeed. The education systems in most LDCs, being direct transplants of the systems of the colonial rulers of the region, and thus designed with the overriding goal to prepare students to pass standard "qualifying" examinations (apparently judged adequate for clerical and administrative services in colonial governments), have a strong urban orientation. The curricula largely neglect the priority needs of the students, namely, the need to live and work in rural and communal settings. Nor do the educational systems make provisions for accommodating major groups with important rural links and rural training needs, namely, members of the peasant subsistence sector, women and female youths from poorer rural communities, and out-of-school youths. Thus, the educational systems that most LDCs inherited from their *colonizers* failed to successfully fit their graduates for the peculiar needs of their regions' social and economic development.

Formal education in most LDCs has rather succeeded mainly in arming the educated with values, ideas, attitudes, and aspirations that are largely inimical to the larger societies' development interests, to the extent that "they are educated away" from the peculiar needs of their economic, social, and political environments. The rural sectors in most LDCs do not have effective demand for large numbers of educated workers. This is mainly because of the still underdeveloped level of agriculture. Therefore, many of the educated persons simply end up being dislocated in the sector. It will require a tremendous amount of time and complementary physical capital resources to raise the sectors' limited absorptive capacity for educated persons. What the rural (agricultural) sector needs is the quality of labor that would allow the use of more modern techniques (equipment, seeds, insecticides, etc.). Clearly, the education required to fulfill this need is not the academic-diploma type that dominates educational programs in most LDCs today.

Where it offers effective productive skills, education in LDCs is oriented almost entirely toward preparation for work in the urban sector of the society and fails to sufficiently prepare people for aspirations in the rural (agricultural) segment, thereby greatly distorting the aspirations of the individual away from the needs of the rural sector. Many LDCs abound with university graduates (some of whom possess "first-class honors") in areas such as mathematics, English, physics, political science, or chemistry, yet employers might be seeking workers skilled in areas such as air conditioning and refrigeration services, cotton-wax printing, plumbing maintenance, or even automotive technician services. Employers must then rely on apprenticeship and on-the-job training to obtain the required workforce -- a time-consuming and costly alternative for both parties, while the graduates remain unemployed in the urban areas.

For most LDCs, and especially those of Africa and South Asia, the extent of their social and economic development is inextricably linked to the extent of their rural development. Rural development encompasses a broader perspective: it reflects the major transformations of social and economic structures, processes, relationships, and institutions in the rural sectors. It reflects the measures to enhance more equitable distribution of income to promote higher levels of living in the rural sector: the creation of more productive employment opportunities, not only in agriculture, but also in social infrastructure such as health, housing, nutrition, and utilities. In addition, and more importantly, these measures must be complementary to agricultural development, as the agricultural sector occupies the largest economic segment of these societies. Unfortunately, however, the past few decades have witnessed the focusing of most priority projects of modernization and development on the urban sectors of most LDCs, to the detriment of the rural sectors.

The Diploma Disease in LDCs

The perennial problem of unemployment of educated people in developing countries has been is termed the diploma disease. LDCs spend substantial portions of their national investment resources on formal education, but after nearly a half-century of rapidly pursuing educational expansion with billions of dollars of educational expenditure, massive unemployment and underemployment of the educated have chronically characterized most underdeveloped countries. The benefits of concerted efforts to expand formal education in developing countries should not be underemphasized. Potential benefits include many of the traditional claims made on behalf of unfettered expansion of educational opportunities: that it would raise living standards and offer unrestricted avenues for the poor to improve their social and economic status, that it would offer equal opportunities to all, and thus serve as a means of achieving a more egalitarian society, and that it would bridge the gaps existing between ethnic and tribal groups in society.

Evidence in many LDCs, however, indicates that the diploma disease has become a major development policy bottleneck. The orientation of the educational drive in LDCs has not been adequate for their employment and productivity needs, as is demonstrated by the existence of the high unemployment rates of educated persons in most LDCs.

In exploring the underlying factors behind this disturbing scenario, one needs an understanding of the peculiar nature and characteristics of the labor markets of LDCs, and of the links (if any) between the needs of the markets and the educational programs and educational infrastructure in society. These prevailing circumstances constitute the legitimate assumptions upon which any effective diagnosis of the diploma disease can be based.

Labor markets in LDCs generally conform to *dualism,* and the dualism also conforms to the observed wide disparities of income among the members of the society: wage-employment in the organized private and public (primary) sector, and wage- and self-employment in the unorganized (secondary) sector (encompassing small-scale informal activities and rural agriculture). Differences in skills among the members of the different segments and differences in technology in the different segments of the labor force only go to widen the disparities further. The workers of the primary segment tend to be more skilled and to engage in capital-intensive activities which require that they be relatively far more trained or "educated." The secondary segment workers undertake casual-type work and require very little capital and virtually no formal education.

For most LDCs, population grows at an average yearly rate of about 2.5 percent. But new entrants into the labor force are absorbed primarily in low-wage employment of the small-scale and informal type. The average household income in the small-scale informal sector (of the secondary segment) has been generally lower than that of the formal (primary) sector, despite the fact that the informal segment has greater access to the services of unpaid apprentices and family workers. The secondary segment of the labor market (rural and urban together) is the largest in terms of employment, but it is also the weakest in terms of productivity and earnings. The bulk of the population is still in agricultural employment at the peasant-subsistence level (engaged in food crops for household consumption and local petty trading) or the commercial (and sometimes wage mployment) level (engaged in cash crops for local distribution and exports).

Within the secondary segment is the urban informal sector which is the next largest employer of labor (to agriculture), notwithstanding the preponderance of underemployment in it. It is very dynamic and adaptable regarding its employment-absorbing capacity. This sector is characterized by relative ease of entry, reliance on indigenous resources, unregulated competitive product markets, flexibility of operation, and the ability to blend well with the society's traditional values and social practices.

The volume of wage employment and the growth in real household incomes have been the greatest, however, for the primary (formal sector) members, namely, the medium-scale to large-scale private and public enterprises, as well as the medium-scale self-employment category. Employment in the primary sector is characterized by relatively higher productivity, higher wages, and lower turnover rates, as the sector is dominated by multinational firms and capital-intensive technology (which explains the relatively high productivity and wage levels).

Entry criteria into the stable primary-sector employment are based principally based on the acquisition of formal education (proven by possession of the requisite credentials). Experience and relevant skills are often stated as important, but they are not given priority in preparations for the job market.

Most employers prefer at least a secondary school education for new recruitment, even for the lowest category manual jobs.

Combined with increasing rural-urban migration and the relatively small size of the primary sector in terms of labor force absorption, a typical underdeveloped country's high rate of population growth has led to a large increase in unemployment and underemployment. Redundancy of agricultural manpower in the secondary sector is a major source of the unemployment problem. Such redundancy has particularly damaging effects on the economy because of the dominance of agricultural occupation in the economy's total employment.

The dual labor market phenomenon presents special challenges for educational programs in LDCs. In most of these countries, the educational evaluation process takes the form of nationwide or subregion-wide examinations that are given at the relevant stage of education to determine the student's preparedness to undertake the subsequent higher levels of education or for employment. Because of the overwhelming importance of these examinations, students and teachers focus their efforts on the task of passing the examinations rather than actual acquisition of knowledge or skill. This system certainly perverts the true purpose of education, not only in the tremendous financial and physical resources entailed, but also in jeopardizing the alternative opportunities to which efforts might have been more fruitfully channeled.

The overall effect of disproportionate investment in formal education in an LDC, especially at the secondary and postsecondary levels, has been the diversion of scarce resources from important socially and economically productive activities in the secondary segment. For example, direct job-creating pursuits in agriculture, handicraft, artisanship, tradesmanship, and the like are forestalled, thereby retarding rather than stimulating contributions to national development from the secondary segment.

These shortcomings are not to be blamed on formal education itself. The problems are due to the mismatch and poor fit between educational curricula and the needs of the employment market in the LDC concerned. They are also due to the failure of African societies to adapt for educational changes to reflect the reality of their circumstances, namely, employment and labor market dualism.

The Demise of Development Initiatives in LDCs

Most LDCs adopted rather impressive looking plans of action toward economic development after independence from colonial rulers. That such steps failed in many cases has continued to baffle many a scholar of international economic development. The fact, however, remains that in pursuing the ambitious development objectives of the postindependence periods, many LDCs embraced policies that were not conducive to growth, and thereby ultimately reduced their flexibility in responding to unpredictable economic shocks that were imminent in a world of unpredictabilities. African and Latin American countries were especially vulnerable in this regard. We examine a few of these and their respective impacts in the demise of their respective development initiatives.

Structural Adjustments, Maladjustments, and Readjustments

Economic development initiatives in most LDCs were heavily based on emphasis on government intervention rather than free-enterprise market forces. However, by the early 1980s it had become evident that those other developing countries (in East Asia, notably) that had effected less economic controls and had their economies rely on the international market forces were experiencing more remarkable economic performances. Nevertheless, most LDCs realized that they had not made the best use of their resources. They had not successfully channelled their resources into producing goods in which they either had (natural) comparative advantage (such as agricultural products or minerals) or in which they had better experience and expertise, and then trade these for goods more efficiently produced elsewhere (as, say, Japan did during the nineteenth century). Generally, they had not been able to align with the fundamental structures of their economies: their economic structures had been maladjusted.

Economic failures in LDCs could therefore be traced to a number of fundamental errors related to their immediate postindependence development posture. From the start, most of the newly independent countries in Africa and South Asia, for instance, possessed only a handful of the requisite management personnel, especially those skilled in government interventionist economic management and planning. Only a few university graduates that trained in medicine, engineering, law, and the natural sciences existed. In African LDCs, the economic advisers of the time who manned the government ministries and institutions were trained in Western economics with heavy emphasis on the efficiency of (competitive) markets. Thus, these countries' planning-led development initiatives had to falter.

The interventionist policies had severe long-term debilitating consequences. In the agricultural cash-crop sector, the marketing boards that passed on very low percentages of the world market prices of the produce to the domestic producers had succeeded only in discouraging private-sector investment in the sector. The governments did not use the accumulated funds to invest in productive activities; instead, it often went for consumption and the establishment of "white elephant" projects. Large parts were also used to finance government recurrent budget deficits, a bit of it was used to finance consumption of foreign conspicuous consumer good imports, and yet another significant portion was corruptly placed in the foreign personal bank accounts of government ministers and other officials.

In Africa, for example, many export marketing boards, far from adding to government revenue, incurred losses that increased government budget deficits. Those marketing boards responsible for domestic foods paid high prices to food producers ostensibly to encourage self-sufficiency in food supply, but they sold the food products at subsidized prices to consumers in urban areas, thereby operating at losses. These policies drove agricultural producers to shift their investments to the domestic market food production and away from the export market cash-crop production.

Exchange rate and import license controls in most LDCs proved unfavorable. High rates of inflation were rife in most of these countries because of huge levels of public-sector (government) spending. Together with fixed exchange rates, the domestic currencies became overvalued, and the official rates could only be maintained by rationing foreign exchange and restricting imports through import licensing. Therefore, foreign exchange black-marketing emerged, and by the mid-1970s the economies of Ghana, Togo, Zambia, Uganda, Mauritania, Sierra Leone, Tanzania, Gambia, and so on, in Africa, were reeling under the effects; Cambodia, Vietnam, Sri Lanka, Burma, and so on, in South Asia, were involved in civil wars and economic decline; while the major countries in Latin America were saddled with runaway inflation and external debt crises.

Overvaluation of the domestic currencies resulted in the reduction of the relative revenues of export crop producers, and this encouraged smuggling. Furthermore, relatively cheaper imports strangled domestic manufacturers. These together contributed to severe adversities in the balance of payments, as the situation was worsened further by the lack of initiatives to implement corrective measures to arrest the situation. Under the weight of the severe hardships emanating from having maladjusted economic structures and diminished prospects for recovery, most LDCs accepted the suggestions for change (reform) being pressed on them by international (creditors) institutions during the 1980s: *structural (re)adjustments*. The group of countries that instituted the most extensive economic reform policies around 1981-1991 did achieve median GDP per capita growth of about 2 percent by 1993, while those that did not adopt the structural adjustment programs had their median GDP growth decline by about 2.6 percent.[8]

The Dutch Disease Syndrome in LDCs

The Dutch disease is a term emanating from the experience of the Netherlands after its 1960s natural-gas discovery, export boom, and balance-of-payments surplus, which promised new prosperity. The result for the Dutch economy during the 1970s was rising inflation, rising unemployment, declining manufacturing exports, and lower income growth rates. The upsurge of oil wealth in the 1970s produced similar paradoxes for many LDCs.[9]

The Dutch disease attacks with massive increases in primary export revenue that result in a temporary appreciation of the exchange rate of the country's currency. The immediate impact is to reduce the world demand for other exports of the country concerned in response to their price increases implicit in the currency appreciation. Since the country is not likely to adjust the nominal exchange rate downward to maintain the previous level, the booming primary export results in domestic inflation in excess of the rest of the world's inflation rate, and this causes profit declines for exporters (as wages and other domestic input prices rise faster -- due to the domestic inflation -- than the world prices of exports). As exporters' profits fall, they produce less for exports, and this will reduce incomes and employment in export industries.

In Indonesia and Nigeria, for example, the booming oil exports and influx of foreign exchange from it created a surplus of foreign currency while driving down the domestic price of foreign exchange. The result, of course, was extraordinary increases in imports, while exports declined. Because the high oil incomes created greater demand for all goods and services in the economy, this demand translated into more imports (whose prices were stable since their prices depend on the entire world market and not solely on Nigerian demand). As a good portion of the oil-boom demands were for domestic nontradable goods (goods such as utilities, transport, construction, food-crops, and staples) which were heavily protected and insulated from external competition, there would be significant increases in the prices of these nontradables, leading to domestic inflation, because there was a limited supply of these nontradables, especially in the beginning years of the boom. One would expect the rising prices of the nontradables to attract more investment from profit-seeking entrepreneurs. This was not realized in the case of domestic agricultural produce because of the vast gap between urban-sector facilities and earnings. In the case of utilities, central control precluded any private-sector enterprises. Residential construction appears to be the only domestic nontradable that benefited.

The Dutch disease paradox afflicted, to varying degrees, the economies of Ivory Coast (Cocoa in the 1980s), Ghana (Cocoa in the 1970s), Zambia (minerals in the 1970s), and Zaire (minerals in the 1970s), in each case of which the export boom not only stimulated more rapid domestic inflation but also caused the country's exchange rate to increase, thereby rendering other exports less competitive and hence less profitable. Although these African LDCs suffered, Indonesia's experience demonstrates a case of an LDC turning its resource windfalls to foster sustained growth and development, though on a limited scale (Glassburner, 1988). The degree of vulnerability to the Dutch disease seems to correlate to the degree of a combination of the network of domestic flaws: corruption and ineptitude in government, misguided priorities in policy choices, and general inability to break a vicious circle of sociopolitical fallacies inimical to economic progress.

External Indebtedness in LDCs

Most LDCs approached the onset of the foreign trade and exchange rate crises with the initial passive policy reaction of allowing it to work itself out and be over. Meanwhile, the authorities helplessly watched as the accumulated foreign exchange reserves of the country concerned were rapidly depleted to meet current and capital developmental needs. Then, short-term trade debts were incurred and soon piled up, thus preparing the ground for the debt crises.

Many LDCs had tended to develop near-insatiable obsessions with quick economic expansion, which led to the contracting of all kinds of commercial loans and supplier credits. Such credits were quite easy to obtain because many of these countries had good credit ratings arising from previous boom times that usually accompanied positive demand shocks in the international markets of primary produce. Their governments received most of the foreign loans, a great deal of which were spent on capital-intensive public projects, military hardware, as well as financing of government recurrent budget deficits.

Calculations from the World Bank's *World Debt Tables* (various issues) indicate that in the twenty-one low-income Sub-Saharan Africa countries, for example, long-term debt (disbursed and outstanding) increased from US$3,320 million in 1970 to US$38,478 million in 1986. In 1986, Argentina, Venezuela, India, Brazil, and Mexico were heavily indebted. Preliminary data in the World Bank's *Annual Report*, 1992, indicate that the nominal value of the external debt of Sub-Saharan African countries together is about US$178 billion, which represents a 3.1 percent increase from the figure of $172.6 billion at the end of 1990. The region's debt-service-to-exports ratio, which stood at 20 percent in 1990, declined only slightly in 1991.

Much of the borrowed resources in the LDCs had been set for consumption and the establishment of projects with negative net present values. Most of the loans contracted by these countries' governments were built into the fiscal structure and were scarcely used to directly finance the production of exports, manufactures, or staples. It is precisely because of this misguided debt orientation that a debt-servicing problem would later emerge, for the situation was inevitably created whereby continued fiscal expansion and amortization of debt could only be sustained by further indebtedness. The result of the huge accumulation of external debt by most LDCs is a situation in which many of them are currently compelled to allocate over 30 percent, on the average, of their individual total foreign-exchange earnings for servicing external debt. This means increasing difficulties in meeting debt-servicing requirements on an ongoing basis.

While high debt-servicing ratios would tend to be consistent with rapid economic expansion and development in some other low-income countries of the world, they have always proved to be a negation of economic development in others. In Algeria, Malaysia, and South Korea, for example, debt servicing in 1986 were between 9 percent and 13 percent, while between 1980 and 1986, total output in these countries grew at annual averages of 4.4 percent, 4.8 percent, and 8.2 percent, respectively. Yet, these countries have performed relatively well. By contrast, in Sub-Saharan Africa, heavy debts in particular have been inimical to the development effort. This leads us to state that the effects of indebtedness are determined by the uses to which the incurred debt resources had been put. In Sub-Saharan Africa, these effects cannot be surprising, given the foregoing account of the ultimate use of their debt funds.

Many of the indebted LDCs have been compelled to adopt structural adjustment economic (reform) programs (as discussed above), partly in an attempt to forge a longer term solution to their debt problems (but mainly in fulfillment of International Monetary Fund conditionality). The outcomes have not been encouraging on the whole; the often-drastic economic "adjustment" measures embarked upon, *albeit* reluctantly, have tended to cause the entire development process to retrogress.

The general results in LDCs have been prolonged poverty, unfulfilled expectations, and massive disappointments. These have led to frequent changes of governments through coups d'etat as rulers have been blamed for mismanagement of resources. The ensuing political instability has worsened the already gloomy environment for any meaningful economic development initiatives. Many LDCs resorted to devaluation of their relatively fixed and overvalued exchange rates in attempts to repair the damages that the overvaluation had caused. These measures, which have often been carried out halfheartedly, appear to have been too little too late. The devaluations prompted severe economic hardships among the populace through its erosion of real wages, spiraling inflation, and continuing social and political unrests.

Human Factor Depravity and Economic Development

The *human factor* encompasses the fundamental spectrum of personality characteristics and dimensions of human performance that enable social, economic, and political institutions to function, and remain functional, over time.[10] Based on this notion, human factor depravity is expressed in Ezeala-Harrison (1995d) as the situation where the society fails to instill such visions as honesty, respect for the rule of law, individual innate self-discipline, and social accountability into the basic training and development of its human resources. These are the most fundamental pillars on which social and economic development efforts rest, and it is these attributes, or the lack of it, that contribute to the successful or unsuccessful economic development of societies. This situation appears to present the most formidable obstacle to economic development in LDCs.

The elements of honesty, respect for the rule of law, individual innate self-discipline, accountability, and commitment to patriotic vision, are the key dimensions that account for and sustain the workings of the sociopolitical institutions on the the smooth functioning of society is based. These are the most fundamental pillars upon which social and economic development efforts rest, and it is these attributes, or the lack of it, that contribute to the successful or unsuccessful economic development of societies. The question, however, is how far have the educational systems in LDCs succeeded in inculcating these rare quality needs of economic and social development in their "educated" people.

It has been easier to see the problems of unemployment, poverty, and inadequate health and educational facilities as legacies of colonial rule and to focus on the technology of development strategies, rather than identifying and emphasizing a human resource aspect that must be developed if LDCs are to make wise choices from among the alternative proposals being offered, and to find the means to make them work through a sustained plan of action.

The prevailing sociopolitical and economic conditions in the majority of LDCs are characterized by intellectual bankruptcy, discontent, persecution, apathy, and stagnation. Such a situation cannot generate or sustain socioeconomic development and national harmony. This sorry state of affairs is largely attributable to the nature and quality of the society's leadership.

Greater effort needs to be invested in indigenous leadership development. It has simply proved not to be good enough to present LDCs' leaders with the results of research, no matter how good that research may be, and then expect these ruling elites to make and implement wise decisions. Throughout history, nations without strong leaders have had no enduring philosophy and commitment to the national goal. These countries therefore need strong and self-confident leaders who are dedicated to honest and disciplined leadership, are loyal to their countries and are totally committed to their development.

These are imperative if LDCs are to enter the next century with any hope of the political stability necessary for economic prosperity. Skillful leadership is the key to the reforms and policy actions that LDCs need in order to reverse their declining economic trends. Their leaders must be ready and willing to hand over political power to prospective successors rather than resorting to coups d'etat, subversion, and treachery in order to perpetuate themselves in political power. They must eschew selfishness and greed, and thereby allow the process of orderly intergenerational succession to establish a foothold in their countries.

Most of the LDCs' postindependence leaders were off to an unfortunate start because of their excessive interest in fame, power, money, and adventure, which caused them to fashion networks of corrupt patronage and brokerage that were sustained by military force. In its 1988 study of Africa, the United States Council on Foreign Relations concluded that in the post-colonial era "the countries enjoying the most solid growth have all been fortunate in strong and continuous leadership or relatively smooth successions and virtual freedom from rending civil upheaval." The countries referred to were supposedly Ivory Coast, Cameroon, Kenya, Malawi, and Botswana. But when economic development and stability were obstructed by conflict and upheaval, even strong authoritarian-style leadership by itself could not assure progress, as has been evident in these countries.

Current social and political indications in Sub-Saharan Africa seem to suggest that tribalism is stronger now than even during the slavery and colonial times. Conflicts over resources have heightened the need to join together with "kinsmen or tribesmen that one can trust." In history, this contributed in part to Nigeria's 1966-1970 crisis and civil war, and to Congo's 1964-1965 bloodshed. In recent times, this has led to Uganda's bloodletting, as well as to disastrous civil war and genocidal-style massacres in Ethiopia, Liberia, Somalia, Rwanda, and Burundi. In Central America, internecine wars have devastated many countries over the past fifty years. In Asia, Sri Lanka, Afghanistan, Vietnam, Cambodia, and many others have been torn by incessant and ongoing conflicts.

At the heart of almost all of the LDCs' ethnic rivalries has been control over the nation's resources that were appropriated as the basis on which to build ethnic strength rather than as a common property resource that should be utilized for equitable national development. In all cases, leadership was lacking that ought to have provided the guidance toward national harmony and concerted effort toward progress. That is to say that the *human factor* has been lacking in LDCs, and this lack has been a major development constraint in these countries.

On the whole, the major problematic issues in the economic development of the LDCs revolve around the deepening economic crisis characterized by weak agricultural growth and declining industrialization in Africa, poor export production, inadequate and disorganized infrastructural base, disintegrated social and economic institutions, international indebtedness, and incessant political instability in all underdeveloped countries as a whole. The result of this situation is the ongoing economic crises and increasingly deteriorating standards of living.

This chapter has dealt with the historical and circumstantial factors that surround the economic plights of some of the underdeveloped regions of the world. The major development constraints have been discussed. Structural factors ranging from resource endowment, structure of the population and labor force, and the political economy of these societies have been expounded. An exposition on the emerging issue of the *human factor* in economic development is given. It is envisaged that the various proposals, policy suggestions, and lessons will go a long way toward shedding more light on the understanding of the current worldwide development problem. This chapter is designed to serve as a prelude for stimulating even more provocative inquiries into what needs to be done in order to alleviate the constraining issues in economic growth and development in LDCs.

NOTES

1. See Ezeala-Harrison and Adjibolosoo (1994), Fieldhouse (1986), Frank (1969), Gillis *et al.* (1992), and Todaro (1994).

2. Many other studies that support this view can be found in Solow (1985), Darity (1982, 1990), and Inikori (1989).

3. See also O'Brien and Engerman (1991), and Inikori (1977). This led to the development of the notorious West African slave-gun cycle: slaves were exchanged for firearms whose acquisition encouraged the initiation of conflicts in which these firearms were used to procure more slaves, to be traded for more firearms, and so on (Darity, 1992).

4. As stated earlier, many writers have strongly argued that the pace of economic development in Europe, and Britain in particular, was accelerated greatly by slavery and

the colonial exploitation of Africa. Most notable among these are Williams (1966), Rodney (1972), Inikori (1977, 1989, 1992), and Darity (1982, 1990, 1992). These authors therefore contend that the slave trade system and the ultimate colonization that followed in its wake lie at the heart of the origins of the vast economic disparity between Europe and Africa (in particular), and the other underdeveloped regions, in general.

5. The avowed mission of the colonizers was to "... open Africa to Christianity and civilization." Mungo Park in West Africa, David Livingstone and Henry Morton Stanley in Central Africa, and, Baker and Sparks in East Africa and the Nile Valley were the pioneering "explorers" of the African hinterland.

6. These were usually fledgling import-substituting light industries that produced relatively simple consumer goods such as matches, plastic shoes, textiles, and beer and soft drinks. These industrialization efforts were minimal and were designed to be far from promoting industrialization in Africa or making African economies self-sufficient (Amin, 1973; Rodney, 1972).

7. The theory of economic dependency in the development literature was applied to Latin America in explaining how perpetual underdevelopment could be attributed to colonialism and imperialism. It stresses that economic exploitation of the former colonies by the former colonizers tended to continue at a massive scale through operations of multinational corporations, the world's financial institutions (such as the World Bank and the International Monetary Fund, controlled by the former colonizers), and political manipulations (see Chapter 6).

8. The Structural Adjustment Program of economic reforms (SAP) was adopted by most LDCs by the mid-1980s. It is a term given by the World Bank to the package of measures designed to direct an economy away from central planning and control toward a well-functioning free market system based on competition, liberalization, deregulation, and an enhanced private sector. For the list of some of the countries that adopted the structural adjustment programs, see Hodd (1992); for evaluation of their relative performances, see Jones and Kiguel (1994).

9. See Ezeala-Harrison (1993) Gelb (1988), and Glassburner (1988).

10. See Adjibolosoo (1994) and Ezeala-Harrison (1995d).

Part II

THEORIES OF ECONOMIC GROWTH AND DEVELOPMENT

4

The Classical Theories of Economic Growth and Development

This chapter presents a set of growth and development models advanced in the pioneering era of economic thought. These theories have been the basis of many development policy formulations across the world during the twentieth century. The classical theories are those formulated on the basis of the works of Adam Smith, David Ricardo, John Stuart Mill, Jeremy Bentham, Jean-Baptiste Say, and Thomas R. Malthus, on the one hand, and Karl Marx and Friedrich Engels, on the other.[1] The major tenets of classical doctrine have frequently been referred to as "liberalist" economic thinking. Apart from the ideological departure of Marxian thinking from it, classical ideas are based on personal liberty, individual initiative, private enterprise, private property, and minimal government intervention.

The term *liberalism*, considered in its historical context, indicates a contrast to feudal and mercantilist restrictions on individual choice of occupations, land transfers and ownership, trade, movements, and property rights. The classicists believed that the individual's economic behavior is guided largely by self-interest, which is basic to human nature. That is, producers and merchants provided goods and services out of profit motives, and workers offered their labor services out of a desire to obtain wage payments, while consumers purchased goods and services in order to satisfy their needs and wants. There is a natural harmony of these various interests as they interact in a free market setting: by pursuing their own individual interests, people serve the best interests of others.

Traditional classical economic analysis presumes that the decisions made by individual economic agents acting in their own self-interest can be relied on to take national output and employment to their potential (full-employment) levels. According to classical economic analysis, income, wealth, output, and employment are determined entirely in the supply side of the economy. The explanation of these variables is based firmly on a microeconomic foundation: quantity of output and level of employment depend on factor market decisions made by profit-maximizing producers and utility-maximizing workers (consumers) constantly interacting in free and competitive markets. The stock of capital used in production evolves over time as the result of optimizing saving and investment choices made by individuals, households, and businesses. The economy was supposed to work as though an *invisible hand* guided the actions of self-interest-seeking capitalists, merchants, landlords, workers, and consumers toward maximum economic growth and public interest. The working of this system, however, was subject to the natural order of the universe, a key tenet of which was Ricardo's *law of diminishing returns*.

Two classical sets of ideas in economics are the theory of *stationary state* and the Marxian theory of *evolutionary economic determinism*. The common strands of thinking that make these two theories "classical" can be outlined as follows: (1) capital accumulation is the prime mover behind economic growth and development, (2) the investors' quest for profit provides the key incentive for them to accumulate capital, (3) over time, recessionary growth overtakes the free market economy, resulting in its eventual demise, in one way or another, and (4) technological progress can postpone the ultimate decline of profits but not eliminate it. The contrasting idea between them is that whereas the stationary state model expected the economy's breakdown to come from within and for purely economic reasons, the Marxian model posited that capitalism's breakdown would be imposed through external force, and for sociological reasons, and only after some degree of advanced level of economic growth and development had been attained.

THE CLASSICAL STATIONARY STATE MODEL

The basic premise of the classical theory of economic stagnation was that, *over time, a progressive economy would ultimately tend to a stationary state.* That is, recessionary "growth" would definitely overtake any economy over time. This is a long-run model: an economy cannot experience perpetual growth in the long term, and this is not because of the effects of the "business cycle," nor would there be the tendency for any built-in mechanisms to gradually guide the economy out of a cyclical downturn toward an upswing. The economy would, in the long run, simply recede into a stationary state in which the rate of growth of capital accumulation, and therefore, output and incomes, employment, savings, and investment, would be zero.

As already mentioned, this theory singled out capital accumulation as the prime mover of economic progress. The assumption was that the pace of capital accumulation determined the pace of investment and productivity, and could thus not only be taken as proxy for economic growth and development but indeed was synonymous with economic growth and development. This is because capital accumulation is the only potential means of production which creates wealth and the infrastructure required for structural transformation of the economy. Therefore, if capital accumulation is increasing, economic growth and development will be feasible and positive, and if capital accumulation is decreasing, economic growth and development will be negative.

The model states that the economy's rate of growth of capital stock over time (capital accumulation) depends solely on the savings capacity of the economy: it is a function of the economy's *will to save* and *ability to save*. By will to save is meant the desire and determination with which savers pursue savings in the economy, per time period. Ability to save refers to the amount of resources that entrepreneurs are able to save out of their profits, per time period. The model is represented by the equation expressing the rate of growth of capital stock, K, over time, t, as a function of the ability to save and the will to save:

$$dK/dt = f(Y - R - wL, \pi - z) \qquad (4.1)$$

where

Y = the gross domestic product (GDP)
R = total rent earned by landlords
w = average level of real wages
L = total labour force employed
π = real profit returns
z = normal profit

This equation simply states that capital accumulation is a function of the economy's ability to save, $Y-R-wL$, and will to save, $\pi-z$. The ability to save is defined as what is left from GDP after meeting the payments for rent and the labor force. Thus, this is the ability of landlords and workers to save out of GDP. The will to save is defined as the amount kept from current consumption by entrepreneurs. If the entrepreneurial class wishes to save more, it will reduce the level of normal profit, z, and if it wishes to save less, it will raise its take in form of normal profit.[2]

Classical thinking recognized that the economy comprises of the private, business, and public sectors, all of which together determine the total level of savings on which the level of capital accumulation depends. However, it assumes a state of *laissez faire:* an overriding principle of free-enterprise in which there is virtually no government intervention in the workings of the economy.

The essence of the classical model is that over time both the ability to save and the will to save will tend toward zero, and thus causing capital accumulation to steadily decrease and the economy to stagnate. We turn to the detailed analysis of this process that would lead the economy towards stagnation.

The Ability to Save

The ability to save is defined as $Y-R-wL$. Y is the GDP, which tends to decline over time because production is subject to the phenomenon of diminishing returns. The law of diminishing returns was a major Ricardian tenet stating that there would be successively lower extra outputs from the steady addition of equal extra input to a fixed level of another input (land).[3] As a result of the economy's limited ability to continually apply larger amounts of capital to production in the long run, total output would decline, thereby lessening the ability to save.

The level of output declines further with the growth of the economy's population. The Malthusian population theory states that whereas population tends to grow at a geometric rate (that is, in multiples), food production can only grow at an arithmetic rate (that is, by additions, because of diminishing returns to the fixed amount of land). Thus, as each member of the population actually has less land to work, his or her marginal contribution to food production actually starts to decline, and as a result, the food supplies cannot keep pace with the expanding population level. Production and per capita incomes will then fall. Technological progress might offset or postpone this outcome, but cannot eliminate it. Even if it could, technological progress could not keep pace with the rapid tendency with which (unchecked) population can grow.

Rent is another parameter that determines the ability to save. Rent is defined as the payment accruing to land for its contribution in production. The classical position is that rent increases over time, for several reasons. First, with rising population growth, land becomes more scarce relative to other factors. Second, landlords need higher returns from their land in order to meet rising costs of subsistence. Prices of food and other consumer goods tend to increase over time because of increasing demand due to rising population. Third, as this rising demand also translates to rising derived demand for land, then rent, as the price of land, must rise (as illustrated in Figure 4.1).

In Figure 4.1, rent (R) is measured on the vertical axis, and the quantity of land (N) is measured on the horizontal axis. S_0 represents the supply curve of the original fixed quantity of land the society has, that is, the supply of land. $D_0(P_0)$ represents the corresponding level of demand for land at society's population level P_0. The level of rent at this stage of the society's population and land acquisition is R_0 established at the equilibrium point A. However, as population rises from P_0 to P_1, the demand for land also rises from $D_0(P_0)$ to $D_1(P_1)$, resulting in a corresponding increase in rent from R_0 to R_1 established at the equilibrium point B.

Similarly, a further population increase will result in establishing the equilibrium point C where the fixed supply curve of land S_0 equals the demand curve D_2, yielding the level of rent R_2. This gives a simplified illustration of why and how rent rises over time in the classical model.[4]

Figure 4.1
Determination of Rent

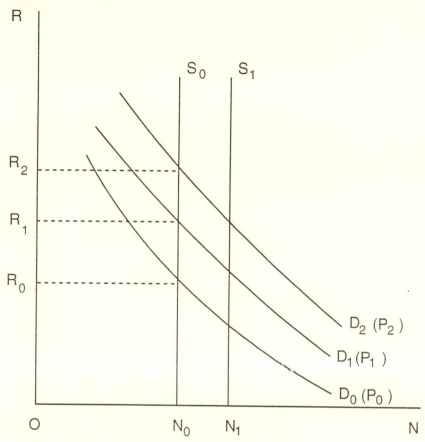

In the long run, the supply of land may increase through such events as improved land reclamation methods, expansion in the country's borders, or discovery of more territories. Such a development would result in increasing the supply of land from S_0 to S_1. This would yield equilibrium points E, F, G with lower rent levels, but further increases in demand as population rises would ultimately outstrip these effects, and rent would still increase over time.

The classical ability to save is also affected by the economy's wage bill - what Ricardo terms the *wage fund*. The Ricardian wage fund theory, or iron law of wages, provides the basis for understanding how and why an increasing population and labor force might not always (if at all) have positive effects on economic growth and development. According to this theory, as wages increase through increasing productivity prior to the onset of diminishing returns, workers are able to achieve improved living standards. This enables them to provide better lifestyles for their dependents and not only maintain larger family sizes but also increase them. Hence, over time, population would increase.

Ricardo's explanation of the iron law of wages did draw a distinction between a *natural wage* level and a market wage level. Labor, as it is bought and sold like any other commodity, has its natural price and its market price: the natural price of labor is the price that enables workers to subsist and to perpetuate themselves without increasing or decreasing their numbers, under the given habits and customs of the people. The natural (wage) price depends on the price of necessities of life. In the long run, the natural wage is the subsistence wage, that is, the minimum wage that would cover the cost of perpetuating the population and labor force. The current wage may rise above the natural wage, in which case the means of sustenance increases beyond what is essential for maintaining the population, leading to an increase in population. The current wage may also fall below the natural wage, in which case, through the process explained above, the population would decline. In any case, over time the going wage tends to equal the natural wage (subsistence wage).

Rising population over time would mean an increase in the labor force over time. However, the wage fund would tend to increase over time not only because the size of the labor force increases but also because the level of the (subsistence) wage must increase. As the population increases, the wage rate must increase in line with rising subsistence demands arising from rising costs of living. The wage fund is the element wL in Equation (4.1) and enters that equation as a negative. Increases in either w or L, or both, thus lowers the *ability to save*.

The Will to Save

The classical model assumes that the economy's will to save rests entirely with the entrepreneurial class. The determinants of the will to save are the (average) real levels of economic profits (π) and normal profits (z): it is a positive function of the level of economic profit and a negative function of the level of normal profit.

The model postulates that the average level of economic profits tends to decrease over time owing to rising costs of production. In fact, the classical model presumes that the level of economic profit is zero because the economy is inherently competitive. However, should any economic profits arise to firms in certain sectors of the economy where there might be imperfect competition, such as natural monopolies, such profits will disappear over time because of declining revenues resulting from diminishing returns. In addition, rising wages will tend to erode any positive economic profits over time.

Just as the average level of economic profits decline over time, normal profit levels increase over time. The normal profit is the minimum amount of payment required for the entrepreneur to undertake the economic functions of risk-bearing, administration, and the critical decision making involved in production. Rising costs of living would mean that the entrepreneur must receive higher remunerations in order to maintain their sustenance. Therefore, the level of normal profit must increase over time. Furthermore, the level of normal profit must increase over time in order for entrepreneurs to meet the rising costs of living resulting from increasing population and dwindling output in the face of diminishing returns.

Ricardo believed that entrepreneurs require minimum profits and interest payments in order to increase or even maintain the level of capital stock. But because average economic profits and interest payments decline over time (and rents increase as population grows), the tendency is for surplus returns to diminish. This decline will also mean a decline in the inducement to entrepreneurs to accumulate capital. This situation is not helped by the constant expansion of the labor force, which leads to a lower average level of capital per worker, and hence lower productivity and income per head.

The classical explanations make clear how, over time, capital accumulation in economy tends to zero. The right-hand side of Equation (4.1) tends to zero as the two elements in the bracket, namely, $Y-R-wL$, the ability to save, and $\pi-z$, the will to save, tend to zero. Thus, we can state that, the classical theory of economic stagnation implies that

$$\underset{t \to \infty}{Lim}\ dK/dt = 0 \qquad (4.2)$$

This implies that in the long run, as time approaches infinity ($t \to \infty$), the limiting value of capital accumulation will be zero. This is the stationary state.

Graphical Analysis of the Stationary State

A graphical analysis easily summarizes the classical stationary state model. Starting with population, as population increases, diminishing returns in agriculture and the increased demand for food will result in higher prices of food, thereby increasing pressure on land as more fertile land is worked intensively while poorer land is brought into cultivation. Consequently, rent will rise; the nominal wage will also increase in order to maintain the natural (subsistence) wage, and profit rates and the profit share of national output will fall. Eventually, the stationary state is reached at which the wage per worker stays at the subsistence level and no further capital accumulation occurs.

Figure 4.2 depicts the production function of total output (Q) produced by the size of the labor force (L). The total product curve (Q) is shown to be subject to diminishing returns. Because rent rises as population grows, the curve labeled Q-R, showing total product minus rent, flattens out faster than the curve Q; the vertical distance between the two curves is the amount of rent accruing to landlords. The slope of the line OE at any point on the production function represents the amount by which total wages will rise with each additional worker.

Figure 4.2
Theory of Rent

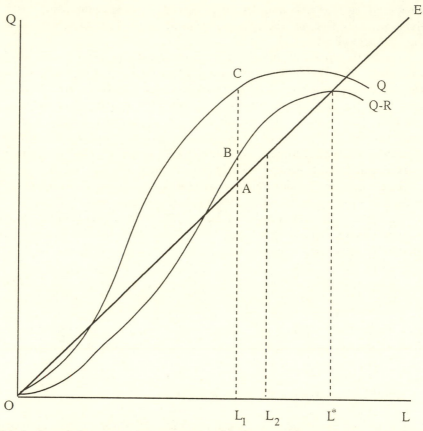

This is the subsistence real wage rate, and it does not change as the labor force increases, although total wages do increase.

Consider an initial size of the labor force L_1. At this level, wage is L_1A, profit AB, and rent BC. The relatively high profits will allow for higher investment and increases in the wage fund, resulting in a temporary increase in real wage. This will stimulate an increase in population and labor force to, say, the level L_2 which will then drive the wage rate down to its subsistence level. However, at L_2 the profit share is lower than it was at L_1, and rent share is higher. But because profit is positive (though smaller than the previous level), the process will repeat itself. This will continue until the profits are reduced to zero at point P with the size of the labor force L^*. No further capital investment will be forthcoming, workers only receive a subsistence wage, economic profits are zero, rents are high, and population and labor force growth will be zero. This stationary state continues as the long-run steady state of the economy.

Critique and Policy Implications of the Classical Stationary State Model

The classical theory has been usefully applied to develop other theories and formulate further policy guidelines that have been used to promote growth and development in various parts of the world today. This model drew attention to the need to pursue technological progress that is required to overcome the constraining effects of diminishing returns. The classical model also warned about the potential problems of high population growth rates that exceed the rate of economic growth: it is believed that population growth averaging about 3 percent per year has contributed to famine, malnutrition, disease, and ecological degradation in parts of Africa. In predicting the potential adverse effects of high unchecked population growth rates, the classical model did serve as a catalyst in fashioning population control policies in many contemporary underdeveloped countries. Seventy percent of the world's present population live in low-income developing countries in which the Malthusian predictions seem all too real.

The key assumptions on which the classical model is built are not very tenable. The first assumption is that capital accumulation is to be considered as the prime mover of economic growth and development. If this assumption is valid in all cases, then the question arises as to why many countries that have accumulated massive amounts of capital are yet to achieve high levels of economic growth and development. An example of such a case would be the former Soviet Union where capital accumulation was pursued and maintained for many decades. In addition, many contemporary LDCs have achieved very high levels of capital accumulation, yet the required rate of GDP growth and structural transformation of the economy have scarcely occurred. It seems, therefore, that the classical view regarding the overwhelming importance of capital accumulation in economic development may have been exaggerated.

The important role that ascribed to profits may not be warranted. The evidence seems to support the fact that entrepreneurs do not always save and reinvest their total profits. A significant proportion of the share of profits is spent on conspicuous consumption rather than being saved. Profits may also be removed from the economy and saved or invested abroad. The classical notion that increases in population and the labor force would result in lower profit does not always seem to hold. One wonders whether a growing labor force would not increase the supply of labor and result in lowering the wage rate, which would then mean a lower cost of production and increased profit.

The classical model also rests on the assumption of diminishing returns in production. Although the phenomenon of diminishing returns does apply in production processes, the advent of a high pace of technological progress has tended to negate it, even over the "long run." Thus, the classicists underestimated or even failed to foresee the impact of technological advances in offsetting the phenomenon of diminishing returns. Moreover, most LDCs have an abundance of arable lands that have not been utilized for agriculture, and rental rates in these LDCs have not risen in line with the classical prediction. That economic growth and development could occur without necessarily being based on private ownership of land and capital seems to have completely escaped classical thinking. State ownership of land and capital has meant that growth and development could occur without rents and interest being paid.

As for the classical *iron law of wages*, one can see that it failed to anticipate the extent to which population growth could be effectively checked through medical advances that gave rise to voluntary birth control methods. Furthermore, positive population growth is not always necessarily detrimental to economic growth and development. It is not population growth *per se*; rather, if a society is able to achieve a pace of economic growth that outweighs the rate of population growth, it would significantly improve and increase the means of sustenance for the growing population. In such a case, population growth would accelerate the pace of growth in creating stable market demand that would support higher productive capacity for the economy. In some instances, an inadequate rate of population growth could hamper the rate of economic growth. In applying the Malthusian theory of population, the classical predictions about the role of population growth in reaching the stationary state have appeared to be highly questionable.

The classical theory is a supply-side long-run theory. Issues of demand are not dealt with. The stationary state could never be reached in a world of high wages and stable demand for large-scale production. It seems that the bulk of the policy implications which the classical model has for present-day development efforts would be irrelevant. This is not to say that the model lacks intellectual insight and originality in its analysis of growth and development. Indeed, the classicists are unequaled in their pioneering contributions and advances in economic theory and analyses, but the bulk of the assumptions on which their models are premised have proved to be rather suspect. As a result, the policy lessons of their model would be limited in today's world.

THE MARXIAN THEORY OF ECONOMIC DETERMINISM

The theories of Karl Marx (1818-1883) basically sought to replace classical economic analyses with historically based evolutionary economic dynamism. The Marxian model of economic growth and development treats the developmental process as a social phenomenon by examining where it was and where it is going, as well as its processes of change over time. It believes that the economy moves from one stage to another. Thus, the classical system of "capitalist" production relations would be simply one of the series of stages in the evolution of society that began at the *primitive economy* and would end at the *socialist state*.[5]

Marx did draw a distinction between the "forces of production" and the existing "production relations" in the society at any point in time. Production relations are defined as the appropriation and distribution of output within a given societal mode of thinking, ideology, and global vision. The former is defined as the organization of production, the state of science and technology, and the development of human skills. According to Marxian theory, there is always bound to be a constant conflict between the forces of production and the relations of production in society, the interactions of which would shape the society's political, legal, moral, religious, cultural, and ideological positions in the world.

In Marxian thinking, the system of free-enterprise economic relations that is governed by private ownership of the means of production and self-seeking profit pursuits is merely one of a series of stages in the evolution of society toward the highest (utopian socialist) state. This state would be the inevitable final stage of economic, social, and political organization. We could summarize the Marxian theory of economic growth and development in the following statement: it states that every society would undergo a *metamorphosis* of transition from a primitive society to a communist utopian and highly developed state economy.

The evolution of the state will take the form of self-transformation of the economic and social arrangements. Each stage of the economy will have its own peculiar characteristic technology and organizational styles, and this will give rise to its own particular kind of "class struggle" that will result in its decay and "breakdown" from within. From that breakdown, the next and "higher" order of social organization will emerge, until the highest order of economic and social relations has been reached: socialism. At this "highest" form, poverty would disappear as unemployment would not exist. The society would be without "conflict" in a utopian economy in which each individual would contribute to the national income and output according to his or her abilities and receive from it according to his or her needs. In order to fully appreciate Marxian thinking and how his prognosis for the economy arises from it, we begin with a closer examination of the evolutionary processes of the economic relations of the state.

The Theory of Evolutionist State

Marx advanced the theory of the *evolutionist state* of society by which he saw the beginning of the organizational state of the economy as the *primitive* society. In the primitive society, the economy is characterized by subsistence production. Factors of production and modes of production would be in their most archaic forms. The scale of production would be limited by the needs of the immediate family and locality. Society would just be economically self-sufficient and self-reliant, as there would be no demonstration effects, nor would there be any need for emulation of consumption patterns.

Marx saw that the society would ultimately evolve from that of a self-sufficient peasantry to a *communal exchange* economy (or primitive communism). This would arise by way of economic exchanges through trade by barter. The peasants' needs to acquire more resources to support growing family sizes, coupled with their aspirations toward greater individual self-fulfillment, would compel them to sell their labor and mortgage their lands to an emerging class of wealthy "lords." The system of *feudalism* would develop: through a "class" of wealthy *feudal lords* virtually enslaved "dispossessed serfs" who worked for them. The feudal system would lead to a struggle between serfs and feudal lords, out of which a class of "emancipated" serfs would became merchants. Moreover, the craving to expand would lead some of the feudal lords to commercialize, hiring the peasantry as "servicemen" of sorts. Thus, feudalism was undermined by the migration of serfs to towns, where competition emerged between factory and handicraft production forces. With these, transportation, trade, innovation, and internationalization of markets arose together with a new business class. This was the *mercantilist state*.

According to Marxian theory, the state of mercantilism gave way to the higher state of *capitalism*. Indeed, the first and earliest phase of the capitalist state was mercantilism. Capitalism would be a very high stage of technological advance characterized, on the one hand, by mechanization, large-scale production, high growth rates of output, and huge possessions of wealth by a capitalist class. On the one hand, capitalism would be characterized by high levels of unemployment, poverty, economic exploitation, and, of course, massive unequal income distribution across the population.

Capitalism would face incessant crises because of the deficiency of the market that depended largely on the consumption of workers but whose demand was inadequate to match productive capacity. This unused capacity would create a *reserve army of unemployed* in the economy. This arrangement would eventually give rise to a bitter class struggle between the workers (the working class, or *proletariat*, of the capitalist economy) and the capitalists (the entrepreneurial and propertied *bourgeoisie* class), from which the proletariat would emerge victorious and thence establish the "dictatorship of the proletariat": a working-class-controlled economy. This *socialist* society would then develop into a full-fledged *communist* society, the ultimate utopian social and economic order. We now present the Marxian model in some detail.

The Marxian Model

Marx appropriated quite a great deal of classical economic theories. His system incorporated all the circularities of the classical model: capital accumulation, diminishing returns, and investment and technology as the prime mover of economic activity, although he disagreed strongly with the classical (Malthusian) population theory. The central assumption of the Marxian model is that capitalists have greater opportunity and undue advantage in controlling the economy because of their access to capital.

The Marxian model is premised on the *Labor Theory of Value*, which states that "use values constitute the substance of all wealth." The theory argues that the value of a commodity is determined by the socially necessary labor time embodied in the commodity. The socially necessary labor time would include the direct labor in producing the commodity, the labor embodied in the machinery and raw materials that are used up during the production process, and the value that is transferred to the commodity during the process. Thus, a product's value is measured in units of simple average labor, while the market determines the prices that are based on the underlying labor cost.[6]

A key implication of the labor theory of value is that labor must duly receive all returns that are created in the production process; if it does not, then there is *exploitation* of labor. Therefore, payment of wages on the basis of profit maximization of the entrepreneur, under the principles by which the wage rate is determined, and the employment level set at the point where the marginal productivity of labor equals the marginal factor cost (the wage rate in a competitive labor market setting), amounts to exploitation. The short expository analysis that follows will help us fully grasp the implications of the Marxian labor theory of value.

Analysis of the Marxian Labour Theory of Value

To fully understand the major developmental implications of the Marxian labor theory of value, we consider the following micro-theoretic application. Figure 4.3 has two quadrants, with the vertical axis measuring the money value of output Y and wages w, and the horizontal axis of both quadrants measuring the amount of labor, L. The left quadrant represents the competitive labor market, with labor supply curve S^L, and labor demand curve D^L, showing the equilibrium wage rate w^*. The right quadrant gives the standard neoclassical production function, showing the total product curve, TP, together with its corresponding average product of labor (AP_L) and marginal product of labor (MP_L) curves.

The Marxian labor theory of value would imply that, for a typical firm in a free market system, the profit-maximizing level of labor demand (employment) L^*, with wage rate w^*, is exploitative of labor. This is because a worker's contribution in the production process is supposed to be the average product of labor, AP_L. Consequently, the amount EF ought also to have accrued to the worker. However, since the worker receives only the wage rate w^*, the amount EF that is withheld as a unit *surplus* for the (capitalist) firm represents an exploitation of labor.

In fact, a more socially optimal situation is for the firm to hire every unit of labor with a positive marginal productivity. This will bring employment to the level L_0 where $MP_L = 0$. At this level of employment, the wage rate would be the w_0 (set at the level of AP_L), but the society is better off because employment is maximized, yielding the maximum national output, Y_0.

Figure 4.3
The Socially Optimal Labor in Marxian Theory

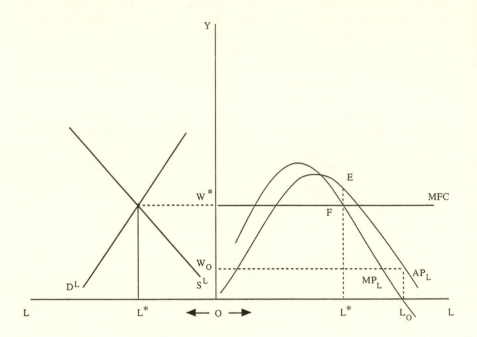

It is in this sense that the Marxian model presupposes that there would hardly be any unemployment in a society governed by, and *regulated* for, social welfare maximization, rather than one left in the hands of private-sector free-enterprise-driven profit maximization.

This is a major strand of thought that fashioned much of Marx's views on economic issues, and an understanding of this analogy would greatly help us to come to terms with most of the Marxian policy prescriptions that would emerge from the model that we now expound.

The Marxian model of Falling Rate of Profit (FROP)

Marx believed that the capitalist system creates profit for the entrepreneur through the institutionalized exploitation of labor, which allows for the purchase of "the commodity that creates value greater than its own," namely, *labor power.*[7] The exploitation of workers was construed as taking the form of extraction of surplus values by capitalists. The surplus value is the extra value that labor produces, which the firm appropriates without due compensation to the workers. The *rate of surplus value* is defined as:

$$s^R = s/v \tag{4.3}$$

where

$$s^R = \text{rate of surplus value}$$
$$s = \text{surplus value}$$
$$v = \text{variable capital}$$

The parameter v, termed *variable capital*, is designated as the portion of capital (investment) expenditure that goes for the purchase of labor power, that is, wages (or rather, the wages fund or wage bill).

Marx depicted Equation (4.3) as the *rate of exploitation* (or the intensity of exploitation). Being the ratio of the surplus value to the variable capital involved in production, it can also be seen as the ratio of unpaid labor time to paid labor time in production. Marx then formulated the rate of profit as:

$$\pi^R = s/(c+v) \tag{4.4}$$

where

$$\pi^R = \text{rate of profit}$$
$$c = \textit{constant capital: the portion of capital invested in}$$
$$\text{machinery and raw materials (capital stock accumulation)}$$

Equation (4.4) shows that the rate of profit received by capitalists is depicted as the ratio of surplus value to total capital invested.

Marx believed that the rate of profit has an inherent and inevitable tendency to fall over time. This assertion is often referred to as the *falling rate of profit* (FROP) syndrome. That is, $\partial\pi^R/\partial t < 0$, where $t =$ time. This can be shown by a simple manipulation of Equation (4.4), which can be rewritten in its implicit form as

$$\pi^R = \pi^R(s, c, v) \tag{4.5}$$

Using this, the time growth rate of the rate of profit is given as

$$d\pi^R/dt = \partial\pi^R/\partial s.\partial s/\partial t + \partial\pi^R/\partial c.\partial c/\partial t + \partial\pi^R/\partial v.\partial v/\partial t \tag{4.6}$$

To verify the FROP proposition, we may deduce Equation (4.6) from Equation (4.4), and show that it is negative. From Equation (4.4),

$$\partial\pi^R/\partial s = 1/(c+v), \ \partial\pi^R/\partial c = -s/(c+v)^2, \ \text{and} \ \partial\pi^R/\partial v = -s/(c+v)^2$$

and substituting these into Equation (4.6), we have

$$d\pi^R/dt = 1/(c+v).\partial s/\partial t - s/(c+v)^2.\partial c/\partial t - s/(c+v)^2.\partial v/\partial t$$

and factoring, we have

$$d\pi^R/dt = s/(c+v)^2\{(c+v)/s.\partial s/\partial t - \partial c/\partial t - \partial v/\partial t\}$$

or

$$d\pi^R/dt = -s/(c+v)^2\{\partial c/\partial t + \partial v/\partial t - (c+v)/s.\partial s/\partial t\}$$

and substituting back $\pi^R = s/(c+v)$, we obtain

$$d\pi^R/dt = -\pi^R/(c+v).\{\partial c/\partial t + \partial v/\partial t - (1/\pi^R).\partial s/\partial t\} \tag{4.7}$$

It is easy to see that, given Marx's assumptions about the various parameters, $d\pi^R/dt < 0$; that is, Equation (4.7) would have a negative sign, thus confirming FROP over time. The term $\partial c/\partial t$ is the time rate of change of constant capital, that is, the growth rate of capital accumulation, which Marx assumed to be positive and high. The term $\partial v/\partial t$, being the time growth rate of variable capital (the wage bill), is assumed to be negative because of exploitation. The term $1/\pi^R$ would be very small as the profit rate tends to be high. Thus, the highly positive rate of capital accumulation ($\partial c/\partial t$) would dominate the weaker negative rates of $\partial v/\partial t$ and $\partial s/\partial t$, resulting in Equation (4.7) having an overall negative sign.

We will now examine the processes involved in FROP. Marx explained the FROP phenomenon as the result of the very nature of the capitalist operation itself. Capital accumulation, as the prime mover of the capitalist system of production, is the capitalist's central pursuit because it is the only means to ensure higher profit. Over time, constant capital must further increase through capital maintenance and technological innovations. As can be seen from Equation (4.4), increasing capital accumulation would lead to reduction of the rate of profit. Moreover, the surplus value, s, would at best remain constant over time, although it tends to fall over time because production is subject to diminishing returns. Therefore, the capitalist must face FROP, except the surplus value can be raised. However, the only effective way of raising the surplus value, and indeed, remedy the FROP, is to reduce the value of v, the variable capital. Reducing v would be used to offset the negative effects of the rising c and falling s.

According to Marxian theory, the main practical ways of reducing the variable capital is through layoffs that result as the capitalists adopt labor-saving innovations that substitute capital for labor. As technological progress increasingly displaces labor over time, a *reserve army* of displaced (unemployed) workers is created and grows over time.

The Marxian Theory of Contradiction and Breakdown

Marxian theory posits that capitalism faces its own internal inconsistencies or *contradictions* that really ensure its demise. This occurs in at least two ways:

one from the supply side and one from the demand side. From the supply side, the drive toward greater capital accumulation reduces the profit rate, workers (laborers) are the source of all value, and as workers are displaced and fewer workers are used, lesser value is created and surplus value falls, and profit rate falls. From the demand side, the creation of massive unemployment would result in a state of *underconsumption* in the economy, whereby the economy would not have the purchasing power to provide effective demand for the produce of capitalist industries. This would lead to reduced rate of profit.

To demonstrate more clearly how and why the capitalist system of operation is inherently contradictory and potentially self-destructive, we examine Marx's concept of the *organic composition of capital* (OCC). Because of the drive toward increasing efficiency through mechanization and labor-saving inventions and innovations, there would be large increases in the OCC. Marx posits the OCC as the ratio of constant capital, c, to total capital investment, $c+v$. Letting the OCC be symbolized by K, then:

$$K = c/(c+v) \tag{4.8}$$

The question is, how would the rate of profit be affected as the OCC increases? That is, what would be the sign of the differential $\partial \pi^R/\partial K$? We know, by definition, that

$$\partial \pi^R/\partial K = \partial \pi^R/\partial c . \partial c/\partial K \tag{4.9}$$

and using Equation (4.4):

$$\partial \pi^R/\partial c = -s/(c+v)^2$$

while from Equation (4.8):

$$\partial K/\partial c = v/(c+v)^2$$

from which we obtain

$$\partial c/\partial K = (c+v)^2/v$$

Substituting these results into (4.9), we have

$$\partial \pi^R/\partial K = \{-s/(c+v)^2\}.\{(c+v)^2/v\}$$

and simplifying, we obtain

$$\partial \pi^R/\partial K = -s/v < 0 \tag{4.10}$$

This shows that the rate of profit varies inversely with the OCC: as capitalists invest relatively more in machinery and less in labor power, OCC rises and the profit rate falls. This is the central axiom of utmost importance to the Marxian theory of *contradiction*.

Recall from Equation (4.3) that the rate of surplus value, s^R (the intensity of exploitation), is the ratio of surplus value to variable capital. This is precisely what we have in Equation (4.10), except that this equation has a negative sign attached. This is to say that the effect of rising OCC on the rate of profit is the negative of the rate of surplus value:

$$\partial \pi^R / \partial K = -s^R < 0 \qquad (4.11)$$

In other words, any unit increase in the organic composition of capital (or the degree of capital concentration) would reduce the rate of profit by an amount equal to the rate of surplus value. So, the very process of capitalist operation constitutes its very undoing.

With regard to how the contradiction will result in the breakdown of the capitalist system, we examine the capitalists' means of offsetting the inherent FROP. To do this, we provide an alternative equation of how the rate of profit would relate to the OCC. This is easily obtainable from Equation (4.11):

$$\pi^R = \int (\partial \pi^R / \partial K) \, dK = -\int s^R \, dK$$

which gives

$$\pi^R = -s^R K + \mu, \quad \mu = \text{constant}$$

This may be rewritten as

$$\pi^R = s^R(\mu_1 - K), \quad \mu_1 = \mu/s^R \qquad (4.12)$$

As Equation (4.12) indicates, the rate of profit varies inversely with the OCC. The capitalist must find a way to offset this effect, and the intensity of exploitation, s^R, remains the only parameter that can be manipulated. s^R can be raised by forcing the workers to increase their pace of work, or by working more hours in the day and by cutting wages. Furthermore, as population grows in relation to jobs, and as technological unemployment increases, conditions become conducive to establishing new labor-intensive industries, with high rates of profits. This is where and when foreign trade and expansionism enter into the capitalist system's array of operations.

Foreign trade mainly takes the form of *colonialist imperialism* and raises the rate of profits because capital invested in colonies yields higher profit rates as the exploitation of colonial labor is far more intense than that of home labor. Moreover, the ratio of constant capital to variable capital is lower in the colonies.[8] The rate of exploitation is raised further by reducing the value of labor power through increased efficiency of production. Over time, therefore, as these factors offset the FROP, *albeit* partially, the ever increasing rate of exploitation heightens the misery of the working class (proletariat), *class consciousness is awakened and promoted*, and a *revolution* becomes imminent.

Policy Perspectives and Critique of the Marxian Model

The Marxian model represents a worthwhile contribution to the analysis and understanding of economic growth and processes of development. The evolutionist theory is particularly illuminating. Although most economists in Western countries do not share this view, it is generally agreed that the model led the way toward understanding the issues of income distribution, resource allocation, business behavior, the business cycle, and development planning, all of which remain the central topics of focus in studying the economic growth and development of free-enterprise economies.

Rapid cyclical swings of the business cycles and incessant crises are necessary accompaniments of the capitalist economy. Rising investment levels must result in higher wages and demand for goods and services. The higher wages, however, reduce the rate of surplus value and profit, pushing for a reduction in investment, exploitation, and a countercyclical downturn. As the depression results in fallen wages, fallen prices of commodities, and fallen monetary value of fixed capital stock and closure of some factories, larger capitalists buy up smaller ones at low prices, the rate of surplus value and profits begin to recover, and investment rises again, for a cyclical upswing.

A major implication of the Marxian model is that, to avoid the inherent fluctuations of the capitalist economy, the means of production, notably capital, must be centralized. The concentration of capital in the hands of a few capitalist profit-seekers is at odds with the prospect of smooth economic growth and development. Centralization of capital would mean centralization of wealth: exploitation, poverty, and inequality in the distribution of income and wealth, as well as class conflicts, would disappear.

The Marxian theory seems to believe that an economy would have attained a significant level of development only when it had reached the *communist* utopian state. What this implies for contemporary policy makers is that societies in the transition stage of capitalism - that is, most developing countries today which are far from attainment of full-fledged capitalism with its attendant strong capital and infrastructural base - would simply have to wait until they attained such final stages of capitalism before they could expect the "egalitarian" and "revolution-ary" outcomes predicted by Marxian theory. Most LDCs appear to be in the *mercantilist* stages, while others may even be at the *feudal* or *communal exchange* stages. Many of them operate a combination of the capitalist, mercantilist, feudal, and communal exchange stages. Thus, the application of centralized planning in fostering economic growth and development in such LDCs amounts to an untimely misapplication of the Marxian model, at best, and to a naive misuse of the predictions of the model, at worst.

One of the major shortcomings of the Marxian model hinges on its preoccupation with capitalism to the detriment of more complete analyses of the other stages of economic development, including socialism and communism. The most damaging flaw in Marxism has been that its prediction of doom for capitalism (presumably in the West) rather applied to socialism (in the East - in the Soviet Union, East Germany, Poland, Romania, Bulgaria, and others) during the late 1980s and early 1990s. Modern Marxian proponents, however, do have an interesting explanation as to why the Western capitalist system has not yet been overthrown and socialism and communism established in their wake, although they seem to be still at a loss as to why the "revolution" instead took place in the Marxist systems of the East.

With regard to why capitalism still thrives in the West, modern Marxian theorists are quick to point out that Western capitalists, having realized the dangers of creating an oppressed working class within the domestic economy, have rather shifted their exploitative designs abroad, namely, onto developing countries. In this way, the revolutions would be affecting these developing countries rather than the Western countries. This is one way Marxists would explain the frequency of political instability in developing countries. Furthermore, Western capitalists have been able to use the social and political institutions such as the news media, educational institutions, religion, and the legal institutions to create a "social consciousness" that supports capitalist ideologies and ruling classes. The capitalist state has at its disposal the powerful legal, law enforcement, military, administrative, and political machinery to put down any potential resistance from the ever exploited "proletariat".[9]

Marx's flaw lay in his oversight regarding the possibility that the interests of the workers and capitalist may coincide rather than conflict. Workers might support capitalism as they realized that they stood to achieve long-run gains from constant share in a rapidly growing output. This brings us to the rise and power of labor unions.

Karl Marx failed to anticipate the enormous power and influence of unionization and collective bargaining between the labor force and the "capitalists." Through collective bargaining, labor has been able not only to deter "exploitation", but also to receive a larger share of output through promotions, cost-of-living allowances, fringe benefits (that is, non-wage benefits such as health-care subsidies and vacation pay), retirement and pension benefits, and gratuities. These developments were entirely lost to Marx.

The theory also lacked foresight regarding the explosion in the number of high-wage jobs during the twentieth century. Significant research evidence that has emerged from the theory of *efficiency wages* supports the fact that "capitalist" firms themselves have voluntarily maintained high wages as a way of increasing productive efficiency and profit rates in the face of rising capital intensity of production (Marx's OCC).[10] What this means is that the Marxian notion of the falling rate of profit, and the dependence of the rate of profit on surplus value and the OCC, is totally flawed on the basis of both technical soundness as a concept and empirical validity in practice. The evidence shows that profit rates have rather tended to increase rather than decrease, together with the intensity of innovations and capital accumulation.

The Marxian model apparently has more problems with empirical substantiation than with intellectual appeal. Even where the model had been observed to seem to be working, particularly in China and Soviet Union, anything like a *utopian* state has hardly been realized. Rather, the "exploitation" has appeared to be meted out by the "ruling proletariat" against the rest of society through massive political repression, economic denial, and central authoritarianism. Nor have we witnessed the transitional metamorphosis of the society in the LDCs. On the contrary, some of the LDCs have tended to be stuck at one stage of the developmental transition indefinitely, thereby raising serious questions about the validity of the theory of *evolutionist state* for developmental policy actions in today's world.

One of the most troubling problems surrounding the soundness of the Marxian model is in relation to the theory's prediction about the role of the state. In positing the state as an instrument of exploitative oppression by the capitalist *bourgeoisie*, the Marxian model showed the state as a potential enemy of the generality of its own population. But even in the most capitalist of all capitalist societies, the state has proved otherwise. There is no historical evidence that seem to support the theory of class conflicts. What is more, the state could be, and has been, an important agent for ameliorating the economic conditions of a society for quicker economic growth and faster development. Twentieth-century Western Europe has witnessed the operation of "welfare statism" which guarantees minimum levels of acceptable income distribution within "capitalist" systems. Capitalist states have operated public utility regulatory controls, laws that establish the right of labor unions to organize and function with strikes. Capitalist states have effected monetary and fiscal policies for economic stabilization.

Generally, we would conclude that the dramatic collapse of Marxism in Eastern Europe and the Soviet Union, as well as in the developing countries of Marxist-leaning Cuba, Ethiopia, and Nicaragua, so exposed a disdain for Marxism that contemporary development policy makers would not likely look at any Marxian models with seriousness. But the study of the theory has helped us get a good picture of the economic development "question" from a slightly radical standpoint. We can appreciate Marx's remarkable zeal and tenacity in, no doubt, advancing what proved to be an "evolutionary" theory for only as long as it worked.

Having said this, we should observe that the present-day incessant layoffs and apparent obsession with "downsizing" in firms in Western capitalist economies, may well vindicate Karl Marx's theory, especially as it relates to the creation of the "reserve army" of unemployed. Much of today's layoffs are the result of capital-labor substitution that displaces labor. Downsizing simply means the reduction of the size of the work force, amounting to the reduction of variable capital as Marx explained.

There is an ever increasing pursuit of profit accumulation among capitalist firms in today's Western societies. This objective is almost always sought through systematic dispalement of workers and substitution of advanced technology in their place. For example, Automatic Teller Machines (ATMs) have taken over most of the jobs of bank-tellers, while high-performance computers and fax machines have displaced many corporate secretaries. Although the argument is often made that "higher-paying positions have been created in place of these relatively low-paying positions" (such as bank tellers and secretaries), there is no question that such replacements create more inequality in income distribution. It remains a question of time whether Karl Marx will be vindicated.

NOTES

1. These are found in the writings and formulations of: Adam Smith. *An Inquiry into the Nature and Causes of the Wealth of Nations* (New York: Modern Library, 1937, first published 1776). David Ricardo's nineteenth- century work was entitled *Principles of Political Economy and Taxation*, published in the year 1817. His work also appears in David Ricardo. *Works and Correspondence*, Edited by Piero Sraffa (Cambridge: Cambridge University Press, 1951-1955). Also included is Thomas R. Malthus's contribution entitled *Essay on the Principle of Population*, published in 1798. The theories of Karl Marx are also considered to fit within the classical label, for they were based on orthodox classical economic thinking that prevailed during the nineteenth and twentieth centuries.

2. The original classical proposition was that workers and landlords did not save; only entrepreneurs saved in the economy. It viewed individuals as willing to produce essentially for sustenance and nothing more. Therefore $Y-R-wL$ is the ability of the individual and households to save whatever is left after sustenance needs $(R+wL)$ are met: they do not voluntarily save. Only entrepreneurs of the business sector save. Their willingness to save is measured by what remains after removal of what is required for sustenance as well.

3. For Ricardo, diminishing returns from population growth on a constant amount of land threatens economic growth in a world of fairly constant technological know-how. If a technological change brings improvement in production techniques, it can only temporarily check diminishing returns and not eliminate it. Therefore, increasing the amount of capital stock would be the only way of offsetting the inevitable long-run threat of diminishing returns.

4. This analysis explains the concept of *quasi rent*: the payment made to a factor of production whose supply is fixed in the short run, and which is over and above that factor's opportunity cost.

5. The original Marxian theory can be found in: Karl Marx. *Capital* (Harmondsworth:

Penguin Books Edition, 1976); K. Marx and F. Engels. *Manifesto of the Communist Society* (New York: International Publishers, 1948 (written in 1848). Some of the earlier analyses of the model were conducted by Joan Robinson. 1967. *Essay on Marxian Economics* (New York: St. Martin's Press, 1967) and M. Sweezy. *The Theory of Capitalist Development* (New York: Oxford University Press, 1942).

6. That the Marxian *labor theory of value* is different from the Ricardian version. While in the Marxian variant labor time determines the *absolute* value of goods and services, the Ricardian version states that the *relative* value of different commodities is proportional to the labor time embodied in each.

7. Marx distinguished between labor power and labor time. Labor power refers to the worker's productive effort and ability to work and produce goods and services; labor time is the actual activity and duration of work task. Labor power was seen as a commodity that is bought and sold, and is what capitalists need to make profits.

8. This thinking is the source of the contemporary Marxist position on imperialism, which is viewed as a natural outgrowth of exploitative undertakings inherent in capitalism.

9. Greater details of these proposals can be found in: D. K. Foley. *Understanding Capital: Marx's Economic Theory* (Cambridge, Mass.: Harvard University Press, 1986); J. E. King. (ed.). *Marxian Economics* (3 vols.) (Brookfield, Vt.: Edward Elgar Press, 1990); and M. Blaugh. (ed.). *Karl Marx.* (Brookfield, Vt.: Edward Elgar Press, 1991).

10. Some of these studies include: G. A. Akerlof and J. Yellen. *Efficiency Wage Models of the Labour Market* (New York: Cambridge University Press, 1986); A. Weiss. *Efficiency Wages: Models of Unemployment, Layoffs, and Wage dispersion* (Princeton, N.J.: Princeton University Press, 1990). See also Ezeala-Harrison (1988a, 1992a, 1992b).

5

The Neoclassical Theories of Economic Growth and Development

This chapter deals with the theories of economic growth and development that utilize some of the basic classical tenets outlined in Chapter 4. However, as these theories are built on fundamental Keynesian ideas, we may refer to them as Keynesian-type models of growth and development. These theories stress the role of the *demand side* of the economy (aggregate demand) in determining output and employment in the short run. Their policy implications involve active (interventionist) roles for government in tackling short-run countercyclical economic difficulties.[1]

The neoclassical Keynesian-type growth models rely on market forces to propel the processes of development, but they emphasize that actively pursued and directed (fine-tuning) policies can accelerate the pace of growth and development. That is, governments can, and should, push development faster than market forces (which are rather sluggish) might have allowed. Various policy instruments are at the government's disposal to pursue this objective, and the market economy and its competitive, self-regulating qualities can be complemented by some degree of government controls to guide and quicken the development process. We present three of the leading models of the neoclassical growth theories - the Harrod-Domar growth model, the Hansen Secular Stagnation thesis, and the Solow growth model - and assess their key policy implications for development and underdevelopment.

THE HARROD-DOMAR GROWTH MODEL

The growth theory that is named after its originators, Roy F. Harrod and Evsey D. Domar, was developed separately by these two early twentieth-century economists.[2] These authors established their theories on the Keynesian framework. The theories are highly complex but essentially reach similar conclusions. We present a simplified version of the Harrod-Domar model here and explicate the two versions separately in the *Appendix* to this chapter.

The basic Harrod-Domar (HD) model assumes that the economy's potential level of GDP is a function of the level of net investment spending, under a given state of the productivity of capital. It also assumes that the economy's level of total savings is the ultimate generator of the capacity to invest: that is, *ex-ante* savings (a savings level generated for purposes of freeing resources for investment) equals *ex-post* investment (actual level of investment realized). In symbols, letting S = savings and I = investment, we may write this equality as

$$I = S \tag{5.1}$$

As long as the economy maintains this equality, there will be no tendency for instability to occur; that is, neither severe inflation nor chronic unemployment will be imminent. However, should investment demand in the economy exceed the amount of savings generated (possibly, say, due to excessive foreign investment or an unexpected increase in autonomous investment), excess demand will occur in the economy and inflation will result. If, on the other hand, savings become greater than investment, deficient demand will obtain, resulting in unemployment. This is an assumption of a *knife-edge* path for the economy over time.

The HD model also assumes a given state of the productivity of capital in the economy. The productivity of capital, defined as the average product of capital (under a given state of technology) is given by

$$\sigma = Y/K = 1/v \tag{5.2}$$

where

        σ = average product of capital
        Y = GDP
        K = level of capital stock
        v = K/Y = capital-output ratio (a measure of how much capital units
            it takes to produce one unit of output)[3]

As net investment spending adds to the economy's capital stock and raises productive capacity and potential output, then any changes in productive capacity, being dependent on investment level, would be given by

$$\Delta Y = \sigma.I = (1/v)I \tag{5.3}$$

For the economy to remain in steady-state growth equilibrium, $I = S$. But total savings in the economy is generated ex-post (that is, the amount of savings out of total GDP). Presumably, it is this volume of ex-post savings that gives rise to the next period's ex-ante savings required for investment in that period. Thus,

$$I = s.Y, \tag{5.4}$$

where s = marginal propensity to save (out of GDP). Substituting Equation (5.4) into (5.3), we obtain

$$\Delta Y = (1/v)sY \tag{5.5}$$

from which it follows that

$$\Delta Y/Y = g = s/v \tag{5.6}$$

The left-hand side of Equation (5.6) defines the growth rate of GDP, or economic growth, g. This indicates that the rate of growth is given by the ratio of the savings rate and the capital-output ratio. Equation (5.6) is termed the *warranted growth rate* of the economy. This term is used because this is the growth rate that is warranted by the economy's capacity to save (as measured by the savings rate, s).

Policy Implications of the HD Model

The major policy implications of the HD model are very clear from its underlying assumptions and analyses. As pointed out earlier, the HD model is premised heavily on Keynesian thought. Its strongest Keynesian aspect lies in the implicit assumption it embodies regarding the stability of the consumption function: additional demand and consumption expenditures would be forthcoming only if GDP expands. Therefore, since investment spending is the source of increases in aggregate demand needed to raise income from one period to another, investment spending in the new period must exceed investment spending of the preceding period in order for the economy to realize the added potential income arising from that preceding period.

Following the Keynesian postulate of the tendency for the economy to be characterized by inherent instability over time (since investment spending depends on autonomous investment which is dependent on the state of what Keynes termed the *animal spirits* of investors), it is realised that annual investment growth cannot automatically be sufficient to ensure the achievement of (full employment) potential GDP. Therefore, this *knife-edge* growth path of the economy is apt to result in incessant instability (spells of inflation or unemployment) unless it is actively managed or "fine-tuned" by an active interventionist government (demand management) policy.

The model implies that the rate of savings is the principal determinant of the growth rate of an economy under given levels of productivity of capital (capital-output ratio) and state of technology. Thus, the capacity to grow depends on the ability to save, a conclusion that is analogous to that reached by classical theories. Also, falling capital-output ratio is needed for increased growth. This implies that the economy must be increasing its productivity of capital over time, a technological requirement.

Critique of the Harrod-Domar Model

The HD model was a major innovation in the study of growth and development. It helped further understanding of the problems of economic fluctuations and cyclical swings. The novelty of the HD theories led to renewed scholarly interest in the theory of growth and development, and the analysis stimulated further study and research toward development of alternative theories of growth. However, the HD model seems to have limited applicability to the growth and development problems of LDCs. Generally, the model seems to apply mainly for relatively large economies that have attained a significant level of capacity to generate high levels of savings, investment, and technological know-how. Most LDCs would not belong in this category.

Specifically, the model's prescription that increased savings would raise the pace of economic growth is suspect. Mere accumulation of savings need not translate into growth. An economy must have the required *absorptive capacity* in order to effectively utilize the saved resources to generate growth. Most LDCs lack this absorptive capacity; huge capital resources have flowed into many LDCs without having led to growth, and at times the resources saved have been transmitted outside the economy, thereby sapping the economy of both the saved resources and the potential demand it would have created if it had been consumed rather than saved. The HD model fails to incorporate ideas of how to channel savings to generate growth.

The assumption of the equality of savings and investment need not be tenable in LDCs. Most LDCs are "open economies" that are subject to rapid and substantial inflows and outflows of capital resources at all times. The constant disequilibria that would be introduced by such movements makes the "knife-edge" analysis of the HD model unrealistic. And the theory fails to address how such disequilibrium conditions may be contained within the economy's steady state growth path over time. Moreover, owing to the inflexibility of interest rates, the capital markets in most LDCs rarely function smoothly enough to yield equilibrium. Therefore, the bulk of the flow of investment in such economies would be of an autonomous nature, outside the control of authorities to manage. This implies that the basis of an active government policy designed to influence the volume of investment for development is weak.

The assumption of a constant capital-output ratio also implies constant technology. Technology, however, changes over time. The model does not provide for the effects of changing technological know-how, and this limits its usefulness for policy formulation. Nor does it consider the implications of a growing population and labor force, and how these might affect the productivity of capital and therefore the capital-output ratio. But it is important to note that despite these shortcomings, the HD model has continued to be seen as a major breakthrough in the annals of development economics, especially in representing the earliest theoretical formulation of growth theory that departs significantly from the predominantly classical traditions of the time.

HANSEN'S THEORY OF SECULAR STAGNATION

In 1938 Alvin Hansen advanced his stagnation thesis and used it to endorse active and continuous government stabilization policies toward the achievement of economic growth and development.[4] Hansen used the Keynesian argument that investment spending would increasingly be inadequate for driving the economy toward its potential output and growth level. He believed that the economy's productive capacity tends to increase with the addition of new capital stock and application of technological progress. Therefore, in order for national income (actual level of output) and national output (potential GDP) to grow at the same pace, new investment spending must increase to prevent planned saving (which is a function of income) from exceeding planned investment. Otherwise, the economy's actual level of output will fall below its potential level.

Hansen's view on the inability of new investment to keep abreast of the level required for continued growth was based on the belief that the population would not be growing at the rate it had grown previously to support economic growth, and that the pace of technological progress would slow down, together with the availability of new and unexploited natural resources. Moreover, according to Hansen, the growth of those major industries such as iron and steel, railroads, and automobiles, would have abated. Consequently, increasing growth in investment spending would be unlikely. Therefore, the economy tends to gravitate toward secular stagnation over time, unless the government intervenes through *compensatory financing* and increases its expenditures to offset the inadequacies of investment spending. By so doing, the government uses its expenditures to fill the gap between the private-sector demand and potential output.

Trends of Potential and Actual Output

The essential tenet of Hansen's model is that the economy will deviate from the path of sustained growth over time and tend toward stagnation. For even though the economy's potential output (supply) may have steady growth, its actual output (demand) would tend to decline over time. The economy's potential output is specified as the production function of total resource endowment:

$$Y_p = Y(N, L, K, E) \tag{5.7}$$

where

Y_p = potential level of output
N = level of natural resources
L = level of the labour force
K = level of capital
E = mix of entrepreneurial abilities and technological know-how

The growth potential of the economy over time is defined as dY_p/dt, which can be obtained from Equation (5.7) as

$$dY_p/dt = \partial Y_p/\partial N.dN/dt + \partial Y_p/\partial L.dL/dt$$
$$+ \partial Y_p/\partial K.dK/dt + \partial Y_p/\partial E.dE/dt \qquad (5.8)$$

This indicates that the time rate of increase of potential output is given by the sum of the products of resource productivities and their respective time growth rates. Hansen believed that the right-hand side of Equation (5.8) would always be positive. That is, the economy's potential output has the tendency to grow positively over time. This would be valid only if the following conditions hold: (1) there must be, at the least, a constant state of technology that guarantees a constant level of input productivities - that is, $\partial Y_p/\partial N$, $\partial Y_p/\partial L$, $\partial Y_p/\partial K$, and $\partial Y_p/\partial$ are, at least, constant over time; and (2) there must be continuous increase in the rate of discovery and exploitation of resources ($dN/dt > 0$), population and labor force growth rate ($dL/dt > 0$), capital accumulation ($dK/dt > 0$), and technological progress ($dE/dt > 0$). We might observe that as long as the population grows at a positive rate under a given state of technology, then dY_p/dt will be positive.

Hansen's actual output (Y_a) is based on the Keynesian aggregate demand model that posits the economy's aggregate demand as the sum of the private individual and household-sector consumption spending (C), private business-sector investment spending (I), and the public-sector spending (government expenditure, G).[5] This is stated as

$$Y_a = C + I + G \qquad (5.9)$$

Total private-sector individual and household consumption consists of autonomous consumption (C_0) and the propensity to consume out of disposable income. Disposable income is given by total income (Y) minus total income taxes (T). With the marginal propensity to consume, c, the consumption function is

$$C = C_0+c(Y-T), \ 0<c<1 \qquad (5.10)$$

and with tax rate, τ, total income taxes is given by

$$T = \tau Y, \ 0 < \tau < 1$$

According to Hansen, the economy's total level of investment is given by the sum of *autonomous investment* (I_0) and *induced investment* (I_i). The level of autonomous investment depends on the growth rate of the combined effects of resource discovery and exploitation, population growth, and entrepreneurial innovation. This combined effect may be denoted by R, and its growth rate and functional determinants are defined as

$$dR/dt = f(dN/dt) + f(dL/dt) + f(dE/dt)$$

The level of induced investment, on the other hand, is a function of the growth rate of income dY_a/dt. Thus, total investment in the economy is

$$I = I_0(dR/dt) + I_i(dY_a/dt). \tag{5.11}$$

Public-sector spending is constituted of government expenditure, G, which is largely autonomous. Equation (5.9) may now be written as

$$Y_a = C_0 + c(Y_a - \tau Y_a) + I_0(dR/dt) + I_i(dY_a/dt) + G$$

or

$$Y_a(1 - c + c\tau) = C_0 + I_0(dR/dt) + I_i(dY_a/dt) + G$$

or

$$Y_a(s + c\tau) = C_0 + I_0(dR/dt) + I_i(dY_a/dt) + G$$

where s = marginal propensity to save

From the above, the level of actual output (aggregate demand) is solved as

$$Y_a = \{1/(s + c\tau)\}[C_0 + I_0(dR/dt) + I_i(dY_a/dt) + G] \tag{5.12}$$

The Secular Stagnation of Actual Output

According to Hansen's model, the growth rate of actual output can be found by differentiating Equation (5.12) with respect to time:

$$dY_a/dt = \{1/(s + c\tau)\}[\partial I_0/\partial(dR/dt).d^2R/dt^2$$
$$+ \partial I_i/\partial(dY_a/dt).d^2Y_a/dt^2 + dG/dt] \tag{5.13}$$

Hansen then demonstrates how the right-hand side of this equation would tend to zero over time; that is, the economy's actual output would stagnate. In doing so, each of the parameters of Equation (5.13) is examined in turn.

Declining Size of the Multiplier

The term in the first bracket of this equation, $1/(s+c\tau)$, is the Keynesian (expenditure) *multiplier*. Presumably, Hansen felt that the value of the multiplier would tend to zero over time because of the tendencies of its parameters, s, c, and τ, to rise over time. The marginal propensity to save, s, would tend to increase over time because of the increasing propensities to save on the part of people as time goes on, due to rising uncertainties and increasing feelings of financial insecurity. The marginal propensity to consume, c, would tend to increase over time because of the role that *International Demonstration Effects on Consumption (IDEC)* plays in consumption patterns.[6] The tax rate, τ, rises over time because of the increasing size of government and the need for government to raise more revenue to meet the rising costs of administration and provision of *public goods* as population rises.

Disappearance of the Frontier and Falling Population

Hansen further explains that, except dG/dt, the parameters inside the larger bracket of Equation (5.13) will also tend to zero over time. As for the growth of induced investment, $\partial I_i/\partial(dY_a/dt)$, it will progressively decline as the size of actual output, Y_a, declines over time and dY_a/dt falls. The parameter $\partial I_0/\partial(dR/dt)$, which denotes how changes in the combined effects of the growth rate of R would influence autonomous investment, would tend to decline over time because the factors that determine R would themselves taper off over time. That is, $\partial(dR/dt)$ approaches zero over time because dR/dt tends to zero. The factors on which dR/dt depend are as follows.

1. Changes in dN/dt: over time, the pace of resource discovery and exploitation will diminish because of a phenomenon that Hansen termed the "disappearance of the frontier." The "frontier" referred to new areas of fertile soil and abundant mineral resources characterized by a relatively high-yielding rate of return to investment. Such frontiers tend to disappear as they are increasingly explored and utilized; moreover, the amount of existing and exploitable natural resources will decrease owing to increasing (over) use. Consequently, entrepreneurs adopt more cautious attitudes in taking risks on their investments involving new resources. Therefore, dN/dt declines over time, tending to zero.

2. Population growth: Hansen saw population growth as a periodic pattern that depended on the stages of development attained in the society in particular eras. At the initial stages of low levels of development, the society's population pattern would be characterized by a low birth rate (LBR) and high death rate (HDR) stage. LBR is due to the low means of sustenance resulting from low incomes, whereas the HDR is due to lack of adequate nutritional and medical facilities. As incomes grow, however, the population pattern enters the stage of HBR and LDR (low death rate), as higher incomes make children more

affordable and improvements in nutritional standards and advances in medical technology produce higher life expectancy and survivability of children. Subsequently, as the desire for greater individual economic attainment and material well-being leads to reduced family sizes, the stage of LBR and LDR is reached. In Hansen's view, this stage will remain the long-term population pattern of the society, causing the population and the labor force growth rate, dN/dt, to decline over time.

3. Falling rate of innovations: first, Hansen believed that innovation had been facilitated by the development of the *Great New Industries*: iron and steel, the railway system, the automobile, electricity, and the like, that typically accompany industrialization and development. However, as this infrastructure is established and generates growth and development, it does not increase in size. Only obsolescence and maintenance encourage new innovations in them. Therefore, the number of innovations decline. Second, Hansen believed that the risks of innovation and investment would become greater over time, ultimately choking off new investments flowing into innovations. This is because of the rising degree of competition that characterizes the free market economy. As a result of the combination of these factors, dE/dt declines over time.

Public Sector Spending

Declining dR/dt causes the actual output, Y_a, to fall over time. Whether or not the economy actually stagnates eventually depends on the size of the remaining parameter in the right-hand side of Equation (5.13), namely, dG/dt, the growth rate of public-sector spending. Hansen therefore demonstrated that the rate of growth of actual output would amount to the rate of growth of government expenditure. In advancing this model, Hansen forcefully projects his strong Keynesian leanings and convictions regarding the potency of active government interventionism in promoting economic growth and development.

Policy Implications of the Secular Stagnation Thesis

Hansen's thesis became one of the most cogent studies of its time to lean unequivocally toward Keynesian policy prescriptions. Its linking of economic growth to the growth of public-sector spending meant that market-based policy approaches to development would miss the mark, at best. It indicates that the government must actively be involved in using the appropriate policy tools open to it to promote the economy's resource exploration and exploitation, entrepreneurship and technological development, human capital and manpower development, and infrastructural development. This would necessitate the use of both *macro* (monetary and fiscal) and *micro* (sector-specific) policies.

Active macro (demand management) policies would be needed to increase and sustain the multiplier to preempt its natural tendency to decline. Active micro policies would be needed to direct investment into exploration and utilization of natural resources to deter the onset of the *disappearance of the frontier*. It would also be required to develop social and economic infrastructure in order to compensate for the decline of the *Great New Industries*. Thus, Hansen's work inadvertently pointed to the need for interventionist micro policies as well as macro policies at a period when the role and efficacy of micro policies were hardly known.

The Hansen thesis clearly implies a positive role for population growth in economic development. Since population growth is correlated with induced investment, rising population will promote economic growth. This marked the first time that population growth had been postulated as anything other than negative to a country's development effort, and represented a notable difference from the classical theories that preceded Hansen's theory.

THE SOLOW GROWTH MODEL

In a major breakthrough into the then relatively scanty world of neoclassical theories of growth, the 1987 Nobel Prize winner, Robert M. Solow, developed his seminal work on the theory of growth in 1956.[7] This model is widely referred to as the *neoclassical* growth model because Solow employed a good mix of both the orthodox classical and Keynesian tenets in its formulation. We present the essential details of the model in a simplified version.

The growth of national output is presumed to depend on the combination of the sizes of resources possessed: physical resources (presumably) encompassing natural and capital resources, which are together denoted as K, and human resources encompassing labor and entrepreneurial abilities, together denoted as L. These resources are related to national output by the technologically augmented implicit production function:

$$Y = A.f(K,L) \tag{5.14}$$

assumed to be homogeneous of degree one.[8] The parameter A represents an index of technological change, indicating that technological progress is a shift parameter in the production function. That is, technological progress raises the capacity of output.

Solow's model also assumes the equality of savings and investment similar to the Harrod-Domar assumptions. Thus, defining savings as the total amount saved out of GDP and defining investment as the time rate of growth of capital stock:

$$S = s.Y$$

and

$$I = dK/dt$$

where

      S = savings level
      s = marginal propensity to save (out of GDP)
      I = investment level
      t = time

we have

$$sY = dK/dt$$

Substituting the production function (Equation 5.14) into this, we find that

$$dK/dt = sAf(K,L) \tag{5.15}$$

The model presumes that the amount of capital per worker in the economy is of crucial importance in determining the capacity of output. The *capital-labor* ratio is defined by

$$k = K/L$$

which means that the total level of capital stock is given by

$$K = k.L$$

To determine the rate of growth of the capital-labour ratio, this relationship is differentiated with respect to time, t, to obtain

$$dK/dt = k.dL/dt + L.dk/dt \tag{5.16}$$

As Equations (5.15) and (5.16) both define the economy's level of investment, depicting the rate of growth of capital stock over time, they are expressed together as

$$sAf(K,L) = k.dL/dt + L.dk/dt$$

Dividing through by L (since the production function is homogeneous of degree one), we have

$$\{sAf(K,L)\}/L = k(dL/dt)/L + dk/dt$$

or

$$sAf(k) = k(dL/dt)/L + dk/dt$$

from which

$$dk/dt = sAf(k) - gk \tag{5.17}$$

where $g = (dL/dt)/L$ = the growth rate of (population) labor force

Equation (5.17) is the popularly acknowledged *Solow growth equation*, which depicts the rate of growth of an economy's capital-labor ratio as a function of savings rate, s, the state of technology, A, the existing level of capital stock per worker, k, and the labor force and population growth rate, g. Viewed altogether, the equation indicates that the proportional change in the level of capital per worker (dk/dt) equals the total level of savings out of GDP ($sAf(k)$) minus the level of investment required to keep an initial level of capital per worker constant (gk). This means that the economy's capacity (or ability) to grow will depend on what is left from the total level of current savings; and what is left from the level of current savings depends on the level of population growth (which needs to be sustained by the level of resources saved).

Policy Implications of the Solow Model

In Solow's model, economic growth is proxied by the level of capital per worker. Thus, the rate of population growth enters as an obstacle to economic growth. This model represents one of the earliest pointers to the supposed threat that the high rate of population growth poses to economic growth and development. This model has become a leading policy tool that guides development economists in their vigorous clamoring for population control as a way of fostering growth.

The role of savings in economic growth is again emphasized in Solow's model. Unlike the Harrod-Domar model (which emphasizes the *rate* of savings), The Solow model stresses the economy's *level* of savings. Applied to LDCs, for example, this means that increasing domestic and foreign investment, and thus the rate of capital accumulation, would have a similar effect as raising domestic savings, which enhances the level of capital per worker and therefore GDP per head. The capacity to grow therefore depends on the ability to save, a conclusion that is analogous to that reached by the orthodox *classical* theories as well.

APPENDIX

In this Appendix we present separately the Harrod's and Domar's theories of growth.

Harrod's Model

Harrod's model assumes that total savings at any given time period in the economy is equal to the amount saved out of the total GDP of the preceding period. That is,

$$S_t = sY_{t-1} \tag{A5.1}$$

where

S = Total savings
$s = dS/dY$ = marginal propensity to save
t = time in years

Investment at any time period is assumed to be equal to the total amount of capital produced from resources saved from one period to another:

$$I_t = \kappa(Y_t - Y_{t-1}) \tag{A5.2}$$

where

$0 < \kappa < 1 = dI/dY$ = the accelerator coefficient
I = volume of investment

In equilibrium, $S_t = I_t$, therefore

$$sY_{t-1} = \kappa(Y_t - Y_{t-1})$$

or

$$\kappa Y_t - \kappa Y_{t-1} - sY_{t-1} = \kappa Y_t - (\kappa + s)Y_{t-1} = 0$$

that is

$$Y_t - [(\kappa + s)/\kappa]Y_{t-1} = 0$$

or

$$Y_t = [(\kappa + s)/\kappa]Y_{t-1} = (1 + s/\kappa)Y_{t-1} \tag{A5.3}$$

Equation (A5.3) is a first-order difference equation whose general solution is given upon substituting t = 1, 2, 3..., as

$$Y_t = B(1 + s/\kappa)^t \tag{A5.4}$$

where B = constant.

Equation (A5.3) is Harrod's growth path of output over time. It indicates that income at any time is growing at a steady state rate of s/κ, the *warranted rate* of growth. This gives a dynamic equilibrium for the economy as long as there is equality between savings and investment. We note that the difference between Harrod's equation and the HD equation (Equation 5.6) lies in the denominators of both equations. The HD equation assumes a constant capital-output ratio

(K/Y), while Harrod's equation assumes a constant *incremental capital-output ratio* (dI/dY). This difference lies in the dynamic nature of Harrod's approach as against the static nature of the HD (re)formulation.

Domar's Model

Domar's model deals with a continuous process of GDP growth in which investment plays a dual role of increasing productive capacity and increasing aggregate demand. Defining

Y_a = actual output
Y_p = potential output
$\sigma = Y/K$ = potential average productivity of investment
I = volume of investment

we can write

$$dY_p/dt = \sigma.I$$

Substituting $v = K/Y = 1/\sigma$, this becomes

$$dY_p/dt = 1/v.I$$

(A5.5)

This depicts the productive capacity aspect of investment.
On the demand side,

$$dY/dt = dC/dt + dI/dt = cdY/dt + dI/dt = (1-s)dY/dt + dI/dt$$

where

C = consumption,
c = marginal propensity to consume

This gives

$$dY/dt - (1-s)dY/dt = dI/dt$$

or

$$sdY/dt = dI/dt$$

that is

$$dY/dt = (1/s)dI/dt$$

(A5.6)

Again, this gives the second of the dual effects of investment: the effective demand-creating capacity of investment (through the multiplier process).

For full-capacity utilization equilibrium, aggregate supply equals aggregate demand; that is, Equation (A5.5) equals (A5.6):

$$1/v.I = 1/s.dI/dt$$

This gives

$$dI/dt = s/v.I$$

(A5.7)

Equation (A5.7) is a first-order differential equation, which is solved, upon integrating both sides, to obtain:

$$I_t = I_0 e^{(s/v)t}$$

(A5.8)

This gives Domar's growth path of investment required to achieve full-capacity utilization over time. It indicates that investment must grow at the warranted rate of s/v.

To verify that if I grows at the rate s/v then GDP will also grow at the rate s/v, we integrate both sides of Equation (A5.6):

$$Y_t = (1/s)I_0 e^{(s/v)t} + B, B = \text{constant}$$

Given that $Y_0 = (1/s)I_0$, then, $I_0 = sY_0$, and substituting this into the above, at $t=0$, we have

$$Y_0 = (1/s)I_0 + B = Y_0 + B, \text{ implying that } B = 0.$$

Thus,

$$Y_t = Y_0 e^{(s/v)t}$$

(A5.9)

This again gives the (warranted) rate of growth of income over time.

NOTES

1. Although the Keynesian system of economic ideas arose out of the neoclassical school of thought, it differs from the neoclassical model in many respects. These range from the degrees of government intervention in the economy to the length of time period that may be regarded as the short run. These differences have shaped the ever-raging "monetarist-Keynesian" debate in (macro)economic policy. For details on the differences and similarities between Keynesian and (neo)classical ideas, see Brue (1994).

2. These ideas were published in R. F. Harrod, "An Essay in Dynamic Theory," *The Economic Journal*, March, 1939: 14-33; and R. F. Harrod, *Toward a Dynamic Analysis*

(London: Macmillan, 1944); and Evsey D. Domar, "Capital Expansion, Rate of Growth, and Employment," *Econometrica*, 14, (1946); and Evsey D. Domar, "Expansion and Employment", *American Economic Review*, 37, (1947): 34-55; and also Evsey D. Domar, "The Problem of Capital Accumulation", *American Economic Review*, 38, (1948): 77-94.

3. σ may be seen as the potential average productivity of new investment, in which case it measures the amount by which each unit of investment spending would increase the economy's capacity to generate future output and income.

4. Alvin Hansen (1887-1975) easily became the leading Keynesian economist of his time in the United States. He extended the work of Keynes in macroeconomic analysis, earning the reference "the American Keynes" because of his strong advocacy of government intervention to promote full employment and growth. He trained such eminent economists as Paul Samuelson, James Tobin, Evsey Domar, Paul Sweezy, Richard Musgrave, and John Dunlop. Together with John R. Hicks, Hansen developed the unified macroeconomic model that bears their names: the Hicks-Hansen IS-LM model, which synthesized the Keynesian and classical perspectives, leading to the resolution of the apparent indeterminacy of interest rate between the real and monetary sectors of the economy. In his 1938 *Full Recovery or Stagnation*, Hansen developed his thesis on Secular Stagnation, by which he argued that it is unlikely that investment spending would expand sufficiently from one period to another in order to keep the economy fully employed and growing at a healthy rate.

5. As the economy's aggregate demand is really made up of the total domestic sector demand (given by Equation 5.9) and the net foreign sector demand (total exports minus total imports), Hansen presumably assumed either a closed economy or that the economy's foreign trade is always balanced.

6. Myrdal (1957) used this term, IDEC, to qualify the emulation of consumption patterns of the DCs within the LDCs. He propounded that the income-elasticity of demand for imported goods of the DCs in the LDCs is highly influenced by the IDEC. According to *Engels's law*, the demand for manufactured goods is income-elastic (income-elasticity is greater than one), while for (agricultural) primary products, demand is income-inelastic (less than one). Therefore, rising incomes will be accompanied by greater proportionate increases in the demand for manufactured goods rather than primary products.

7. The model has been simplified in many ways since its formulation. For the original work, see R. M. Solow, "A Contribution to the Theory of Economic Growth", *Quarterly Journal of Economics*, 70 (1956): 65-94.

8. This means that production is characterized by constant returns to scale. It implies that if all inputs are augmented (increased or decreased) by a given proportion, output changes by a similar proportion.

6

The Structuralist Theories of Economic Development

The essence of *structuralism* is that the LDCs should focus their development efforts within themselves by mobilizing their internal potentials and resources. The structuralist school of thought in economic development is premised on the ideas put forward through a United Nations agency established in 1947: the *Economic Commission for Latin America* (ECLA).[1] The thinking was that prevailing orthodox and neoclassical theories of development had little or nothing to contribute to the understanding of the peculiar development problems of peripheral countries. In fact, structuralism tended to blame the increasing income disparities between the DCs (*the center*) and the LDCs (*the periphery*) on the legitimacy accorded to the existing pattern of world economic order by neoclassical models and tenets. Thus, some Latin American economists and sociologists worked together for a set of alternative constructs, using the institutional forum and infrastructure provided by the ECLA.

The leading tenets of structuralist ideas were propounded by Raul Prebisch.[2] These ideas gave the problem of economic development a greater regional perspective. The center-periphery propositions gave greater and direct attention not only to Latin America but also to the entire underdeveloped world as a whole. The originality lies in the proposition that the process of economic development and underdevelopment is a single process involving the center and the periphery, two layers of the world developmental sphere that are very closely interrelated and that form part of one global economy. It is proposed that the disparities between the center and periphery are reproduced and sustained through the ongoing mechanism of international trade.

Structuralist economic thinking is driven by notions of the peculiarities of particular economic systems and their structural circumstances. It is based on the notion that development must be fashioned in accord with the economy's particular situation: level of development at the time, historical circumstances, geographical conditions, political setting, and the prevailing and overall global economic environment. Structuralist theories are based on the belief that orthodox classical and neoclassical models may not be suitable for LDCs because these models are premised on assumptions that are largely invalid for LDCs. Therefore, certain peculiar aspects of an LDC, for example, may prevent certain economic policy actions from being effective, although such a policy would function smoothly in DCs.

Classical and neoclassical ideas presume the flexibility of markets and prices, as well as the harmonious functioning of a country's economic, social, and political institutions. Structuralism sees such assumptions as not only unrealistic but also naive when projected to LDCs. Static equilibrium analysis, for instance, presumes that the paths to attainment of equilibria are clear, free from hindrances and indivisibilities. But this is untenable in LDCs where markets are largely imperfect and structural rigidities and indivisibilities abound. In LDCs, economic agents and actors may not necessarily be very responsive to small changes in prices and opportunities, nor would prices and quantities necessarily be as responsive to relative changes in each other, in the same degree that they might be in DCs. Producers in LDCs may not be as responsive to price and profit incentives if the society is rife with moral, religious, or cultural values that shape individual lives, beliefs, and aspirations.

Structuralist views on the state of development and the application of appropriate policy instruments toward development in LDCs can be predicated on the following observations.

The Center-Periphery Paradigm

The main cornerstone of structuralism is the center-periphery paradigm. It is used to explain the imbalanced nature of the world economic order. According to this notion, the world economic order is based on a dualistic structure created and maintained by the industrialized sectors of the world (the center) as they developed their industrial capital-goods sector used in spreading the improved technology throughout all sectors of their economies. This resulted in the development of a homogeneous and closely integrated economy. The periphery is the sector created and maintained solely as the source of raw materials and cheap labor, and as a market outlet for the mass production of the industrial center (the LDCs of the world, most of which had been colonized at one time or another for that purpose). In the periphery, new technologies are largely imported (from the center, of course) and confined mainly to the primary-product export sector. The industrial sector is kept small and inefficient in order to forestall its potential competition with exports from the center, while the capital goods sector is kept rudimentary.

The Industrial Revolution transformed the center countries into industrialized and developed economies, while at the same time assigning the peripheral countries the role of primary-product producers. Where industry became the most dynamic economic sector in the center, the most dynamic sector in the periphery has been the raw-material producing primary-product sector geared solely to exports, namely, agriculture and mining. Structuralists term this export-led growth orientation of the periphery the *outward-looking development model*. This development policy approach may be dynamic and effective as long as export earnings grow quickly and highly enough to sustain an adequate pace and rate of growth for the economy.

The result of the center-periphery policy is that the economy of the periphery is made dependent and dichotomized - dependent on the degree to which it could receive imported technology from the center, and dichotomized by having a gulf develop in its domestic economy: the export sector (the so-called modern sector) and the subsistence sector (see Chapter 1). The subsistence sector constitutes a sizeable noncapitalized and low-productivity segment that continues to survive or even dominate the economy of the periphery, producing a continuous surplus of unskilled and low-income labor.[3] This labor surplus and its low productivity keep wages low, and prevent the periphery from gaining the benefits of technological progress since productivity increases (in the export sector) are largely transferred to the center through the imbalanced terms of trade in favor of the center. In this way, international trade not only perpetuates and deepens the center-periphery asymmetry, it also serves as an instrument of the *underdevelopment* of the LDCs.

The Perpetual Terms of Trade Imbalance

The structuralist terms of trade position, especially the thesis of the perpetual deterioration of the periphery's terms of trade, has generated much controversy and produced a clash of ideas between structuralism and neoclassical doctrines.[4] The focus on the terms of trade issue challenged conventional (neoclassical) economic theories of international trade and its pivotal premise of international division of labor. Structuralists argue that, according to **Engels' law**, the income-elasticity of demand for manufactured goods is greater than one, while for agricultural primary products, the income-inelasticity of demand is less than one. Therefore, rising incomes will be accompanied by greater proportionate increases in the demand for manufactured goods rather than primary products. Hence, in the international market, the prices of manufactured goods would always tend to rise relative to that of primary products, resulting in a relative deterioration of the terms of trade of primary product exporters, the LDCs.

Structuralism argues against the conventional (neoclassical) international trade theoretical proposition. This proposition holds, in essence, that there are significant mutual benefits for all trading partners as each enjoy's *comparative advantage* in its respective area. This is because, over time, the effect of international trade would be to reduce income inequalities between trading countries as free factor mobilities (perfect mobilities of labor, capital, resources, and technology), on the one hand, and products, on the other, would equalize prices (the rates of exchange). This would then distribute the benefits (of technological progress) more equally between the trading countries.

The main argument in the structuralist arsenal is that specialization in primary raw-materials production limits the growth prospects of the periphery countries, as has been evident in Latin American countries, owing to the inevitable exhaustion of whatever export-led growth potential the primary sector had. Prebisch observed that the economic gap between the DCs and the LDCs continued to widen mainly because incomes tended to grow much faster in the industrialized (center) countries than in the LDCs (periphery). And this, in turn, is due to the prevailing international division of production and trade which confines the periphery to primary production (with its exceptionally low valued-added potential for development).

Structural Heterogeneity and Rigidities

A typical LDC lacks a sufficiently developed level of market networks that provides the effective signaling required to closely knit the various players in the economy together, in order to foster productivity growth (or keep productivity from faltering). The agricultural sector in LDCs, characterized by severe lack of communication and transportation, particularly suffers a lack of coordination in this regard. In this sector, the direction of prices and quantities is separated by long time lags that do not permit the effective development of the sector. For example, massive price reductions on consumer goods might not cause their demand to increase because of pervasive low-income levels among the population.

The money market does not function freely: rigid monetary and interest rate controls tend to preclude free flow of funds and finance to accommodate the growth of commerce and industry. Stock markets are not very functional; therefore, capital movements are restricted, and investment capacity is limited.

Role of Multinational Monopolies

The commercial and industrial sectors of most LDCs are dominated by monopolistic subsidiaries of multinational corporations (MNCs) whose activities are often inimical to the country's overall economic development. The (usual) small size of the domestic market and stiff competition from international competitors in the world market compel these industries to operate at wasteful excess capacity levels. The larger proportions of their profits are repatriated abroad rather than being reinvested in the LDC. In many instances, these firms obtain huge tax exemptions from the LDC's government as part of an incentive package used to attract them. In other cases, they establish "white elephant" projects that are not essential for development, while some MNCs are involved in extensive corrupting influences on some LDC's governments.

Legacies of Colonialism

Most LDCs have inherited economic, social, and political institutions from their colonizing powers that have been largely deterrent to their development. Such transplanted institutions (such as in the educational, legal, and political facets) only result in the LDC's cultural dependence on foreign values, and these do not function successfully in the LDC. This situation often gives rise to the growth of a small elite of a privileged segment among the population (such as the military or the academically educated), who acquire the foreign culture and lifestyle, rendering the economy import-dependent rather than geared toward mass production of domestic produce for industrialization and export. The economy experiences what structuralists refer to as *inward directed development*.

For purposes of organization, we consider the paradigms treated in this chapter as the "structuralist-type paradigms of development." Under this banner, we include the *Rostow Stage theories of economic development, the Balanced and Unbalanced growth (Big-Push) theories, the Prebischian Circular Deterioration hypothesis, Arthur Lewis' (Two-Sector) Dual economy model, and the Dependency theory of development.*

THE STAGE THEORIES OF GROWTH AND DEVELOPMENT

The stage theories of economic development are considered *ahistorical* in structuralist circles, for these theories do not take into account the external factors and different structures and dynamism that the center-periphery interaction brings into play. These theories propose that the economic development of a society involves a series of evolving stages through which the society must pass. Thus, all developed countries were once undeveloped (underdeveloped?) and the present-day LDCs, like the DCs, will evolve through their own respective series of stages into developed countries. The stage theories are eminently represented by the Rostow stage theories of growth.

W. W. Rostow (1961) developed a synthesis of the various historical and evolutionary ideas on the development of society, and formulated the stage theories of economic growth. Five stages are explained: the *traditional society*, establishing the *preconditions for takeoff*, the *takeoff*, the *drive to maturity*, and the final stage of the *age of high mass consumption*.

Stage 1: The Traditional Society

This stage is depicted as the earliest stage in the economic state of society. In this stage, the society is presumably characterized by agrarian production, predominance of unskilled labor, and limited productivity. Technology would be "pre-Newtonian," and social structure would be hierarchical, with little scope for vertical mobility.[5] At this stage the economy is not yet ready for self-sustained growth and development. Apparently, many present-day LDCs are still locked up in this stage.

Stage 2: The Preconditions for Take-off

Rostow saw this as the stage that was developed in Western Europe during the late seventeenth and early eighteenth centuries. In this period, modern science, as ushered in by the massive applications of Isaac Newtons's scientific formulations, was massively applied to develop industry and agriculture. Two case illustrations were offered: one in which this stage was attained through gradual metamorphosis from the traditional society, and the other in which this stage was effectively transplanted to form the basis for the economic development that was later achieved. The first case is Europe (much of Western Europe) and Asia (ostensibly Japan), while the second case is the "settler nations" or "born-free nations" (including the United States of America, Canada, Australia, New Zealand, and South Africa).[6]

Rostow thought that the preconditions stage required an "effective political coalition" that had strong interest in modernization and economic development, as well as a population that had a strong desire for economic progress, driven by an effective "urban-based modern society." In these circumstances, a strong entrepreneurial drive sustains investment in commerce and industry: risks are taken to convert inventions to innovations, creating productive enterprises.

Rostow's *leading Sector theory* states that some sectors of the economy have greater potential in leading the economy toward sustained growth. These sectors are found within the primary sector, notably, agriculture (especially food production, or cash crops (exports) such as wool, cotton, silk, timber, and rubber, or even, minerals (such as crude petroleum oil). The "spread effects" of growth in these sectors would "drag on" the rest of the economy toward self-sustained growth and development. Therefore, according to Rostow, it is the primary sector that would set the preconditions for takeoff.

Stage 3: The Takeoff

The takeoff stage is a stage of self-sustained, self-reinforcing growth, during which the economy finally overcomes the internal constraints and resistances to steady economic progress. According to Rostow, this stage is characterized chiefly by increases in savings and investment rates (the ratios of savings and investment to GDP) from about 5 percent or less to about 10 percent or more. Other features of the takeoff stage include the development of at least one major substantial manufacturing industrial sector. In Britain, this was the cotton textile industry which expanded rapidly, having wide spinoff (direct and indirect) effects on the demand for coal, iron, machinery, transport, and social infrastructure. Similarly, in France, the United States, Germany, Canada, and

Russia, the railroad sector grew rapidly to widen markets, providing powerful stimuli for the coal, iron, and engineering industries.

The takeoff stage is also characterized by the existence or emergence of a stable social, political, and institutional framework that harnesses the expanding economy. The institutional framework would include the banking, insurance, and capital markets. Stable legal institutions would emerge to support the social and political order, ensuring a the conducive atmosphere for entrepreneurial risk-taking and innovation, thereby fostering economic progress.

Rostow states that the takeoff can be defined as an industrial revolution. He assigns specific time spans for the takeoff stage and suggests that it covers an average period of twenty to thirty years for most countries. For Britain, the takeoff stage was the twenty-year period 1783-1802 (the beginning of the Industrial Revolution); for France, the thirty-year period 1830-1860 (preceding the French Revolution); for the United States, the eighteen-year period 1843-1860 (the railroad and manufacturing expansion era prior to the Civil War); for Japan, 1878-1900 (the twenty-three years just after the Meiji dynasty was restored); and for Canada, the twenty-year period 1896-1914. It would also refer to the twenty-fife-year period of rapid growth of the railroad, coal, iron, and heavy engineering industries leading to the 1917 Bolshevik Revolution in Russia.

Stage 4: The Drive to Maturity

Although Rostow does not clearly state the differences between them, the drive to maturity stage of economic development involves an extended period following takeoff, during which economic growth and development is sustained and becomes a regular feature of the economy. There may be fluctuations and cyclical swings, but the economy has finally achieved self-propelling growth. Rostow associates this stage with the investment of 10 to 20 percent of national income, permitting the GDP growth rate to regularly outstrip the growth rate of population. This era of maturity is expected to be achieved in about sixty years after takeoff, although the interval generally varies from country to country. It was obtained in Britain around 1850, in the United States around 1900, in France around 1910, in Japan around 1940, and in Canada around 1950.

At this stage, it is expected that the economy has finally been *structurally transformed*. The nation has acquired the mastery of existing technology as new leading sectors supplant the older ones in sustaining the growth and development process, and enables the economy to produce anything it chooses. The society is predominantly urbanized, and the labor force is largely skilled and highly productive.

Stage 5: The Age of High Mass Consumption

The economy's self-propelled growth and development continues until it reaches the final stage of high mass consumption, such as that attained in the

United States in the 1920s and Europe in the 1950s. The interval between the achievement of "maturity" and high mass consumption is apparently the longest. In this stage, the society may choose to be a welfare state (such as Britain, Canada, or Sweden), a world (militaristic) power (such as the United States), or simply an international pacifist (such as Switzerland or Austria).

The age of high mass consumption is the stage characterized by unlimited consumption of consumer durable goods and services on massive scales, for it symbolizes regular social and economic life. The automobile, electronic communication and entertainment gadgets, music, and the theatrical arts feature as prominent items in such a society's daily living.

Critique of Rostow's Stage Theories

The stage theories offer some pertinent insights into the key structural characteristics of different levels of economic development. They present perceptive indications of the changes that must occur in an economy if development is to be attained. Rostow offers some degree of dynamic, *albeit* quasi-evolutionist, perspective through which an economy's progress or lack of progress through the course of economic development may be measured. With its implied hope for sustained growth and development for those LDCs possessing the right conditions and showing the right signs, the stage theories represent a major body of thought that served useful purposes for American policy on international development during the 1960s.

Over time, however, the stage theories have been severely criticized as mere descriptions of characteristics that may be associated with various levels of economic achievement, without stating how they may be created. They are, therefore, not *theories* in the true sense of the word, but merely, observations. As such, Rostow's descriptions do not really offer any lessons or policy guides as to how to achieve the "stages" defined. The stages are simply definitions of various levels rather than explanations of the reasons for those levels of economic development, and as such they cannot possibly be proved wrong.

A major flaw of the stage theories is their observed circularity. They seem to be stating that in order for an LDC to achieve, say, takeoff, it must possess the conditions of takeoff. This is very vague indeed. Without question, Europe's economic development took a rather "natural" course driven by a mix of agricultural and industrial development in a series of stages. This pattern of development may not realistically be expected to be emulated by present-day LDCs. In this connection, Rostow's contribution becomes irrelevant.

Rostow failed to explain cases where instances of "takeoff" were not *preconditioned* as described. Nor does he explain the phenomenon of *economic dualism* in present-day LDCs. To what extent can the modern manufacturing industries of India, Indonesia, Mexico, Argentina, Nigeria, or Egypt be qualified as "pre-Newtonian"? Why would the stage of "high mass consumption" (of the

U.S. type) be a desirable level of economic development that a society may aspire to achieve? Would many societies not simply hold their levels of development at the "maturity stage" owing to cultural, political, and even environmental differences? As these questions seem to suggest, many of Rostow's conditions are highly irrelevant to most modern LDCs, and the stage theories appear to hold extremely limited usefulness to development policy-making today.[7]

THE BALANCED AND UNBALANCED GROWTH THEORIES

The balanced growth and unbalanced growth debate confronts the question of the *demand problem* in the economic development of LDCs. The demand problem arises from the lack of effective demand in the LDCs, which therefore constrains the ability to generate market-led economic growth. This idea is summarized in the concept of the *vicious circle of poverty*. This concept implies that poverty and underdevelopment exist because they are driven by underlying conditions of poverty and underdevelopment.[8]

Simply stated, the vicious circle of poverty has two dimensions: the demand side and the supply side. On the supply side, the condition of very low income results in low capacity to save and low savings, which gives rise to a low level investment level, small capital formation, limited productive capacity and low productivity, and low income. On the demand side, low income results in low market demand for output, which limits production and investment, and in turn limits incomes and market demand.

The balanced growth and unbalanced growth theories are propounded as ways to overcome the demand problem posed by the demand side of the vicious circle of poverty. The idea was advanced by Ragnar Nurkse (1953) and Rosenstein-Rodan (1957), among others. These writers presumably likened an LDC to a "stalled automobile" that needs to receive a massive jolt in order to enable it gain momentum and move again. This is the theory of the *Big Push*. Because the LDC's development is stagnant, a big push (or big pull) might be required to get it off the ground. It is important to understand clearly how balanced growth would provide the required big push for such an economy to be placed on a growth and development path.

The Balanced Growth and Big Push Theory

Balanced growth is the simultaneous establishment of a wide range of industrial projects across the major sectors within the economy, in a concerted effort to stimulate economic activity. Nurkse (1953) saw this approach as the most viable for an LDC, given that its exports face inelastic demand in the world market. Besides, an export-led strategy would amount to a gradual approach to overcoming the inertia inherent in a stagnant economy, which would not work. It needs a massively applied big push.

Apart from the apparent unsuitability of gradualism, the prevailing conditions in an LDC are less than adequate to initiate and sustain any viable economic activities that are capable of fostering growth and development. A big push needs to be exerted to initiate growth. Among the major problems of the LDC are the sluggishness of key market parameters such as prices, interest rates, bond prices, exchange rates, and the like. Moreover, the LDC has inadequate infrastructural facilities such as transportation systems, hydroelectric power, water and sewerage, and communications systems. The balanced growth advocates believe that investment in these infrastructural facilities create indivisibilities that spill over to the economy as a whole, rather than to the specific sectors and individuals involved in them. This occurs by way of creating demand for other sectors and services.[9]

The stagnant economy would need a big push by way of a comprehensive investment program that establishes a set of projects undertaken simultaneously. This would create an initial surge of demand stimuli in the economy, which is precisely what the economy needs. Thus, the maintenance of a balanced growth among several sectoral projects simultaneously would provide the *big push* that would jolt the stagnant economy into, presumably, the "preconditions" stage.[10]

Among the balanced growth advocates, Rosenstein-Rodan strongly believed that external sources of capital, combined with internally available cheap labor, would provide the required impetus for the big push. The projects would support each other by providing the demand for each other, thereby overcoming the demand problem. Such complementary demand would reduce the uninsurable risk of limited size of market and inadequate demand inherent in an LDC, which have been behind the lack of incentive for entrepreneurs to invest in such an economy.

Unbalanced Growth: Critique of the Balanced Growth and Big Push Thesis

The balanced growth and big push ideas are sound in theory, but their practical validity is questionable. The LDC lacks the resources to establish several simultaneous investment projects as recommended by the balanced growth strategy. Rosenstein-Rodan's expectation that the required capital resources would be obtained from abroad is unrealistic. The LDC may not easily find a willing and able donor of sufficient resources in the amount needed. International creditors may be less than liberal in their lending conditions; moreover, foreign technology may not be adaptable to the needs of the LDC. There also is the export incapability of LDCs, given the adversities in their terms of trade and their export price fluctuations.[11]

By implying and emphasizing that investment decisions are mutually reinforcing, and implying implicitly that overall "supply creates its own demand",[12] the balanced growth theory has a strong intuitive appeal as a prescription for initiating development. However, as account is taken of the fact that a poor LDC hardly possesses the capacity to attain the type of balanced investment over a wide range of industries as envisaged in the balanced growth recommendations, the balanced growth idea increasingly appears unrealistic.

Albert Hirschman (1958) and Hans Singer (1958) proposed an alternative to the balanced growth thesis: the strategy of *unbalanced growth*. They argued that unbalanced growth, rather than balanced growth, should be deliberately created to spur economic growth. Given its resource constraints, the LDC is more likely to be capable of establishing one major investment project than a number of various projects. In addition, one major project would be more apt to elicit not only demand, but also supply responses from the rest of the sectors of the economy. Therefore, Hirschman argued that the Big Push could easily come from a well-selected single project that is used to create an unbalanced growth.

Advocates of the unbalanced growth alternative argue that the method of balanced growth cannot bring about as high a rate of development as can unbalanced growth. Instead of striving for balanced investment, they propose the creation of strategic imbalances that will set up stimuli and pressures which are needed to induce investment decisions (Meier, 1976, p. 630). Hirschman (1958) believes in the deliberate creation and maintenance of "disequilibria of which profits and losses are symptoms in a competitive economy, for if the economy is to be kept moving ahead, the task of development policy is to maintain tensions, disproportions, and disequilibria."

According to the unbalanced growth doctrine, a development strategy must be addressed primarily to overcoming the lack of appropriate decision making in the economy. Therefore, unbalanced growth is necessary to induce investment decisions and thereby economize on the LDC's major resource constraint, namely, genuine and relevant decision making.

Hirschman's Principles of Linkage Effects

In explaining the potentials of the unbalanced growth strategy and how to determine what kind of unbalance would likely be the most effective, Hirschman advanced the principles of *linkage effects*. According to Hirschman, the total linkage effects of a project are the sum of its *forward Linkages* and *backward linkages*. The forward linkage of a project is the total (potential) number of other projects that are established because they demand its (initial project's) output for their own operations. The backward linkage of a project is the total (potential) number of other projects that are established because they supply their outputs to it (initial project), which it needs for its own operations. In other words, a project's forward linkages are those projects that it feeds, and its backward linkages are those projects that feed it. Thus, a project would ultimately have a total linkage effect of giving rise to a number of subsequent industries, some of which supply it with its needs and some of which needs it supplies.

Hirschman proposed that a project with the highest total linkage effect be selected and established to create the unbalance for the big push. As the projects with the highest linkage would vary from society to society and from time to time, such a project could only be determined by empirical feasibility studies involving input-output models. Hirschman's own studies indicated that iron and steel had the greatest total linkage effects while agriculture had the lowest total linkage effects. It showed that while primary production is relatively low in backward linkage, mining and agriculture are relatively low in forward linkage.

Critique of the Unbalanced Growth Theory

The LDC's major development problems lie in both supply and demand. In focusing solely on how to use unbalanced growth to overcome the demand constraint, Hirschman's theory fails to suggest how to tackle the supply problem, namely, the severe lack of investable resources. How does the LDC get the resources to establish the leading project? Moreover, the LDC would likely lack the capacity to fund the preliminary feasibility studies needed to select the leading project, as well as the personnel.

One of the major criticisms of the unbalanced growth theory is its apparent disregard for the potentials of agriculture and its relatively high comparative advantage in the development efforts of many LDCs. The role of agriculture in the economic development of Europe, and Japan, is evident, yet Hirschman believed that agriculture's linkage effects were relatively weak. Undoubtedly, agricultural development could provide significant spillovers to other sectors as a source of cheap food supply, cheap raw materials, foreign exchange, and effective market demand. To the extent that it fails to emphasize the role of agricultural development, the unbalanced growth theory appears to be unrealistic for the needs of most LDCs, many of whom are agrarian societies.

In terms of practical and operational purposes, the crucial question of how to determine the proper sequence of investment decisions so as to create the proper amount of imbalance, and in the most appropriate activities and sectors, arises. It is not surprising, therefore, that people began to look to other paradigms for more relevant approaches to development in LDCs. Among the most widely attractive alternative paradigms are the *the Import Substitution Industrialization* paradigm, the *Dual-sector* model, and the *Dependency* theory. We now examine these alternative paradigms in turn, except the Import Substitution model which is treated more appropriately in Chapter 10.

STRUCTURALIST CRITIQUE OF THE INTERNATIONAL TRADE "ENGINE OF GROWTH" DOCTRINE

Classical and neoclassical thinking proposed that international (free) trade could be the engine for economic growth and development for LDCs, just it was for most DCs. Free trade was thought to offer the following advantages for an LDC.

1. Exports of mass production of primary agricultural produce would create foreign exchange for the purchase of vital capital resources for industrialization and infrastructural establishments. The examples of Britain (wool, cotton), Japan (silk), Canada (wheat), U.S.A. (grain, corn), and Russia (cereal) are frequently cited.[13]

2. Capital acquisition through trade and borrowing are facilitated. The LDC is able to easily obtain the much needed equipment to apply to its own industrial and infrastructural production.

3. Technological transfer is readily available to the benefit of the LDC. It can readily apply ready-made technology that is available through the constant interaction that only international trade allows. The LDC needs not spend huge resources and time on research for technological progress, it simply copies what is freely available and applies them to its own benefits.

4. As it establishes its own industrial base, the LDC has the wide world market to dispose of its manufactured produce. It earns more foreign exchange to reinforce its development efforts.

5. Through international trade, the LDC can assess the borrowing and aid facilities available in international financial institutions and the international community.

International trade's potential for growth is driven by the *comparative advantage* paradigm. According to this principle, a country's economic specialization in the production of, say, manufactured (industrial) commodities, and another country's in, say, primary (agricultural) commodities, the products of which are then freely traded among them, would work greatly to their mutual benefits as each enjoyed comparative advantage in their respective areas. Over time, the effect of this relationship would presumably be that any income inequalities between these countries would diminish as free factor mobilities (perfect mobilities of labor, capital, resources, and technology), on the one hand, and products, on the other, would equalize prices (the rates of exchange). This would then distribute the benefits (of technological progress) more equally between the trading countries. International trade is therefore an *engine of growth* and development.

In theory, adherence to this principle seems to have all the potential to enable a country to achieve development after some time. At least it worked in the case of the present-day DCs. However, when viewed in the light of the experiences of most twentieth-century LDCs, international trade could not be said to have been an engine of economic growth and development. What went wrong? To this question, ready answers have been provided by eminent structuralists: Hans Singer (1950), Raul Prebisch (1959, 1962, 1964), and Walter Rodney (1972). Based on historical studies and analyses of the facts and economic performances of various LDCs, these writers propounded hypotheses, theories, and expositions to prove that international trade has lost its engine of growth mechanism for the LDCs. We examine three of these: Raul Prebisch's circular deterioration hypothesis, Hirschman's hypothesis on lost inter-dependence (linkage) effects, and the impact of colonization.

The Circular Deterioration Hypothesis

Prebisch viewed the twentieth-century world as markedly different from the nineteenth-century world in which the present-day DCs achieved their takeoffs through trade. The twentieth-century world is dichotomized into the economic Northern and Southern hemispheres, the center and the periphery. The center produces and exports mainly manufactured goods by utilizing raw materials acquired from the periphery, which serves mainly as the source of cheap raw-material imports. The periphery also depends on the center as the market outlet of its primary produce. The centre, therefore, essentially exercises a considerable degree of monopsony power in the global international trade arrangement.

The Terms of Trade Adversity Syndrome (TOTAS)

The main argument about how international trade has resulted in a one-sided flow of benefits to the center away from the periphery was advanced by Singer (1950) and Prebisch (1959, 1962). They asserted that the raw-material exports of the periphery are characterized by low price-elasticity of demand and low income-elasticity of demand. The price-inelasticity of demand means that any attempts by the producing periphery countries to raise output would amount to massive price declines and severe losses in export revenues. Moreover, the income-inelasticity of demand would mean that rising incomes in the center (consuming) countries do not lead to rising demand and rising prices for these raw materials. This situation may be referred to as the *terms of trade adversity syndrome* (TOTAS).

As a result of the TOTAS facing the periphery in its international trade relationship with the center, the center (buyers of raw materials) becomes the sole beneficiary from the international trading of these products. Gains from any productivity increases in raw-material production in the periphery accrue solely to the center. At the same time, output and productivity increases in manufactured products in the center remain in the center as these products have high income- and price-elasticity of demand. Thus, twentieth-century LDCs in the periphery could not raise sufficient foreign exchange to finance their capital needs for industrialization and development, as, say, Japan (who did not face the condition of TOTAS) did during the nineteenth century.

Lost Inter-Dependence Effects Hypothesis

It was thought that the LDCs could escape the damaging effects of TOTAS by adopting a policy of processing their primary products and converting them to more durable semifinished products before exporting them. By so doing, the LDCs would (1) initiate industrialization within their economies; (2) create additional employment avenues for their labor force; (3) create additional value-added for their export products; and (4) earn higher prices for their exports as their terms of trade improved. These benefits constitute what Hirschman called the interdependence effects of primary-product processing policies.

The interdependence effects have been largely lost in the twentieth-century LDCs that have pursued the primary-product processing initiative. This is because of the counter-policies and measures adopted by the center to thwart such initiatives. Hirschman believed that during the twentieth century, the center countries adopted the policy of *Selective Tariff Bias* (STB) as a way of discouraging raw-material processing and exportation by periphery countries. The STB is a policy of imposing very high tariffs on imported processed or semifinished products from periphery countries, while at the same time imposing very little or no tariffs on unprocessed raw materials imported from the periphery countries.

To implement the STB, the center countries organized themselves as the *Organization of Economic Cooperation and Development* (OECD), and together with the periphery countries, formed the *General Agreement on Tariffs and Trade* (GATT). Through GATT, the voting power of the OECD (center) countries would be sufficient to operate and maintain their STB policies. As an example of the STB policy, in 1975, the U.S. had a 121 percent tariff on cocoa butter, but only a 0.06 percent tariff on raw cocoa beans.[14]

As a result of the seemingly counteractive attitudes and policies of the OECD-center countries, the LDCs are denied the massive advantages that flow from the interdependence effects through international trade. The lost interdependence effects simply nullifies the well-acclaimed classical gains from trade potentials for twentieth-century LDCs. Developing countries of the nineteenth century did not face as formidable an obstacle to their development as STB.

Impact of Colonization

Colonization was a nineteenth- and twentieth-century undertaking driven principally by the search for international trade expansion. It was a bid to access greater sources of industrial raw materials and market outlets for the manufactured produce of the center. As discussed in Chapter 3, the development potential that international trade possessed and so generously spread across the "developing" world of the nineteenth century quickly evaporated by the turn of that century. By this time, the colonialist and expansionist expeditions led by the countries of continental Europe transformed international trade from an "engine" of growth into a "weapon" of exploitation against the societies of Africa, Asia, and Latin America and the Caribbean.

Colonial domination meant a more complete and effective exploitation of the periphery, through which the center oversaw the continuous and uninhibited massive transfer of resources (raw materials and profits) from the periphery (colony) to the center. By the time colonialism was dismantled, the economies of the colonized periphery countries had become strongly dependent on their colonial "masters." Their production structures had been fashioned on alien patterns as they produced mainly to satisfy the needs of the center's industries. They concentrated on production of cash crops, such as coffee, cocoa, tea, cotton, peanuts, and rubber, for export to the center; and they imported manufactured consumer goods from the center. Such lack of diversity rendered many of these LDCs exclusively dependent on the economic moods and dictates of the center countries, thereby dislodging them prematurely and alienating them from their self-sufficient economic structures.

In the quest for even bolder economic gains, the colonizers also became settlers in many of the LDCs where the climate and environmental conditions were favorable. They selected the best, most fertile land (such as parts of eastern, central, and southern Africa) and established their own economic bases for even more thorough economic exploitation: they exploited the mines of these areas, and they utilized cheap local, and sometimes forced, labor. In such circumstances there could be no long-term commitments to the economic development of the colonies.

Colonialism doubtlessly disrupted production, distribution, consumption, savings, and investment aspirations in the affected LDCs. Colonies provided "captive consumers" for the center countries' expanding economies; many of the resulting center-periphery trade arrangements and special trade preferences still remain strong today. Rodney (1972) presents a candid and complete account of the legacy of colonialism for Africa. The bulk of the feedback effects of colonization (termed *neocolonization*) are still central in keeping most LDCs underdeveloped today. Many LDCs are still highly dependent and concentrate on the production of primary produce for export to center countries.

THE DUAL-SECTOR MODELS OF DEVELOPMENT

The two-sector models of economic development are ascribed mainly to the works of the 1979 economics Nobel Prize laureate, W. Arthur Lewis.[15] The model uses the fundamental characteristics of the LDCs in its formulation of its basic tenets. The most central of these characteristics is the *dualistic* nature of the economy of a typical LDC. The economy is dualistic in being composed of a *traditional* or *subsistence* sector, and a *modern* or *industrial* sector. The traditional sector is mainly agricultural and less capitalistic, characterized by a *labor surplus* situation, with relatively low productivity and abundant disguised unemployment.[16]

The modern sector of the dualistic economy operates like the economy of a developed country: industrialized, capitalistic, and relatively highly productive. Therefore, this sector has a higher average wage level, which serves as a constant pull of labor from the traditional sector into the modern sector, facilitated by the existing free mobility of resources across the two sectors. As a result, the supply of labor is perfectly elastic at the given market wage in the modern sector.[17] The process of economic growth in the Lewisian dual-sector model is illustrated by the following analytical framework.

Let the average modern sector urban wage be W_m and the average subsistence sector wage be W_s. Lewis assumes that W_m is determined by, among other things, the alternative available to potential entrants into the modern sector's capitalist employment - namely, the standard of living in the subsistence sector (of which W_s is an approximate indicator). Therefore, W_m will be greater than W_s by at least a margin that is necessary to induce the transfer of labor from the rural to the urban sector, and represents the amount required for the attainment of a conventional (higher) standard of living for modern sector workers, and to compensate for higher costs of living in the modern sector. This difference, given by $(W_m - W_s)$, is termed the "compensating differential."[18]

There is a perfectly elastic supply of labor at the existing $W_m > W_s$. Assuming the typical firm's operational policies are driven by profit maximization, its profit level at any initial time period, t_1, is given by

$$\pi = pQ(L_1, K_1) - W_m L - rK_1 \tag{6.1}$$

where

π = profit
p = price of output Q (assumed to be constant)
L_1 = labor input in the initial period (period 1)
K_1 = level of capital input in the initial period (period 1)
r = rental rate (price) of capital resources
and subscripts *1, 2,...* denote different time periods.

As the firm chooses its optimal level of employment of labor to maximize profit, the first-order conditions for maximization of profit is

$$\partial \pi / \partial L = pQ'(L_1, K_1) - W_m = 0 \tag{6.2}$$

From this, the firm's optimal wage and employment levels are given respectively as

$$W_m = pQ'_1(L*_1,K*_1),$$ (6.3)
$$L*_1 = L(W_m,r,Q'_1(.))$$ (6.4)

At the wage rate W_m, a perfectly elastic labor supply faces all employers in the sector, and the typical firm then employs $L*_1$ amount of labor. The firm's optimal profit level at this time is

$$\pi*_1 = pQ'_1(L*_1,K*_1)-W_mL*_1-rK*_1$$ (6.5)

According to Lewis, as the firm reaps profits, it would reinvest its profits for expansion. As it does so, the level of investment increases from its previous level in period 1, $K*_1$, to a higher level K_2, which enters into Equation (6.4) to yield a higher level of demand for labor (employment) at this second period (period 2) as

$$L*_2 = L\{W_m,r,Q'_2(.)\}$$

Meanwhile, W_m remains unchanged as result of the existing surplus labor. Again, as the higher amount of capital and employment are engaged in period 2, productivity increases, resulting in higher profit:

$$\pi*_2 = pQ'_2(L*_2,K*_2)-W_mL*_2-rK*_2$$

The process continues with further higher investment, $K*_3 > K*_2$, giving higher employment, $L*_3 > L*_2$, in period 3, and so on.[19]

Figure 6.1 presents the Lewis model's graphical exposition. The vertical axis measures output and wages, while the horizontal axis measures the amount of labor employed. The supply of labor is given by the perfectly elastic curve S^L existing at the initial modern-sector wage level W^n. Q'_1, Q'_2, and Q'_3 are, respectively, the (marginal) product curves of labor in periods 1, 2, and 3, while points X, Y, and Z are the respective equilibrium points of profit maximization and employment, in these periods. In period 1, as the typical firm invests an amount of capital, $K*_1$, its employment level is shown as $L*_1$, resulting in the level of profit, π_1 = area AXW_m. This then leads to higher investment $K*_2$, in period 2, again resulting in higher employment $L*_2 > L*_1$ and higher profit level π_2 = area BYW_m, as shown. The process is repeated for period 3, at which profit would be π_3 = area CZW_m, and so on.

Thus, over time, rising profit levels will lead to higher subsequent capital stock and labor demand, and the process will continue until all available surplus labor supply has been absorbed. It should be noted, however, that the era of unlimited labor supply may never end because labor supply is being expanded continuously through population increase. Unless the labor demand curve shifts out faster than the labor supply rises, surplus labor will persist over time.

Figure 6.1
Economic Growth in the Lewis Two-Sector Model

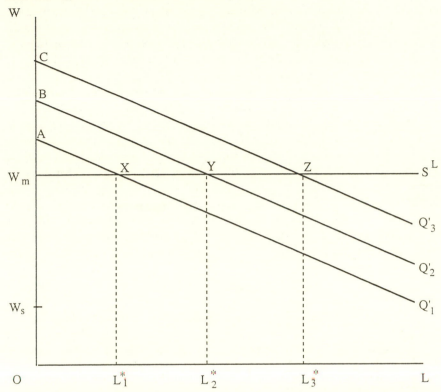

Meanwhile, average agricultural productivity and income in the subsistence sector remain at W_s, and will not decline as a result of the persistent withdrawal of labor from the subsistence sector into the modern sector, because of the prevailing surplus labor and massive disguised unemployment in it. Nor will the level of W_s be affected by the size of the labor surplus, for even though the labor surplus might reduce the subsistence sector's marginal productivity on which the level of W_s depends, this wage will not fall below its "fixed" level that is required for basic subsistence. However, should a time come when the labor surplus is exhausted and labor becomes relatively scarce in the modern sector, the labor supply in the modern becomes upward sloping: all disguised unemployment has been eliminated in the subsistence sector, and the marginal productivity of all labor in this sector has now risen to W_m. This is the point which Ranis and Fei (1964) terms the *commercialization point*.

Upon the attainment of the commercialization point, the economy has gained significant growth and developmental momentum. The subsistence sector must pay labor the value of its marginal product, and must compete with the modern sector for "scarce" labor. The subsistence sector has now vanished by becoming "modern," and both sectors now operate on commercial principles as rural workers are no longer rationed and are able to move between sectors. The structural transformation of the economy would then have taken place, with the bulk of economic activity having shifted from the rural subsistence (agricultural) level to the urban modern (industrial) level. The time it takes for an LDC to reach this stage is not clear from the model's stipulations, but it is clear as to what needs to be done to reach this stage.

For reasons that include noneconomic factors, the modern-sector wage level may have risen (and been rising) prior to the exhaustion of the labor surplus. The main reasons for this would be that modern-sector wages may increase in line with increases in conventional standards of living, voluntary increases granted by capitalist employers on moral grounds, trade union pressure, or government (minimum wage) regulations. Therefore, the modern-subsistence-sector wage gap would still always exist, and labor rationing and rural-urban labor "immobility" would continue to exist in the economy's labor market. Furthermore, it must be noted that W_s is not expected to increase while labor surplus still exists. If for some reason, it does increase, however, the result would be higher W_m and perhaps a further postponement of the attainment of the commercialization point.

Critique of the Lewis Dual-Sector Model of Economic Development

The Lewis model clearly presents an insightful analysis of the probable development path of an LDC. There can be no doubt that it aptly illustrates the development experience of the present economically developed countries. For most LDCs today, this model explains their well-known peculiar and overriding characteristic of economic and technological dualism. It sheds light on our understanding of the persistence of intersectoral wage gaps and disguised unemployment. And above all, the Lewis model helps us, *albeit* implicitly so, to understand the far-reaching implications of unchecked population increases in LDCs. That is, a high rate of population growth would mean greater additions to the "surplus" labor, further postponing the attainment of the "commercialization" point and economic development. Therefore, the rate of population growth could be maintained at the rate of expansion of the modern sector to ensure steady progress toward development.

Although the Lewis dual-sector model has proved highly useful in portraying the development process, it relies on certain questionable assumptions whose invalidity may lead it to crumble. First, the assumption concerning a competitive product market (which guarantees a fixed product price) appears to be untenable in most LDCs. As the product price changes, so will the modern-sector wage rate, which would then not be constant, thereby jeopardizing the predictable employment decisions of firms in the economy. There also is the assumption that capitalist owners of firms would reinvest their profits. The evidence, rather, indicates that most of the profits find their way outside the economy as foreign owners of businesses in LDCs repatriate the greater proportions of their profits. Even many leaders and citizens of the LDCs themselves send their "profits" to foreign banks in the Western DCs for safe-keeping and consumption.

The question of the extent to which modern sector firms are able to readily absorb the migrant "surplus" labor from the subsistence sector arises. If such labor would have to be trained before being absorbed, then the pace of the process of transformation, as depicted by the model, would be rather too sluggish to be relevant as a policy guide in a society seeking to achieve development within a reasonable length of time.

Finally, Lewis obviously did not anticipate the rural-urban migration problem that would later be addressed by the Harris-Todaro model of intersectoral migration. In their famous study of the dilemma of higher unemployment that may result from attempts to create more jobs in the modern sectors of LDCs, Harris and Todaro (1970) hypothesized a two-sector model in which the individual decision to migrate is a function of the urban-rural real income differential and of the probability of finding a modern-sector job. If the present value of the discounted real income gain from migration, after taking account of the chances of being unemployed, is positive, then migration is worthwhile. Several studies have concluded that the Harris-Todaro "dilemma" does, in fact, pose a major development policy bottleneck for LDCs, thereby casting doubt over the ability of the Lewis process to result in the absorption of the economy's "surplus" labor.[20]

THE DEPENDENCY THEORY OF DEVELOPMENT AND UNDERDEVELOPMENT

The dependency theory of development and underdevelopment summarizes the main crux of the structuralist theories. As stated at the beginning of this chapter, advocates of dependency theory do not agree with the conventional paradigms of development analyses which explain economic development as a difficult and cumulative process. They see economic underdevelopment as actively imposed and maintained by the actions and policies of some members of the globe upon others. They point to colonialism, neocolonialism, and imperialism as the key instruments that are used to propagate and maintain underdevelopment. In other words, dependency theory posits that economic underdevelopment exists because of the continued exploitation of the "periphery" areas of the world—Africa, Asia, and Latin America and the Caribbean—by the *imperial* center.

Andre Gundar Frank, a leading proponent of dependency theory rejected the widely-held belief among development analysts of the time that the lack of development in the LDCs could be likened to the earlier transitional stages of the present DCs.[21] Frank contends that, although the present DCs may have been *undeveloped* during their transitional stages, they were never *underdeveloped* in the sense of apparently having underdevelopment imposed upon them through the policies and actions of a powerful external "competitor" occupying the other half of the globe. Underdevelopment, therefore, needed redefining. It does not mean "traditional" or "rural" or "non-modern" or "informal" standards of economic, political, and social life; rather, it means the subjection of LDCs to colonial or quasi-colonial exploitation and imperial domination by foreign powers. Frank (1969) cites concrete examples of the CREATION of underdevelopment: the deindustrialization of India (by British colonialism), the exploitation and enslavement of Africa (by European imperialism and colonialism), and the destruction of Incan and Aztec civilizations (by Spanish imperialism). More specific discussions are offered in Nafziger (1990, pp. 91-95).

The essential tenet of Dependency theory is that the economic development of the rich developed countries of the world necessarily contributes to the underdevelopment of the poor countries. Underdevelopment in the LDCs is an essential element of development in the DCs because development and underdevelopment are the two sides of a single process of the global utilization of earth's human and material resources. That is, the LDCs, as the economic satellites of the highly developed regions of the world, especially Europe and North America, must be poor as a result, and cannot, therefore, self-generate economic development autonomously.

Dependency theory would contend that, although political colonialism may have been overtly dismantled, economic (colonialism) exploitation has always continued on massive scales through the operations of multinational corporations (MNCs) and such powerful institutions as the International Monetary Fund (IMF) and the World Bank. It would argue that activities in the LDCs that conventional thinkers often regarded as developmental, were not developmental at all, but rather, *underdevelopmental*.

Such underdevelopmental policies abound, which include replacing indigenous technologies with more advanced (foreign) ones that were often solely beneficial to subsidiaries of MNCs, and encouraging the formation of mass local unskilled labor for employment in factories, mines, and shops. Colonial policies shaped the LDCs solely for trade and investment in raw materials, in exchange for the DCs' trade and investment in industrial goods. As a result, the LDCs developed elitist consumption patterns on which the bulk of their foreign exchange earnings are spent, to the benefit of foreign industries. In addition, the educational systems established in LDCs produced highly educated persons for unskilled jobs and posts in colonial administrations, and acquainted them with ideas and values that were alien and even inimical to the cultural, social, and economic needs of their environment.[22]

International trade brought polarization as the LDCs were "assigned" the production of primary raw materials through (1) worsening terms of trade and circular deterioration (see above), and (2) the control of their economies by monopolistic MNCs, by which their resources ("profits") flew out from them into the DCs for the continuous economic well-being and development of the

DCs.[23]

Policy Implications of the Dependency Theory

The major policy implication of the dependency theory is that economic underdevelopment is deliberately maintained in the the periphery (LDCs) by the powerful center (the DCs) who stand to benefit by it. Therefore, in order for real development to occur in the LDCs, the DCs will have to permit it through goodwill gestures and acts of benevolence. Thus, in a situation of (international) competition and opportunism (such as the situation that rules today's world), the LDCs cannot possibly achieve development. This is because the power of the center is overwhelmingly overriding, and the center must be prepared to lessen the application of such power and willingly yield ground to the LDCs. This is not likely to happen in an atmosphere of aggressive international competition and rivalry. Therefore, only goodwill and benevolence on the part of the DCs (the OECD countries) can lead to more economic growth and ultimate economic development of the LDCs today.

NOTES

1. Presently known as the ECLAC (Economic Commission for Latin America and the Caribbean), ECLA was originally located in Santiago, Chile. Latin American "structuralism" emerged essentially as ECLA's principal concern - namely, discovering the major obstacles to the region's development and determining appropriate policy suggestions for them (see Kay, 1989).

2. Prebisch was the executive secretary of ECLA during 1948-1962. For a complete profile of Prebisch's structuralist ideas, see Prebisch (1959, 1963, 1964, 1984). In addition to Prebisch, the other key originators of the structuralist paradigm can be found in Kay (1989).

3. In his classic contribution to this theory, Lewis (1954) articulated the low-productivity characteristic of the subsistence sector and used it to explain the preponderance of low wages in the capitalist (export) sector of the dualistic (peripheral) economy. This further explains the perpetual deterioration of the periphery's terms of trade. For an insightful analysis of how the Lewis and Prebisch ideas better explain the fallacies of the orthodox (neoclassical) factor price equalization theorem in analyzing export-led growth and development in LDCs, see Chichilnisky (1981).

4. From the onset, advocates of standard neoclassical theories have attacked the structuralist paradigms on several grounds. Thorough critiques can be found in Viner (1953), Ellsworth (1961), Johnson (1967), and later Powelson (1977). As recent as the early 1980s, Streeten (1981) stated that there was no evidence of the secular deterioration syndrome in the terms of trade of primary-product exporters in relation to manufactured-product exporters. In fact, questions did arise as to whether Prebisch really understood and interpreted the neoclassical factor-price equalization model correctly. For this, see Flanders (1964).

5. This state would be similar to Marx's conception of the traditional society; Rostow's ideas were a skillful synthesis of Marx's, classical, and other social thoughts of the preceding era. Details can be found in another of his classic works: Rostow (1963). See also Rosovsky (1965) or Kuznets (1963).

6. The "settler nations" differ from the others in that they were "created" out of the economic development that had already been established in Britain. Although these countries were occupied, it is important to understand that they were not colonized by Britain in the same sense as African, Latin American, or some Asian countries were colonized. They were not exploited as colonies, and no center-periphery relationships were created. They were, in effect, created as centers in themselves.

7. Further critical evaluation of Rostow's stage theory, especially focusing on some of the suggested structural characteristics of the stages, can be found in Nafziger (1990).

8. This concept is explained in detail in the section: "Characteristics of Underdevelopment" in Chapter 1.

9. This is the phenomenon of positive *externalities* or *external economies*: spillovers that benefit others who are not directly involved in those activities. Economic goods and services that possess this property are known as *public goods*. Many economists believe that such goods should be provided by the public sector through taxation, and should be made available to all members of society at prices equal to marginal cost, and by so doing, social welfare is maximized. This is because a private-sector-based provision of such public goods would result in *market failure* (see Strick, 1994).

10. Although the balanced growth paradigm is often related to the Big Push doctrine, it should be noted that the principle of balanced growth is not necessarily a component of the big push idea. This is because balanced growth neither ought to be dependent on a large amount of public investment nor need it be dependent on the dominance of the public sector (Meier, 1976, p. 630).

11. For further discussions and critique of the balanced growth theory, see Fleming (1955), Singer (1958), and Hagen (1980). For a more modern critique in addition to that offered here, see also Nafziger (1990).

12. This is the classical *Say's Law* of market clearing, by which the classical school of economic thought posits that severe unemployment could not emerge from an overproduction that results from inadequacy of market demand for the output of an economy (see Chapter 1). For more on this aspect of classical (macro)economics, see Brue (1994).

13. Japan is a classic example of an agrarian economy that developed through international trade. By the time it achieved takeoff, over one-third of Japan's export earnings were from agricultural raw materials (mainly silk), and the country financed over 40 percent of its development capital needs with agricultural foreign exchange earnings. Also, some of the modern East Asian Newly Industrialized Countries (NICs) - for example, South Korea, Thailand, Singapore, and Malaysia - also achieved significant successes through international trade, although from agrarian backgrounds (see Chapter 13).

14. A good economic analysis of the impact of the OECD countries' STB structure on LDCs can be found in Balassa (1976). See also Boltho (1988) for a related account covering resources as a whole.

15. See Lewis (1954, 1955, 1979, 1984). Ranis and Fei (1964) developed an extended analysis of the original Lewis model. Todaro (1994) states that many of the basic ideas extended in the Lewis as well as the Ranis and Fei models had been originally expounded

by Nurkse (1953).

16. Disguised unemployment exists if the worker's marginal productivity is close to zero. In such a situation, labor could be withdrawn from the production without affecting total output. Lewis posits this as a situation of labor surplus, and see it as the case in most LDCs, especially in their (rural) agricultural sectors.

17. Presumably, the assumption is that rural agriculture is predominantly at the subsistence level rather than the wage-employment (commercial) level.

18. The role of the compensating differential in determining the permanent intersectoral wage gap as it applies to the Lewis model has been extensively studied. For some of the major findings, see Godfrey (1979) or Leeson (1979).

19. Lewis assumes that firms are monopolists that make positive profits. However, it could be wondered why there should be entry barriers perpetuating the monopolists' prolonged positive profit margins. Arrighi (1973) explains why this could be so by noting that the modern-sector firms are usually foreign multinational oligopolists operating with high capital-intensive techniques.

20. For some of the major studies on this, see Blomqvist (1978), Ezeala-Harrison (1988b), House and Rempel (1980), and Mazumdar (1976).

21. The key ideas are expounded in Frank (1967, 1969, 1992).

22. See Ezeala-Harrison (1995b) for a candid analysis of how this situation has given rise to Africa's "diploma disease", a serious problem of underdevelopment in the region.

23. The MNCs exert formidable control in the LDCs: they intrude into their laws, politics, and foreign policies by often using offers of money and wealth to corrupt the leaders of these LDCs, who, because of low income backgrounds, are often susceptible and vulnerable to such corrupting influences. For the role of MNCs in perpetuating underdevelopment in LDCs, see Sunkel (1973).

Part III

THE PROCESS OF ECONOMIC DEVELOPMENT: THE INTERNAL DIMENSIONS

7

Capital Accumulation and the Process of Development

This chapter deals with the role of capital formation in the development process. This role, together with its accompanying requirements of technological skill and know-how, cannot be overemphasized. Although both physical capital and financial capital are implied, financial capital is deemed to be just a means to acquiring physical capital. Financial capital is based on the savings decisions that finance physical capital, which involves the actual *real* investment decisions. In the LDCs, savings and investment decisions are often combined because of the low level of development of financial markets and institutions. Therefore, it may not be necessary always to draw the line between physical capital and financial capital.

Capital has always been recognized as the single most critical factor determining a nation's ability to develop. In fact, it is regarded as the prime mover of the development process. It is made of the various forms of investment in the development of land and natural resources, construction of residential and industrial buildings, physical plants and equipment, raw materials, and *human capital*. Human capital is the acquisition of knowledge, skill, and technological know-how through investment in human resources.[1]

Within the internal aspects of a country's development circumstances, capital formation, entrepreneurial ability, and technological know-how together constitute the most essential requirements in generating and sustaining growth. In an LDC, capital accumulation would enable the economy to break, and indeed reverse, the *vicious circle of poverty* that tends to constrain the ability to initiate growth. More capital would increase the capital-labor ratio, enabling productivity to increase, leading to higher incomes, higher savings ability, and higher investment and capital accumulation for further growth.

Higher capital formation would enable the economy to be capable of making higher capital consumption allowance, and to facilitate more effective utilization of capital stock, resulting in higher productivity. This is especially essential in the creation and maintenance of the infrastructural base of the economy, especially transportation, communication systems, and utilities. Moreover, capital formation is a prerequisite for forming not only an industrial base for the economy, but also for the development of agriculture. Overall, capital accumulation advances outward an economy's *production possibility frontier*.

To regard economic growth and development as simply a question of capital accumulation alone, would, however, be a serious overstatement. Complementary and cooperant factors are necessary. Other things such as technological know-how, entrepreneurship, natural resources, leadership, and conducive socioeconomic and political institutions are as important as capital resources. The development of these cooperant factors, however, is usually dependent itself on some level of capital formation. Therefore, capital formation may truly be regarded as the ultimate prime mover of the development process.

Before we consider the various sources of capital formation for an LDC, it is important to explain a notion that is related to this need for cooperant factors to capital. This is the concept of an LDC's *absorptive capacity* of capital resources. This concept refers to the ability and preparedness of the economy to actually utilize the capital resources effectively. The ability to do so depends on the economy's acquisition of natural resources, the labor force and its skill characteristics, especially technical, administrative, and managerial skills, and the overall efficiency of the functioning of economic activities. The level of absorptive capacity sets limit to the amount of efficient investment that is physically possible, as well as the pace and amount of development that could arise from it.

SOURCES OF CAPITAL ACCUMULATION

There are various ways and channels by which an LDC can accumulate capital for its development effort. Here we consider the major sources of capital accumulation involving voluntary and involuntary savings, direct and indirect investment, public-sector investment, and foreign investment.

Saving as a Source of Capital Formation

Saving is the main internal source of capital formation. It involves reserving a portion of currently earned income and postponement of current consumption. It therefore frees resources for investment. Saving can be generated voluntarily or involuntarily through the various inducements to save. The level of savings would depend on the size of incomes and the cost of living in the economy. Whereas the *propensity to save* is a cultural or customary parameter whose magnitude will remain fairly stable over time, the amount of savings will generally vary with the per capita income level of the society. Higher incomes mean higher abilities and capacities to save. The levels of tax rates and interest rates also affect the amount of savings generated.

Voluntary Saving for Capital Formation

The pervasive low-income levels in LDCs mean that the volume of voluntary savings is very low. Gross income inequalities abound, and the groups with high incomes have higher propensities to save. The nineteenth-century experience of Japan is a case where severe unequal income distribution allowed for higher savings to flow from the private sector after an initial wave of government investment had been committed to the development effort. However, modern LDCs may not be expected to successfully emulate Japan's case. The spread of the *International Demonstration Effect on Consumption* (IDEC) has meant that, even for those LDCs that are close to the *preconditions stage*, the middle-class upper income earners often assign considerable prestige to conspicuous consumption. As such, the capacity to generate voluntary saving is curtailed.

Arthur Lewis (1955) stated that the voluntary savings ratio is determined by a particular kind of inequity in place. If the inequity is in favour of the entrepreneurial class (profit, interest, and rental incomes), savings may be raised. Savings will be low for societies with higher proportion of wage incomes to GDP.

Forced Saving for Capital Formation

Forced saving involves a combination of measures that are implemented to compel members of society to save in the amounts judged necessary for the economy's development needs, amounts when they would not voluntarily have done so. One of the key ways to generate forced saving involves the use of *inflation*. The government simply runs a budget deficit and finances it by creating new money. This is referred to as *deficit financing* and is apt to be inflationary. All things being equal, the increased government spending that results from this action will bid away consumption activity from the private sector to the public sector. Thus, as the public sector consumes more, the private sector consumes less, and hence saves more. A *forced saving* is therefore imposed on the private sector.[2]

Complementarily, through this inflationary process, a spread is created between nominal and real incomes. Consequently, wage earners, who are less disposed to save, have part of their incomes passed on to firms and businesses (whose owners are the entrepreneurial class in society who are more apt to save). With more resources passing into the hands of the entrepreneurial classes, higher savings are effected in the economy. The success of this approach, however, depends on the validity of the Lewis view on voluntary savings cited above. Also, the imminent problems of inflation are ever present. Moreover, labor unions may not allow for a substantial gap that would be sufficient to generate savings from the entrepreneurial class.

An alternative way to generate forced saving is through *taxation*. The government could raise tax revenue above its spending and save the budget surplus. This is easy to achieve, for the government's tax revenue rises more than proportionately because the tax system is *progressive*. The rise in government tax collection amounts to a reduction in private consumption: forced saving. The danger with this approach, however, is that the private sector might also reduce its own saving level following the higher taxes.

A third approach to generate forced saving is to alter the *domestic terms of trade* in favor of the modern sector. As the subsistence sector tends to save less relative to the modern sector, resources could be appropriated from the subsistence sector by raising the prices of manufactured goods and lowering the prices of agricultural goods. This could be accomplished easily through the operation of Marketing Boards or through legislation.[3] There are obvious disadvantages with this measure. Besides promoting more income inequity against the subsistence sector, this would result in further impoverishment of many low-income members of the subsistence sector. It could even lead to a more difficult problem of "agricultural abandonment" where farmers simply resort to growing just enough crops for their immediate food needs and little or nothing for commercial purposes, as a reaction against the policy.

Related to this measure is that of absorption of underemployed labor into productive work. This generates an internal source of saving through the utilization of the "invisible surplus" of underemployed labor. With the existence of disguised unemployment in agriculture, labor could be withdrawn from the agricultural sector for productive employment elsewhere, especially to work on investment projects such as construction, irrigation works, road construction, housing, and the like without reducing agricultural output. As national output is increased by so doing, tax revenue increases, generating savings for the government. Moreover, through the multiplier process, most of the additional income will be directed toward food, thereby boosting the demand of agricultural output and incomes, which may then also be taxed and saved.

INVESTMENT AND CAPITAL FORMATION

Economics has a straightforward definition of investment: it is the production of capital goods. The various forms of investment include autonomous investment and induced investment, both of which together make up private sector investment. Other forms are public-sector investment, government investment, and foreign investment. We consider each of these separately.

Private-Sector Investment

In Chapter 5 we described the Hansen model in which the main factors that determine the level of autonomous investment are discussed: the combined effects of resource discovery, population growth, and technological progress, and how these factors and their impacts tend to taper off over time. Thus, there is the tendency for autonomous investment to fade away over time, particularly in an LDC. By standard Keynesian economics, however, autonomous investment is more dependent on the subjective perceptions and the degree of "business optimism" of entrepreneurs. For an LDC that is eagerly seeking sources of investment resources for development, these uncontrollable factors could not be relied on.

The size of induced investment depends on GDP levels. The level of GDP is often subject to fluctuations owing to the cyclical movements of the economy. However, the size of profits is the key factor that induces entrepreneurs to invest: low interest rate, high product prices, and low wages. The inducement to invest is very low in LDCs for reason of the low level of incomes. This is compounded by the pervasive low-investment capabilities and political instabilities that present adverse investment climates. In such circumstances, it is doubtful that the private sector could generate the level of investment for capital formation adequate to propel and sustain development. Autonomous investment, on the other hand, would also be low because of weak demand, which means that potential investors do not see the encouraging levels of *prospective yield* as incentives to invest in the economy.

Therefore, to encourage whatever private investment there may be, it seems that the LDC must rely heavily on its financial markets. There should be very attractive interest rate levels in order to attract those who could invest to actually invest. The problem, though, is that the LDCs do not have well-developed and functioning financial markets. It then appears that the LDC must lean heavily on the government sector to generate the bulk of the level of its investment needs.

Public-Sector Investment

Investment that is implemented by the public sector seems to be a promising source of capital formation in the LDC, especially in infrastructure. In the sector of infrastructural development, private-sector investment cannot be expected to be forthcoming because of the nature of the specific projects involved. Infrastructural projects usually involve *natural monopolies*. These are firms whose production circumstances are characterized by *economies of scale*, such that in setting their production policies in accordance with profit-maximizing rules the resulting output and pricing levels would be largely unsuitable for a predominantly low-income economy.[4] Government investment seems to be the only main source of capital formation for infrastructural development in LDCs.

The public sector does participate in general economic activities by establishing and operating various industries and commercial enterprises. In LDCs, public-sector participation has been *complementary* rather than *competitive* with the private sector in generating economic progress. This is mainly because of the lack of sufficient private sector entrepreneurship. The government tends to establish *public companies* or to acquire majority holdings in large-scale joint-stock corporations in various sectors of the economy. The problem with these companies has been that, as *State enterprises*, they lack the profit motive, and are neither properly motivated nor operated with sufficient economic incentives. They often operate very inefficiently, under huge losses and subsidies. However, some could also operate successfully, especially in banking, insurance, air and sea transportation, and tourism.

Foreign Investment

Perhaps foreign investment is the most critical source of capital formation in any economy. The experiences of the DCs indicate that the foreign sector could actually be the most important source of capital for development. Such an outcome, however, may no longer be hoped for in today's world.

Foreign sources of capital could take either of the following forms: direct investment by foreign companies carried out mainly by multinational corporations (MNCs), borrowing from foreign countries, and foreign aid.[5]

Direct Investment by Foreign Companies

Foreign capital could flow into the LDC from foreign companies, mostly foreign direct investment by large transnational MNCs with headquarters in the DCs. These include the flows of financial capital from private international banks. Foreign direct investments in LDCs grew considerably over the 1960-1980 period, although the bulk of it went to Asia and Latin America, with Africa receiving relatively little. Since the primary objectives of MNCs are to maximize their returns on capital investment rather than regional or national economic development, their finances are attracted to regions with the highest financial returns, economic and political stability, and public security.

In order for the MNCs to provide a stable level of foreign capital, the LDC must have a significantly low level of corporate and income tax rate. There must also be no restrictions on the repatriation of profits. Furthermore, the LDC must have a significantly developed and well-functioning infrastructural base. That many modern LDCs could satisfy these conditions, is very doubtful.

The United Nations Development Program's *Human Development Index* (1992) indicates that 83 percent of all foreign direct investment goes to the DCs, while 17 percent goes to LDCs. This indicates that MNCs simply seek and direct their resources to the best profit opportunities and are not concerned with the general issues of development such as unemployment, poverty, income inequality, industrialization, or infrastructural development. They concentrate their locations in the urban sectors of the LDC and usually bring in their own skilled personnel rather than spend additional resources to train local personnel. Most importantly, the MNCs often repatriate the bulk of the profit returns to their parent companies in the DCs, thereby posing some balance-of-payments problem for the LDC concerned. Their overall positive contribution to development in LDCs is highly questionable. In fact, the African region in particular seems to have suffered serious economic development setbacks as a result of the operations of the MNCs.

Borrowing from Foreign Countries

Borrowing could be relied on to generate the needed capital, especially for investment in infrastructure. The problem, however, is that there are not many willing lenders, and the LDC may not be very creditworthy. But the real danger is that a borrowing LDC could eventually create a debt crisis for itself that could, indeed, eventually cripple its development efforts and potential.

The LDC's desire to quickly launch its various development programs could cause the LDC to enter into many kinds of commercial loans and supplier credits. Such credits could be quite easy to obtain for countries with good credit rating (such as those who have oil). For many LDCs, however, a great deal of the foreign loans are spent on capital-intensive public projects and military hardware. Large parts are used to finance government's recurrent budget deficits and importation of foreign conspicuous consumer goods. Significant portions are also placed in the foreign personal bank accounts of corrupt government ministers and other officials. As a result, the borrowed resources often fail to flow into actual economic development activities.

Most LDCs are currently burdened by a foreign-debt-servicing problem. Some of them allocate over 30 percent of their individual total foreign-exchange earnings to servicing external debt. Such a situation can only retard the development effort. Many of the LDCs have been compelled to adopt "structural adjustment" economic (reform) programs, partly in an attempt to forge a longer-term solution to their debt problems (but mainly in fulfillment of International Monetary Fund [IMF] conditionality). The outcomes have not been very successful, for the often drastic economic "adjustment" measures embarked upon (or rather imposed), *albeit* reluctantly, tend to make the entire development process retrogress.[6]

Borrowing may not actually promote faster capital formation; it may, in fact, retard it. The borrowed resources may substitute for, rather than supplement, domestic savings and investment. Moreover, it would certainly create a balance-of-payments adversity as the demands for debt servicing and repayment obligations are met in future.

Foreign Aid as a Source of Capital Formation

Foreign aid refers to all official financial and nonfinancial grants and concessional loans that effectively transfer resources from a donor country to a recipient country, usually for general purposes of development. It is defined as any noncommercial flow of capital with *concessional terms* attached to it, from one country to another. By concessional terms is meant the conditionalities associated with the grant - for example, charging a very low interest rate on some specified sum, or extending repayment periods very liberally, or the so-called *strings attached* to the aid.

Almost unquestionably, most LDCs are eager to accept foreign aid even in their most stringent and restrictive forms because, clearly, foreign aid supplements domestic resources and provides a boost in the effort to overcome the constraints of scarcity of resources. Foreign aid can also help effect the economy's structural transformation. Aid is particularly attractive to LDCs as it comes from the already developed countries, which, if genuinely motivated by the desire to promote development in LDCs, could easily extend their "experiences" to the benefit of the LDCs.

Although foreign aid may represent an important source of development capital for the LDC, it seldom comes without conditions. Ordinarily, well-intentioned foreign aid ought to be bestowed in the form of outright grants or long-term low-cost loans without certain compelling demands attached. That is, the aid should not be linked or *tied* to such conditions as requiring that the recipient spend most of it in buying, say, military hardware, from the donor country. At most, any attached conditionalities should be limited to the minimal requirement that the aid resources be devoted exclusively to pure economic development agendas rather than, say, being diverted to providing greater political leverage to the existing leadership, such as measures aimed at suppressing political opposition and maintaining itself in power. The LDC should be given the flexibility to channel the aid resources into areas of their best development interest.

The real problem associated with foreign aid, however, is the problem of the strings attached with the aid. In particular, the donor country often has a vested interest in extending the aid, and this interest is usually to the recipient's detriment. In many cases, the aid is tied by way of compelling the recipient to spend it on the purchase of the donor country's products or military hardware, or requiring that it be spent on particular specific project such as a steel mill or a modern international airport. Most examples involve the purchase of capital-intensive equipment or new machinery from producers in the donor country. In this way, the actual real value of the aid is diminished because the transaction would likely involve the purchase of expensive products from the donor, or it would involve establishment of a project of little or no development priority for the LDC.

The problem of the LDCs' *absorptive capacity* of the aid resources has limited the usefulness of foreign aid in development. Therefore, the most valuable forms of aid are those that are given in the form of foreign exchange, without "strings attached." Unfortunately, however, the donor DCs are often unwilling to extend aid free of "strings." This is because the reason they give aid in the first place is to pursue and extend their own economic, political, military, and strategic interests. There is no question that some development aid is motivated by humanitarian and moral principles (for example, emergency food lifts to Ethiopia in 1985), but if the main objective of foreign aid were truly to assist the LDC in its development effort, there would be no "strings" attached, nor would such aid be tied.

The impact of foreign aid in the capital formation effort of LDCs is fraught with controversy. Some observers believe that aid has indeed helped promote economic growth and development in LDCs. Critics counter that foreign aid has largely been exploitative and has tended to benefit the donor more than the recipient. Yet others argue that aid has been focused on one-sided development in LDCs, thereby contributing in widening the rich-poor gap in LDCs. They contend that foreign aid resources have been the mainstay of corrupt political leaders and military dictatorships in LDCs, many of whom would not have lasted that long in power without being propped up by the flow of such resources. Aid may have indeed stifled initiative and drive for self-striving in the bid to achieve self-sustained growth and development.[7]

As it is, present-day LDCs can no longer rely on foreign aid as a viable source of development capital formation. The political mood and economic climate in most of the donor DCs indicate that the flow of aid from them may no longer be forthcoming. Most of the donor countries in Europe and North America are saddled with huge national debts, enormous government deficits, and very high tax rates, as well as rising unemployment rates and a myriad of economic problems. These circumstances have rather swayed the voters in these countries away from generosity, especially toward LDCs. Moreover, the amounts that are involved could never be sufficient to provide reliable amounts for capital formation in LDCs.

TECHNOLOGY AND CAPITAL ACCUMULATION IN DEVELOPMENT PROCESS

It is expected that technological progress and capital accumulation go hand in hand. Furthermore, it is supposed that it was the existence of already accumulated knowledge and technological know-how that enabled, say, the United States, or Germany, to develop much more rapidly than Britain did as the pioneer of Industrial Revolution. It may not, however, be totally accurate to suppose that the existence of technological know-how should quicken the pace of development. On the contrary, Hans Singer (1975) has argued that it is precisely because of the accumulation of science (know-why) and technology (know-how), and because of the specific nature of this accumulation, that there have been such widespread failures to achieve real development in present-day LDCs.

Singer shows how disproportions arising from such factors as the high rates of population growth in LDCs and their geographical placement could be at odds with the types of technological progress that exist. Recent studies indicate that most modern technological advances are biased toward the further developmental needs of DCs and have only led to distortions and disruptions in the types of development processes suitable for the LDCs. As new science and new technology are always developed and created within the the developed world, they displace those that already exist. As the LDCs try to readjust to the new technologies, they lose track and become disoriented, as they incur losses in the huge investments they may have already poured into the old technologies. This could only retard development.

Next we examine the various factors that may explain why direct technological transfers have failed to propel development in modern LDCs.

Technological Mismatch to the State of Development

Often the LDCs simply adopt the technologies that are applied to economic activities in the DCs wholesale into their own situations. These fail to be workable and would only, at best, be temporarily applicable. For example, capital is usually more expensive than labor in an LDC, whereas in the DCs labor is relatively scarce and more costly, and capital relatively abundant and cheap. Therefore, capital-intensive production methods and designs that were developed for use in a DC should not be applied to an LDC.

Large-scale mass production associated with the manufacturing industry may not be economical for an LDC with a low-level market demand and highly seasonal and fragmented economic variations, although it would suit a DC well. Much of modern technology, however, is designed for use in large-scale plants. But the operations of such plants in an LDC might require well-organized and already functioning distribution networks and a disciplined factory workforce. Their managerial techniques might involve measures that conflict with accepted customs, cultures, beliefs, and systems of authority and male/female roles in the LDC. Moreover, the availability of occasional service personnel and engineers for regular maintenance of the machines comes to question. The LDC's scarce capital resources are wasted as they invest in technologies that are mismatched to their domestic conditions.

Technological Displacement of Indigenous Producers

As the application of modern technology leads to mass production of goods and services far more cheaply than the going methods, large numbers of indigenous craftsmen and business entrepreneurs cannot compete. These redundant workers are often not absorbed in the new factories because their capital-intensive production methods mean that machinery, rather than labor, is employed. Moreover, these people need to be trained and must learn to adapt to the new methods, and the modern firms would be unwilling to spend more on labor training when they could easily substitute more machinery.

Technology and the Brain Drain

The brain drain is a phenomenon that shows how technological progress has harmed the development efforts in LDCs. Brain drain refers to the emigration of highly educated and skilled persons of the professional, managerial, and administrative (PMA) category from LDCs to the DCs. It occurs in various aspects. First, there is the wave of students who go overseas, especially to Western developed countries, to acquire higher education; eventually they remain permanently in these countries as immigrant workers and citizens after graduating as skilled PMAs. In most cases they are trained at the direct financial expense of their countries of origin. A second aspect of the brain drain concerns the emigration of highly trained PMAs to the developed countries to reside and work as immigrants and citizens (see Chapter 8).[8]

It is more accurate to see the brain drain as a fallout from technological progress. In effect, it amounts to an effective transfer of human and material resources from the LDC to the DC.[9] The problem is compounded in LDCs whose educational systems tend to produce graduates who are not properly suited for their local environments.

Appropriate Technology for Economic Development in LDCs

Hans Singer believes that unsuitable technology seems to be the only option that exists because, other than machinery that has been designed to meet other needs, there is nothing else on the technological market for LDCs. In this connection, several options are immediately available. For example, as highlighted under the brain drain discussion above, LDCs could pursue specially designed technologies to suit their peculiar needs. Technologies that involve the scarcity of capital and the abundance of labor readily come to mind.

Applications of the DCs' modern technological inventions need neither be abandoned altogether nor indiscriminately applied. Rather, they should be adapted to the needs of the LDCs, and then applied. For example, improved understanding of the physical and chemical components of matter and the environment, deeper biological knowledge, and application of extension services in agriculture could easily be tapped from modern technology without acquiring sophisticated capital equipment to attend to them. Research geared toward determining how to make better use of local raw materials under the prevailing climatic conditions, and toward determining the appropriate solutions to familiar local problems, based on first-hand knowledge and understanding of the local situations, must be focused on.

NOTES

1. Human capital development takes various formal and informal forms. Formal education and institutional training constitute significant parts of human capital formation. Informally, human capital is also formed through on-the-job training and experience.

2. This method is referred to as inflationary financing. Studies on the potentials of using inflationary financing to propel development can be found in Meier (1976, pp. 311-330).

3. As immoral as this proposal might sound, it could be very effective and beneficial in several ways. For one, it takes away resources from high-income members of the traditional sector who tend to spend their wealth on unproductive social activities such as lavish marriage feasts and funerals, and channels them toward economic development.

4. To pursue profit maximization objectives, a *natural monopoly* firm, such as a hydroelectric utility company or even a post and telecommunications company, would set output at the point where its marginal cost (MC) equals its marginal revenue (MR). In a low-income economy, the *effective demand* for such utilities is usually not very high, and the demand curve would almost always lie below the average cost (AC) curve. With a continuously declining MC curve that is always lower than the AC curve, the profit maximization point would yield a very high price and low output levels. However, for fear of such uneconomical (especially high price) outcomes, most LDC governments would not allow private-sector monopolists to operate in these sectors. For more on this, see Strick (1994).

5. The MNC is a company that operates business activities in two or more countries. It is usually a large-scale corporation, with bases in Europe, North America, or Japan. For a good discussion of how the MNC could both help and hurt economic development in LDCs, see Todaro (1994, p. 527).

6. A complete analysis of the problems that external indebtedness has posed for African LDCs, and how these problems have impacted on their developmental abilities, can be found in Ezeala-Harrison (1994a, 1995a).

7. Among the most recent studies on this debate are Killick (1991), Riddell (1992), and Cassen *et al.* (1986). See also Chenery and Carter (1973), and Griffin and Enos (1970). Todaro (1994, p.554), in an extended list of the various studies, refers also to Bauer's (1982, 1985) contributions on the subject.

8. See Chapter 8 for some of the major studies on the problem of brain drain in LDCs. See also Ezeala-Harrison (1995b).

9. There are doubtlessly some significant financial benefits from these that flow to the affected LDCs when funds are remitted home from abroad. This point is discussed in greater depth in Chapter 8 under the subject of education and development.

8

Population and Human Resources in Development

Population growth is often referred to as *natural increase*. This implies that population growth is a natural feature of human life and cannot be as easily manipulated as other aspects of economic development such as capital accumulation or technological acquisition. People must demand the natural needs and wants of life and sustenance, not only at a particular time of life, but also over time. Therefore, a given level of population must have an adequate level of living resources, and the extent to which this requirement is or is not met determines the level of development of the society.

The issue of population growth in most LDCs must be clearly understood. In many LDCs, the policy of having large number of children in families is often driven by a mixture of rational choice consistent with maximizing behaviour, and the cultural norm of high preferences for large families. Under rural settings, children tend to be effective *net producers*: they contribute more to the family budget than they consume, over their childhood periods. This is not the case in the urban settings or in developed countries, and hence the divergent attitudes to population control policies among these two settings. Moreover, in many cultures (of many LDCs without well established social welfare programs) children are seen as a type of *insurance* against old-age: they are a kind of investment toward future needs for care and support for the parents and family. These are perfectly rational policy incentives against which any population control policies must be fashioned.

In this chapter, we deal with the subjects of population level and growth, human resource availability, and migration. The importance of these subjects in a society's economic development cannot be overemphasized. The *population problem*, as it is commonly referred to in economic development, can be so diverse that it poses a general economic development problem. On the one hand, an inadequate population level that is small in relation to the country's land area would impose severe diseconomies of scale in production of goods, utilities, transportation, and public services. It would mean a restricted market for goods and services and provision of infrastructure. North America (nineteenth century) and Australia (early twentieth century) are good examples of developed societies where large and rising population levels fostered more efficient utilization of natural resources and growth of wider markets in the promotion of economic growth and development.

On the other hand, a high population level and a high rate of population growth could present a serious economic problem by way of outstripping the food supply, constraining the amount and rate of savings and foreign exchange, and making greater and costlier demands for the provision of infrastructure. Rapid population growth could also constrain the ability to save and retard the growth of physical capital per worker, resulting in lower productivity of labor and low income growth. High population level would lower *per capita income*. The connections between these dual aspects of population level are brought out clearly in a standard theory that attempts to postulate a relationship between population and economic development: the *Malthusian theory* of population, referred to earlier in Chapter 4 in our treatment of the classical theory of economic growth. Before studying this theory and its implications for economic development and underdevelopment, we need a good grasp of what precisely constitutes the population of a country.

THE LEVEL OF POPULATION GROWTH

Population is the total number of people residing within a given society at a point in time. The level of population may be defined over two horizons: the short run and the long run. In the short run (say, within one year), the population level of a society is the sum of the net natural increase and net immigration. The population growth of a country is given as

$$dP/dt = [dB/dt-dD/dt] + [dI_m/dt-dE_m/dt] \qquad (8.1)$$

where P = population level, B = total births, D = total deaths, I_m = total immigration, and E_m = total emigration. The term $dB/dt-dD/dt$ in Equation (8.1), indicates that the growth of total births minus the growth of total deaths gives the net natural increase; the term $dI_m/dt-dE_m/dt$ (immigration minus emigration), gives the net migration. The equation can be rearranged as

$$dP/dt = (dB/dt+dI_m/dt) - (dD/dt+dE_m/dt) \qquad (8.2)$$

Equation (8.2) expresses population growth as a residual in terms of its contributory factors (birth rate or *fertility rate* and immigration) and its depleting factors (death rate and emigration).

It is important to make the distinction between the *growth level* of population over time (dP/dt), and the *growth rate* of population over time [$(dP/dt)/P$]. The society's population *growth rate* would depend on a number of demographic factors, including the society's fertility rate (defined as the number of child births per 1000 women of child-bearing age), as well as the factors defined above.

The importance of distinguishing between the level of population and the growth rate of population is central to an understanding of the key implications of the population question in economic development. As far as it concerns economic growth and development, the level of population bears mainly short-term effects (as it relates to such things as the level of GDP, income, market demand, unemployment, and the distribution of income), whereas the growth rate of the population bears mainly long-term effects, as it affects the economy's growth rate and development potential.

THE MALTHUSIAN THEORY OF POPULATION

Thomas R. Malthus presented his original ideas on population and economic progress in his 1798 *Essay on the Principle of Population*. The theory states that whereas population grows by geometric progression (that is, in multiples), food production grows by arithmetic progression (that is, in additions), so that population would tend to outstrip the means of sustenance for it. Therefore, Malthus stressed, unless checked through such measures as *moral restraint* (presumably late marriages, celibacy, abstinence and birth controls: measures that Malthus considered as *positive* "preventive" checks), the population "explosion" would be checked by *negative* "natural" factors such as famines, malnutrition, wars, epidemics, and high infant mortality.

This theory was based on the phenomenon of diminishing returns. Malthus believed that because of diminishing returns to land as a fixed factor, food production could only be *added to* whereas population multiplies itself; therefore, each member of the population would not only have less land to work but also less food to eat as the marginal productivity would tend to decline. Eventually, the per capita income would be so low as to be close to the subsistence level, at which the population level would then be stable.

Malthus's theory presumably assumes that the state of technology and resource acquisition levels are constant. However, these factors are not constant, and the experiences of the DCs have shown that the Malthusian theory has largely been untenable. Population explosions have been consistent with rapid rates of economic growth in North America, Australasia, and parts of Europe. This is because the phenomenon of diminishing returns in agriculture has been negated through agricultural mechanization and application of advanced technology to farming. Apparently, Malthus did not foresee these developments.

For LDCs, Malthus's model appears to hold some relevance. An *optimum* level of population is apparent. This is the population level that is consistent with maximum level of per capita income, given the economy's resource and technological levels. If the economy's GDP rises faster than population, per capita income will increase as population increases, and if the rate of GDP growth is lower than that of population growth, per capita income will fall as population increases.

The concept of optimum population is illustrated in Figure 8.1. The level of population, P, is measured on the horizontal axis, while the per capita income, y, is measured on the vertical axis. At the beginning stages of economic growth and development, population growth would be consistent with rising per capita income. The maximum level of per capita income, y*, occurs at the population level P*—the optimal population level. Under the existing technology and output conditions, to avoid reductions in y*, the economy must keep the population growth rate from exceeding the current rate and ensure that population level does not exceed P*.

A higher population level, such as P_2 (beyond the optimum), would result in lowering the per capita income level (to $y_2 < y*$); and a lower population level, such as P_1 (below the optimum), would also result in lowering the per capita income level (to $y_1 < y*$). The economy's optimum population is P*, the level that yields the maximum per capita income. As indicated by the arrows pointing toward P* from P_1 and P_2, a less than optimal population level such as P_1 or P_2, is undesirable, necessitating the need for population control measures that should drive the population level toward P*. If an economy's population level is below the optimal level P*, resulting in a less than optimal per capita income y*, it is said to have the problem of *underpopulation*; and if its population level is above the optimal level P*, again resulting in a less than optimal per capita income y*, it is said to have the problem of *overpopulation*.

Figure 8.1
The Model of Optimum Population

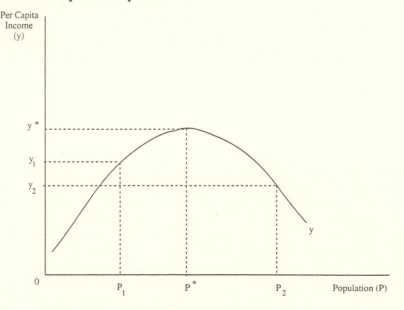

These illustrations show that one cannot ordinarily reach an *a priori* judgment on the absolute size of a population regarding whether or not such a size would pose an economic problem. This is because a population problem does not arise from absolute population size *per se*; rather, it arises from the relative balance of the level of population and GDP, as well as when the growth rate of population is compared with the growth rate of GDP. It is in this connection that we are able to determine whether an economy has the problem of overpopulation or underpopulation.

This simple model, premised as it is on the phenomenon of diminishing returns under fairly constant technology and resource levels, appears relevant for LDCs. As it points to the need to maintain population levels around their optimum, it calls for population control policies by way of "preventive checks" as recommended by Malthus.

THE POPULATION PROBLEM IN ECONOMIC DEVELOPMENT

Present-day LDCs are concerned with the various ways in which high population levels could pose developmental problems. There can be no question that in order to increase the capacity for economic growth and development, there is a need to control population around its optimum level. Among other things, this would enhance the ability to save and generate investment resources for development. The problems of overpopulation or underpopulation could easily become a real economic development bottleneck for an economy, especially an LDC. There are various ways in which these problems could arise; two of the most common ones can be illustrated with the concepts of *dependency burden*, the *growth constraint*, and the *residual growth paradigm*.

The Dependency Burden

A population's dependency burden relates to the *age structure* of the population. It concerns the degree of relative concentration of particular age groups within the population. In particular, an economy must "space" its population with a view to ensuring that the population is not skewed toward either "youthfulness" or "agedness".

A "youthful" population is one in which the majority of people, or a very significant proportion of it, are in the 14 years or less age group; an "aged" population is one with a majority or a very significant proportion in the 65 years and above age group. An economy whose population is either too "youthful" or too "aged," or both, is said to have a high *dependency burden*. The burden arises because of the high demand that these age groups make on the economy's resources for sustenance and training, while at the same time they do not actually "participate" in the labor force in order to engage in direct production.

This imposes severe constraints on the ability to save and invest in capital accumulation for development, a problem that would contribute directly to keeping an LDC in a vicious circle of poverty.

The degree of an economy's dependency burden can be directly measured by the *dependency ratio* (ρ), which is defined as

$$\rho = (P_{15-} + P_{65+})/P \tag{8.3}$$

where P_{15-} = Population below 15 years of age, and P_{65+} = Population above 65 years of age.

The dependency ratio statistic defined by Equation (8.3) could serve as an important indicator of the suitability of the population's age distribution at any particular time. As the ratio increases, due to more "youths" or more "aged," the dependency burden rises, and the economy must devote more of its current resources to maintain these "dependent" age groups. The ratio will fall if the absolute size of population increases while the dependent age distributions remain unchanged. This could happen as a result of increasing net migration that brings in more people in the nondependent age groups. The economy's dependency burden falls.

Important policies that could enable an LDC to reduce the degree of dependency burden that could be imposed on it by its population size can be deduced from this. The Malthusian recommendation of restriction through birth control seems appropriate for curtailing the "youth dependency" ratio, but it may not be enough. In order to also curtail the "aged dependency" ratio, there should be *birth spacing*. By spacing births, the population avoids having to have high concentrations in particular age groups, and thus reduce an imminent high dependency ratio at some point in time. The ability to implement any meaningful birth spacing, however, calls for some degree of relative high living standards. This becomes a problem for most LDCs which are already unable to achieve and maintain living levels above the bare minimum standards.

Jorgenson's Growth Constraint

A central argument against high rate of population growth concerns its potential adverse effects on the productivity of labor. In his dual sector analysis of the economic effects of surplus labor, Dale Jorgenson formulated an important theoretical framework that can be used to demonstrate the growth constraint that high rate of population growth can exert on an economy.[1]

The economy is assumed to be characterized by constant returns to scale production functions of the Cobb-Douglas type, with fixed amounts of land and capital resources:

$$Y = e^{\alpha t} R^{\alpha} P^{1-\alpha} \tag{8.4}$$

where Y = volume of output, Ω = growth rate of technological progress over time, t; R = amount of fixed level resources (land and capital), P = population level. The level of per capita output in the economy is

$$y = Y/P = e^{\Omega t}R^\alpha P^{1-\alpha}/P = e^{\Omega t}R^\alpha P^\alpha \tag{8.5}$$

Over time, the *rate of growth* of per capita output is

$$(dy/dt)/y = R^\alpha\{[e^{\Omega t}(-\alpha P^{-(\alpha+1)}dP/dt)+\Omega e^{\Omega t}P^\alpha\}/e^{\Omega t}R^\alpha P^\alpha$$

or

$$(dy/dt)/y = \Omega-\alpha(dP/dt)/P \tag{8.6}$$

This gives the growth rate of per capita output as a negative function of population growth rate: per capita growth rate is given by the rate of technological progress minus the product of the rate of growth of population and the output-elasticity of other resources. Therefore, as long as the rate of technological progress grows ahead of that of population, economic growth would not be jeopardized by population growth. But the question arises as to how far a country can succeed in achieving a rate of technological progress that outpaces its population growth rate.

As expressed in Equation (8.2) above, the population growth rate itself is assumed to be governed by the birth rate (dB/dt) and the mortality rate (dD/dt), and subject to a biological maximum P'. Following Jorgenson (and also Grabowski and Shields, 1996) this can be written in terms of the per capita output (that is, the birth rate as a proportion of per capita income), as

$$(dP/dt)/P = min[(dB/dt)y-dD/dt, P'] \tag{8.7}$$

This assumes that the growth rate of population would increase as per capita income increases, up to a given biological maximum, and can be expressed as

$$\sigma y - \phi < P' \tag{8.8}$$

where $\sigma = dB/dt$, $\phi = dD/dt$.

At any point in time, any given population growth rate that satisfies Inequality (8.8) can be substituted into Equation (8.6) to obtain

$$(dy/dt)/y = \Omega-\alpha[\sigma y - \phi]$$
$$= \Omega-\alpha\sigma y + \alpha\phi$$

Multiplying through by y gives the time growth level (rather than the growth rate) of per capita output as

$$dy/dt = (\Omega+\alpha\phi)y - \alpha\sigma y^2 \tag{8.9}$$

Using Equation (8.9), we can obtain the so-called *optimum* level of birth (population) growth, ϕ^*, (by setting $dy/dt = 0$), in terms of per capita income and technological progress. Apparently, this quadratic relationship defines the Malthusian optimum population model illustrated in Figure 8.1.

In terms of y, setting $dy/dt = 0$ in Equation (8.9) gives a quadratic expression

$$(\Omega+\alpha\phi)y - \alpha\sigma y^2 = 0$$

which can be solved to obtain two solutions:

$$y_1 = 0, \text{ and } y_2 = (\Omega+\alpha\phi)/\alpha\sigma \tag{8.10}$$

Clearly, $y_1 = 0$ implies that a population growth of zero would obtain if or when per capita income is zero. The solution, y_2, indicates the level of *optimal* per capita income, expressed in terms of technological parameters (Ω and α), and demographic parameters (ϕ and σ).

As the maximum growth level of per capita income occurs where $\partial(dy/dt)/\partial y = 0$, we can determine the appropriate level of per capita income (y^*) that maximizes dy/dt. That is

$$\partial(dy/dt)\partial y = \Omega+\alpha\phi - 2\alpha\sigma y = 0$$

yielding

$$y^* = [\Omega+\alpha\phi]/2\alpha\sigma \tag{8.11}$$

This is the level of per capita income that ensures a steady state maximum growth level of itself. Again, it is a function of technological progress, productivity of resources, and the demographic parameters of population growth.

The *growth constraint* that population growth places on economic growth and development is demonstrated by

$$\partial(dy/dt)\partial\sigma = -\alpha y^2 < 0$$

and

$$\partial y^*/\partial\sigma = -[\Omega+\alpha\phi]/2\alpha\sigma^2 < 0$$

These indicate that higher population growth would reduce the growth of per capita income, as well as its potential maximum level.

The Residual Growth Path

Other key potential economic problems that population growth could present to an LDC can be illustrated by use of the *residual growth paradigm*. The model implicitly applies the concept of dependency burden to express an economy's ability to generate resources for its economic growth after meeting its "maintenance burdens." The residual growth equation is given as

$$G = \delta(dK/dt - dL/dt) + \Omega \qquad (8.12)$$

where

$G = dY/dt - dL/dt$ = residual or net (economic) growth
Y = Gross domestic product
δ = residual-growth-elasticity of "net investment", a positive parametric constant
K = capital resources
L = labour resources
Ω = Impact of technological progress

This equation simply states that and economy's residual growth potential net of the burden of labour force (population) growth ($G=dY/dt-dL/dt$) is given by the sum of the positive function of "net investment" ($dK/dt-dL/dt$) and the state of technological progress (Ω). It posits the high population growth problem in at least two of its most devastating ways: its constraining effect on the ability to save and invest (captured in the definition of G), and its effect on the ability of the economy to have a productive labor force (captured in the functional relationship between G and "net investment."

In depicting the economy's growth potential as a residual, the model implies that, under a given level of GDP and state of technology, high population growth would reduce the growth potential through the high dependency burden it imposes. Therefore, the level of growth will depend on the ability to control the population growth rate dL/dt.

The second term in Equation (8.12) indicates that the economy's ability to achieve and maintain a given growth potential under given technology depends on how much of the rate of investment resources goes to cater for the labor force (a category that is a close proxy to the level of population). This may be seen as the economy's "net investment" population wise. The residual-growth-elasticity of "net investment" is an index that measures the degree to which a unit resource net of labor force growth and productivity would contribute to residual growth net of population. This parameter is particularly important because it captures the overall impact of population growth - that is, its dependency burden and the effects of the dependency burden itself on the economy's ability to invest and the productivity the labor force.

The role of technological progress is seen in considering the state of residual growth when the rate of labor force (population) growth is high enough to outstrip the rate of the ability to invest in capital accumulation - that is, when $dK/dt-dL/dt = 0$. Such a situation will reduce Equation (8.12) to $G = \Omega$; that is, residual growth would simply be given by the state of technology. If we assume that the growth rate of GDP is closely correlated with the rate of capital accumulation, then G may, in fact, be approaching zero or negative, indicating that the country's available technology is essentially devoted to keeping its population alive. Thus, the extent to which the application of technological progress could contribute to economic growth is limited by the size of the population. This highlights an aspect of the population problem that is not commonly recognized.

The application of the residual growth model still points to the same types of policy implications that are discussed above. However, it stresses even further that the population problem is far greater than that presented by the dependency burden. Therefore, population control deserves more urgent attention, especially in LDCs.

Population Policies for Development in LDCs

The link between population growth and economic development is not a very clear one. While Malthus and others who support his theory would argue that population growth does hamper economic development, many others would contend that population boosts demand, spurs innovation, and promotes economic development. So far, the discussions in this chapter have shown that the absolute level of a country's population needs not present a problem until it is matched with the country's resource acquisition and its capacity to produce goods and services to create income and wealth. It is in making such a link that we can determine whether or not a country has a population (or overpopulation) problem.

It is apparent, based on their per capita income levels, that most present-day LDCs indeed have population problems. Since most LDCs have very low and sometimes declining per capita income levels over time, it can only be concluded that their population levels are *beyond* their optimal levels (see the analysis in Figure 8.1). Therefore, the most appropriate population policy for an LDC today is to curtail population growth. Indeed, most LDCs have implemented some kind of population control measures, ranging from government-sponsored family planning programs involving education and material incentives to direct and aggressive birth-control promotional measures involving widespread distribution of contraceptives and surgical devices.

The population situation of a country cannot be separated from the country's overall social and economic conditions, especially the development of such facilities as health, education, employment, income growth, and basic human living conditions. Population control measures cannot successfully achieve their objectives if they are not preceded by significant improvements in the social and economic conditions of society. Official family planning programs, coupled with improved social and economic conditions that lower the benefits and raise the costs of raising children, would result in reducing birth rates.

Given the experience in most LDCs in which family planning programs have been pursued vigorously over the past several decades with only limited success, it appears that population control *per se* does have its limits. For one thing, population control programs have had only limited success in most LDCs because of the cultural and religious clashes between such programs and the members of society in which they are introduced. In some countries, they have been resisted openly, while in others they were ignored at best and met with apathy at worse. Thus, although population control policies may have succeeded in promoting economic development in the DCs, it need not be so in the LDCs.

In this regard, the pursuit of alternative measures to raise productive capacity and economic development seems to be a more viable policy toward the achievement of economic growth and development for the LDCs. Clearly, the measures to control the so-called excess population has failed in the LDCs. Rather than adamantly (and maybe unwisely) continuing to pursue the goals of curtailing population, goals that, as experience shows, would hardly be realized, the best recourse would be to concentrate on getting the existing population properly engaged and productive in the economic life of the society. This takes us to the subject of *human resources development*. In this, we consider the issues of education and training, employment, and migration.

HUMAN RESOURCES

The level of human resources is the central driving force in the achievement of economic development. For the DCs, many economists believe that the key asset that propels their self-sustained growth and development is not their physical capital but the body of knowledge amassed by empirical science, coupled with the ability to train and equip the population to use this knowledge effectively.[2] Involved in human resource development are the issues of human capital formation, that is, education and training, on-the-job skills acquisition, health and lifestyles, and the general attitudes and human and interhuman relations in society. These relate to the issues of employment, location, and migration.

Education and Economic Development

The level of educational attainments in a country is a major contributory factor, both directly and indirectly, to the degree of economic growth and development that is achievable in that country. Education contributes to economic growth and development directly through employment, enhanced productivity, and the composition of a civil population that is apt to promote social progress. It contributes indirectly through the multiplier effects of consumption and savings, and the inculcation of the right kinds of skills, thoughts, and attitudes required for constructive social change and economic progress.

It is believed that weaknesses in educational levels and human resource endowment have been one of the major constraints to the economic development of the LDCs. This comes not only at the aggregate (macro) level of economic performance but also at the individual (micro) level. Education enables individuals to develop and fulfill aspirations aimed at economic progress, by developing their abilities and talents; it also enhances people's development of general reasoning faculties, causes values to change progressively, and increases the receptivity of new ideas and attitudes toward society.

Through such endeavors, people improve their nutritional and health conditions, increase their productivity, and achieve higher incomes and wealth. Education gives individuals specific knowledge and skills for not only creating production but also for enhancing technological progress and facilitating their applications in economic activities. Education equips people with the technical and organizational skills needed for the effective utilization of society's natural resources for the creation and management of wealth, and the promotion and sustaining of economic development.

The contributions of education to economic growth and development have been widely studied and documented. In one of the most comprehensive studies, Psacharopoulos (1988) analyzed a list of potential benefits inherent in mass education that include many of the traditional claims: that it would raise living standards and offer unrestricted avenues for the poor to improve their social and economic status; that it would offer equal opportunities to all, and thus serve as a means to achieve a more egalitarian society; and that it would bridge the gaps between ethnic and tribal groups in society.[3]

In order to better determine the proper place of education in the process of economic development, it is important to analyze the nature of education as an instrument of development. The provision of education belongs in the class of *impure public goods* specifically referred to as *merit goods*. These are goods that involve very high *externalities* in consumption, but are easily *excludable*. As a merit good, education has immense potential social benefits as discussed above, but if left to themselves, the members of society do not take these high potential social benefits into account when planning for their demands for education. Therefore, the actual level of demand of education would be far smaller than the level that would yield the most total benefits to society, a level that society "merits." Thus, the total *private demand* for education and total the *social demand* for education tends to diverge.

On the production side, as public good, educational provision is characterized by *economies of scale*; that is, its production is characterized by continuously declining average cost. These peculiar conditions surrounding the demand side of education mean that education cannot be produced and traded like any other product in the economy. In a free-market driven economy, the profit incentive provides the impetus for entrepreneurs to provide goods and services for distribution, as long as the market does not *fail* as an effective mechanism for the transactions between producers and consumers. For public goods, however, a market failure is encountered in their production and demand. The market fails because, as explained above, on the demand side, education is a merit good, and on the supply side, it is characterized by economies of scale. An example of the production and demand conditions of a semi-public good such as education is analyzed as follows.

Figure 8.2 presents the various conditions surrounding the provision of a merit good such as education in the economy. The quantity of education Q (in, say, the number of school places) is measured on the horizontal axis, and the costs of production (average cost, AC, and marginal cost, MC) and price (P) are measured on the vertical axis. Both the AC and MC curves are continually downward-sloping as a result of economies of scale in production. The market demand curve is D, which is assumed to lie below the AC curve because, as explained above, education is a merit good. The curve MR is the marginal revenue curve.

Under private-sector production, the producer would choose to maximize profit, setting production at the point where MC equals MR, and thus would produce the amount of education Q* and charge the unit price P*. We note that this firm will not charge the price P_1 on the demand curve, which is the price that the buyers would be willing to pay for the quantity Q*. This is because the price P_1 does not cover the unit cost indicated by the point A. The producer of education, therefore, would charge the price P* which covers the cost of production. However, at this price the market demand would be only the amount Q_a indicated by the point B on the demand curve. And at the amount Q_a, the unit cost of production is on the point C, and so on. This shows that the production of education under the private sector would not be efficient in the economy, as the private-sector producer(s) would not only charge relatively very high prices but would also limit production at levels that would not yield the most benefits to the economy.

The social-welfare-maximizing level of education would be the level at which marginal cost equals price. This obtains at the point D, at the unit price P_0 and production level Q_0. At this level, however, the unit cost, indicated by the point E, exceeds the price P_0, resulting in total losses equivalent to the area $FEDP_0$, to the producer. The private sector would not operate under this condition. However, the government could grant subsidies to cover these losses.

Using Figure 8.2, we can easily prove that, besides its massive social benefits, the society would derive a positive net monetary benefit by providing the level of education Q_0.

Figure 8.2
Education as a Merit Good

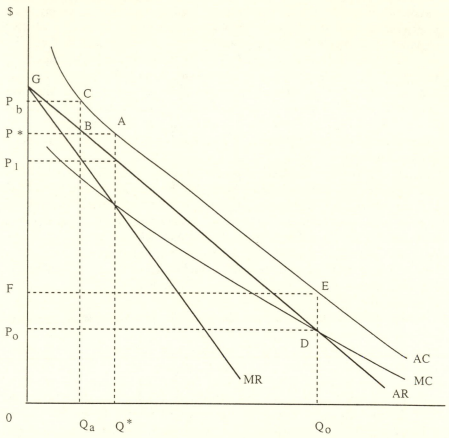

This is done by simply comparing the magnitudes of monetary benefits and costs. At this level, the total monetary benefit that society obtains from education is given by the area under the demand curve: the area $GDQ_0 0$. However, the total monetary cost of providing Q_0 level of education is the area FEQ_0, which is clearly less than the area $GDQ_0 0$. This shows that the total utility (benefits) that accrues to society far outweighs the total cost in providing a given level of education. This alone provides sufficient economic justification for public-sector funding of education.

From the preceding basic model, it can be proposed that, given the relevant assumptions about education as a merit good, the society would derive the maximum social and economic benefits from its educational provisions if education were produced by the public sector and provided to the general population at relatively low prices such as P_0, which makes it affordable to the bulk of the population. This can only be very appropriate for an LDC, given its low-income situation. For in the absence of governmentally supported education, only a relatively small amount of education (such as the amount Q_a) would be available to be rationed to the population according to affordability. And such an outcome is clearly unsuitable for an LDC seeking to develop its human resources to promote economic development.

The evidence indicates that educational policies in most present-day LDCs appear to have been largely guided by this model. Most LDCs provide mass low-cost or free education at the primary, secondary, and postsecondary levels. The problem however, is that most LDCs have not really reaped the most benefits from their educational programmes. It is important to examine the reasons and factors surrounding why most LDCs have failed to obtain the expected economic benefits from education.

Appropriateness of Educational Economic Objectives in LDCs

Many studies on the impact of formal education on the economic development of the LDCs have contended that formal education as an instrument of socioeconomic development has indeed failed in LDCs.[4] The problem of "misconceived educational programs" in Africa had been anticipated by Balogh (1962), while Blaug *et al* (1967) examined the problem in India, and Lewis (1972) expressed some skepticism on the issue of mass formal educational programs involving huge investment expenditures. Thus, the question of the need for LDCs to pursue the appropriate levels of education for their specific circumstances is not a new one. What may be new is wading into the specific designs of educational goals and pursuits, and the delivery of educational programs, with a view to determining how and why they failed in many LDCs. It is important to relate the levels of education to the types of education that an LDC might need for its particular social and economic development.

Studies by Illich (1970) and Dore (1976), both of which referred to the perennial problem of the chronic unemployment of educated people in developing countries as the *diploma disease*, represented the earliest challenging and critical views of the role of education in the economic development of LDCs. As noted earlier, the diploma disease occurs when a country invests a major proportion of its resources in formal education, only to turn out graduates who are not only unsuitable for employment in the economy, but also a social liability in terms of social and political unrest.

The "disease" involves a long-term feedback ramification. As the educated people cannot be utilized productively, they become alienated, and society subsequently loses not only the idle human capital but also the huge opportunity cost of their education. Furthermore, as a result of the unemployment and underemployment of the bulk of educated people, less and less investment would be made in education, leading to long-term human capital deficiencies in both quality and quantity.

Quality of human capital suffers because the private demand for education will be centered on the need to acquire just the "paper qualification" needed to enable one to obtain employment. The goals of *excellence and quality in teaching and instruction, learning, and research*, which are the goals explicitly stated as central to national educational programs, are perceived as "unnecessary" in individual and social educational needs.

This aspect of the disease has an even more damaging symptom, namely, the incessant occurrence of "examination malpractice." Given the perceived importance of "paper qualification", people resort to whatever means to obtain and possess it. This involves students (and in many cases encouraged by parents) resorting to cheating on a very large scale in order to pass examinations. For example, examination officials are corrupted with huge bribes to "leak" examination questions to candidates beforehand. Other forms of the malpractice involve impersonations or outright "buying" of successful examination results. To counter such problems, authorities resort to massive and large-scale cancellations of results, which throw many people and their future into disarray and jeopardy. As a result, the quantity of human capital formation declines with the declining incentives to acquire learning. Dropout rates rise as people channel their priorities elsewhere in order to meet the immediate need for economic sustenance.

The diploma disease has become a major obstacle to development in LDCs. Formal education has failed to meet the special employment needs of the peculiar social and economic environments of LDCs. In most of these countries, formal education has catered more for the academic and intellectual needs of an elitist class in a low-productivity society of massive unemployment and growing poverty, and less for the unique circumstances of an underdeveloped society.

Private Returns to Education in LDCs

The benefits of education accrue both socially and privately. Socially, education brings higher levels of decency and morality, less crime, more honesty and concern for others, greater tolerance, and increased devotion to civic duty. These benefits accrue to the society at large and represent the social returns that may flow to a country from its investment in education. Despite the potential social benefits, private benefits from secondary and university level education (the levels that have the highest social costs in most LDCs) are much more significant. These levels of education are required for job procurement and promotion (credentialism and screening) in LDCs. Wage and salary scales are geared to educational levels rather than to performance and productivity.

Private returns for educational investment are very high in LDCs. Studies by Psacharopoulos and Woodhall (1985) show that private educational returns in LDCs surpass those of DCs. For Africa, the average returns to investment in education between the early 1960s and 1980s were 27 percent per year for primary education (22 percent for higher income countries), 17 percent for secondary education (14 percent for higher income countries), and 12 percent for higher education (12 percent for higher income countries). Evidence from the World Bank's *World Development Report* for 1993 indicates that the rates of return from all levels of education in LDCs are about one and a half times those of DCs.

Individual earnings at higher levels of education relative to lower levels are uniformly higher at every stage of the social hierarchy in most LDCs. Psacharopoulos (1988) indicates that private rates of return to university graduates were on the average 6 times higher than those of primary school graduates in most African countries, while they were only 2.4 times higher in United States, Canada, and Britain. Many LDCs still base their pay scales for various levels of education on the relative scarcity of graduates of the various levels. These levels were set by colonial administrations seeking such graduates during the colonial era, and were not based on the productivity of the skill concerned. Public-sector pay scales are used as the barometer for fixing all earnings levels in the economies of most LDCs. However, the public-sector wages are dominated by the pay scales of government bureaucrats, which are set as a percentage of the per capita GDP outside of labor market and productivity considerations. These scales range from 750 percent of per capita GDP in Cameroon to 1000 percent in Benin Republic and 1500 percent in Burundi.

Given these circumstances, the demands for secondary and university education are artificially inflated, and as a result, LDCs devote enormous amount of funds to these levels of educational provision, *albeit* unjustifiably so. The resulting mismatch is a surplus of graduate job-seekers, and then it becomes only a question of time for the diploma disease to develop. Thus, education has tended to increase inequality in LDCs.[5]

Relevance of the Educational Agenda in LDCs

The lack of relevance in the curriculum is fundamental to the LDCs' educational problems. Educational curricula in most LDCs are still dominated by foreign (colonial) philosophies ranging from the history, geography, literature and classical writings of Western intellectuals to language and cultural arts in English, French, Latin, Greek, and Roman civilization.[6] Although many of these subjects have been replaced with a more indigenous curriculum, the systems and values that they established are still firmly entrenched. The traditions of colonial education that attached more prestige to the liberal arts and law than they did to vocational training in applied fields such as agriculture and artisanship have been prelude to the diploma disease in many LDCs.

Formulation of the required educational curriculum for development in LDCs must be tailored to the region's immediate as well as longer-term socioeconomic needs. Evidence of some success stories exist in Singapore where vocational programs have been implemented to train labor specifically for employment in particular aspects of industry where demand for labor is largest. Singapore's

Industrial Training Board conducts courses in which class time is combined with on-the-job apprenticeship training in sectors where a need is expressed. By focusing on actual needs, the program can avoid the danger of "overproduction" inherent in the diploma disease. Brazil has achieved a relatively milder success by establishing its National Industrial Apprenticeship Agency, which relies on labor market surveys and detailed analyses of job openings in planning and implementing the country's training programs. The program is financed by a 1 percent payroll tax that is waived for any firm that agrees to sponsor on-the-job training.[7]

In order to reduce the artificially inflated private benefits from higher education and bring them closer to equality with the social benefits, key reforms in human capital development policies should be made to accord more closely with an LDC's development needs. In particular, there should be a curtailment of the heavy government subsidization of higher education with, a view to shifting the costs to the individual beneficiary.[8] Furthermore, job specifications may be redrawn to deemphasize high educational attainment, while the tying of wages and salaries to educational levels is modified to conform to labor market supply and demand.

Education for the Dualist Labor Market

The labor market dualism of LDCs (see Chapter 1) conforms to the observed wide disparities of income among the members of the society: wage employment in the organized private and public (primary) sector, and wage and self-employment in the unorganized (secondary) sector, encompassing small-scale informal activities and rural agriculture. Differences in skills among the members of these different segments and differences in technology in them have only widened their disparities further. The workers of the primary segment tend to be more skilled and engage in capital-intensive activities which require that they be relatively far more trained or "educated." The secondary segment workers undertake casual-type work and require very little capital and virtually no formal education.

Given the relatively high rate of population growth, new labor force entrants are absorbed mainly in low-wage employment of the small-scale and informal type, including subsistence agriculture. The average household income in the small-scale informal sector (of the secondary segment) has been generally lower than that of the formal (primary) sector, despite the fact that the informal segment has greater access to the services of unpaid apprentices and family workers.

The secondary segment of the labor market (rural and urban together) is the largest in terms of employment but the weakest in terms of productivity and earnings. The bulk of the population is still in agricultural employment at the peasant-subsistence level, engaged in food crops for household consumption and local petty trading; or the commercial (and sometimes wage employment) level, engaged in cash crops for local distribution and exports. Within the secondary segment is the urban informal sector, which is the next largest employer of labor (next to agriculture), the majority of which is underemployment. It is very dynamic and adaptable regarding its employment-absorbing capacity. This sector is characterized by relative ease of entry, reliance on indigenous resources, unregulated competitive product markets, flexibility of operation, and the ability to blend well with the traditional values and social practices of the particular region.[9]

The volume of wage employment and the growth in real household incomes, however, have been the greatest for the primary (formal sector) members, namely, the medium-scale to large-scale private and public enterprises, as well as the medium-scale self-employment category. Employment in the primary sector is characterized by relatively higher productivity, higher wages, and lower turnover rates, as the sector is dominated by multinational firms, with capital-intensive technology (which explains the relatively high productivity and wage levels).

Entry criteria into the stable primary-sector employment is based principally on the acquisition of formal education proven by possession of the requisite credentials. Experience and relevant skills are often stated to be important, but they are not given priority in preparations for the job market. Most employers prefer at least a secondary school education for new recruits, even for those in the lowest category manual jobs.

Combined with increasing rural-urban migration and the relatively small size of the primary sector in terms of labor force absorption, a typical LDC's high rate of population growth has led to a large increase in unemployment and underemployment. Redundancy of agricultural manpower in the secondary sector is a major source of the unemployment problem. This redundancy has particularly damaging effects in the economy because of the dominance of agricultural occupation in the economy's total employment.

The dual labor market phenomenon presents special challenges for educational programs in LDCs. In most countries, the educational evaluation process takes the form of nationwide or subregionwide examinations that are given at the relevant stage of education to determine the student's preparedness to undertake the subsequent higher levels of education or to obtain employment. Because of the overwhelming importance of these examinations, students and teachers focus their efforts on the task of passing the examinations rather than actual acquisition of knowledge or skill. This system perverts the true purpose of education, not only in the tremendous financial and physical resources entailed, but also in jeopardizing the alternative opportunities to which efforts might have been more fruitfully channeled.

Where it offers effective productive skills, education is oriented almost entirely toward preparation for work in the urban (primary) sector of the society, and fails to prepare people sufficiently for aspirations in the secondary segment's agriculture and rural development, thereby greatly distorting the aspirations of the individual away from the needs of the secondary (rural) sector. The overall effect of disproportionate investment in formal education in the LDCs, especially at the secondary and postsecondary levels, has been the diversion of scarce resources from important socially and economically productive activities in the secondary segment. For example, direct job-creating pursuits in agriculture, handicraft, artisanship, tradesmanship, and the like, are forestalled, thereby retarding rather than stimulating contributions to national development from the secondary segment.

Many LDCs abound with university graduates, some of whom have attained "first-class honors" in areas such as mathematics, English, physics, political science, or chemistry, yet employers might be seeking workers skilled in areas such as air conditioning and refrigerative services, cotton wax printing, plumbing maintenance, or even automotive technician services, most of which are in the secondary sector of the employment market. Employers must then rely on apprenticeship and on-the-job training to obtain the required workforce, a time-consuming and costly alternative for both parties, while the graduates remain unemployed in the primary sector. Even in the primary sectors, empirical evidence suggests that the educated people still lack the skills to satisfy the employment needs. The public service sectors in many LDCs have had to conduct specialized training programs for their own staffs, indicating that the needed skills were not being supplied by the formal education system.

Education for Rural Development

Rural development encompasses the major transformations of social and economic structures, processes, relationships, and institutions in the rural sectors. It reflects the measures designed to enhance a more equitable distribution of income in order to promote higher levels of living in the rural sector: the creation of more productive employment opportunities, not only in agriculture, but also in social infrastructure such as health, housing, nutrition, and utilities. As the educational curricula of most LDCs are overwhelmingly oriented toward urban development, they seem to have succeeded only in arming the "educated" with values, ideas, attitudes, and aspirations that are largely alien to their environment, to the extent that they are educated away from their rural surroundings. The rural sectors in LDCs do not have effective demand for educated people who consequently end up being dislocated in the sector. What the rural (agricultural) sector needs is the quality of labor that would allow the use of more modern techniques (equipment, seeds, insecticides, etc.). Clearly, the type of education required to fulfill this need is not the "academic diploma type" that dominates educational programs in modern LDCs.

A number of research studies on rural-urban migration in developing countries have suggested that an individual's level of educational attainment is positively correlated with his/her propensity to migrate from the rural sector to the urban sector in search of the more attractive urban jobs. The traditional theoretical explanation of this phenomenon is based on the Harris-Todaro (1970) migration model. Basically, educated individuals perceive better (though erroneous) chances of accessing urban sector jobs, which gives them a wider potential urban-rural earnings disparity. Lacking the pertinent skills that may be needed by urban employers, they move to the urban sector in search of employment, only to remain unemployed. Higher education simply results in transforming various kinds of underemployment into open unemployment, primarily through rural-urban migration.

Education and the Brain Drain Syndrome in LDCs

In Chapter 7 we discussed the LDCs' brain drain problem: the emigration of highly educated and skilled persons of the professional, managerial, and administrative (PMA) category from the LDCs to the DCs. This emigration pattern is considered a drain because their home countries incurred considerable expense for their training, directly (governmentally funded scholarships) or indirectly (social costs), while the benefits of their contributions flow to the further economic growth of the already affluent DCs.[10] Since the costs of training are incurred by the poor country where educational resources are already limited, whereas the benefits are received by the developed world, this in effect means that the poorer countries are subsidizing the supply of human resources to the richer countries, creating a severe drain on the human and material resources of the low-income countries.

World Development Report (1983) indicates that the developing countries as a whole lost about $320 million on the average each year between 1970 and 1980 in training PMAs who moved to the United States, which translated into a saving of about $883 million per year in education costs for the U.S. For Britain, Canada, and the U.S. together, the total savings was about $44 billion per year over the period. The data also reveal that on an annual basis, many developed countries receive more from brain drain than they spend in foreign aid: over twice as much for Canada, about 50 percent for Britain, and 50 percent for the U.S.[11]

The brain drain problem of LDCs can be seen as a symptom of the larger diploma disease. As a result of improper coordination, the educational systems have only succeeded in turning out "experts" that are better suited for the foreign countries from which the systems of education originated. Consequently, practising PMAs in LDCs base their performance criteria more on receiving praise and international recognition, and less on contributions to national development. University researchers are preoccupied with research on international issues such as atomic energy and nuclear physics or sophisticated economic models of nonexistent competitive markets in order to be published in international professional journals and attend professional and academic association meetings in London, New York, Paris, or Tokyo.

Solutions to the LDCs' brain drain must be directed at the root causes of the diploma disease itself rather than the symptoms. Proposals that have emerged from previous studies do not seem to be on the mark. Bhagwati (1977) and Hamada (1977), for example, both suggested that the developed countries place a supplementary income tax on the earnings of emigrant PMAs from developing countries and then channel the tax funds through the United Nations to the developing countries concerned to be invested in development. Others have proposed higher foreign student fees in developed countries, a suggestion that has been implemented in Britain and Canada. The United States has implemented the J-visa system which requires foreign students to leave the country they have completed their studies.

The problem with these approaches is that they are only *ad hoc*. They suffer from being only short-term measures that could not lower the brain drain syndrome. Their rationale is simply compensatory to the home country, and fails to address the question of skill shortages in the home-country. Besides, such approaches might even encourage more emigration to the developed countries and exacerbate the brain drain.

The ultimate solution rests in reforming the educational programs and curricula in the LDCs. If the PMAs are trained specifically for their countries' environment, they will remain in their countries where their productivities will be positive, and will stay away from foreign countries where their skills will be less in need. Furthermore, the LDCs themselves must not directly encourage the brain drain through their attitudes to "foreign training." By creating conditions where foreign-trained PMAs are accorded special respect and even higher wages and salaries, the LDCs have tended to push their students overseas for training. Scholarships and training grants should be awarded solely for training within the country, and in fields of particular relevance and applicability to domestic and local economic and social needs.

EMPLOYMENT AND MIGRATION

The main concern with high population growth in LDCs relates to its creation of adequate employment for the growing population. In the LDCs, the *employment problem*, as it is generally termed, is always at the center of the overall underdevelopment question. The nature of migration directly affects the state of employment and unemployment.

The Employment Problem

Employment is the engagement of the labor force (and the other resources) in continuous and productive creation of goods and services to generate flows of income and wealth in the economy. This has been a particularly difficult achievement for most LDCs, and for them, an employment problem is said to exist. The employment problem manifests itself in the following ways:

1. The occupational sector in which the bulk of the population is engaged, namely, agriculture, is not a reliable source of employment because productivity is very low and therefore incomes are low. The sector is still at the *subsistence level*; as such, it does not provide sufficient incentives for labor, and it fails to sustain the workforce.

2. Massive underemployment and disguised unemployment are pervasive in most sectors of the LDCs' economy.[12] This is due mainly to lack of the cooperant factors, notably, capital, with which labor may combine productively.

3. The labor market is dominated by an oversupply of unskilled and semiskilled labor, while there is an acute shortage of skilled humanpower.

4. The majority of the employed people are engaged in informal economic activities in the *informal sector*, in which, although "employed" (usually in self-employment), are still eager to accept wage employment in the *formal sector* if offered to them. The informal sector is unregulated and unorganized, and involves economic activities that are neither registered nor recorded in government statistics.[13]

5. The majority of industries employ capital-intensive technology and have limited demand for labor.

6. The public sector is the main employer of labor, relative to the private sector of the economy. In this sector in particular, productivity is very low and disguised unemployment and underemployment abound.

The employment problem in LDCs is not just a question of unemployment in the sense of unutilization of human and material resources. It also encompasses the problem of low productivity and low incomes for the resources that are employed. It reflects the uneconomical allocation of resources, in that resources are not properly harnessed. It also has a very inticate geographical dimension: the desertion of the rural sector and the development of slums in the urban center, with their broader sociopolitical repercussions.

Migration

The root cause of rural-urban migration in LDCs is the relative unattractiveness of rural living. As we saw in the discussion of education above, most LDCs have tended to channel much of their development efforts to the urban centres, to the relative neglect of the rural sectors. Following the often ambitious drive with which most LDCs pursued their development programs after achieving political independence from colonial rulers, rapid urban growth occurred. This only exacerbated rural-urban income and development differentials as sectoral distribution of income tended consistently to favor the urban-oriented sectors.

Per capita earnings, on the average, in urban-oriented sectors such as manufacturing, commerce, construction, transport, utilities, and services far exceeded those of rural-oriented sectors such as agriculture, forestry, and mining. Most LDCs failed to correct this lopsided situation through, say, adoption of the appropriate incomes policies; therefore, the trend continued and the disparities widened even further.[14]

For most LDCs, the development programs that prioritized industrialization and urban development, while placing relatively insufficient emphasis on agricultural and rural development, tended to signal to the population, rightly or wrongly, that only participation in the urban-oriented sectors provided viable employment opportunities for labor. The result, therefore, could hardly be surprising: a wave of rural-urban migration.

Generally, rural-urban migrants are driven the *push factors* and the *pull factors* that motivate the individual to migrate. The push factors are those adverse conditions in the rural sector that *push* the individual to seek better alternatives. Included in these conditions are the unattractiveness of rural dwelling relative to urban dwelling, lack of high-paying rural jobs, slack business opportunities, and unavailability of utilities and infrastructural facilities. The *pull* factors are the attractions of the urban sector that *pull* the individual to seek urban living. These include higher urban wages, relative ease of securing urban employment, abundant utilities and infrastructure, prestige attached to urban living, and relative independence from family obligations and controls. The extent to which these factors affect the rate of migration, and their economic implications, are fully explored in the following theoretical model.

The Harris-Todaro Migration Model

The problem of rural-urban migration in LDCs is concerned mainly with why the flow of migration continues even in the face of high urban unemployment.[15] This situation simply worsens the urban unemployment problem, with immense social and economic repercussions. In a widely acclaimed contribution, John R. Harris and Michael P. Todaro (1970) developed a two-sector model that explains this phenomenon on the basis of the underlying structural conditions explained above. The model offers pertinent policy implications that may provide important guidelines for rural-urban developmental policy approaches in LDCs.

The model posits the individual's decision to migrate is a function of the urban-rural real income differential and the probability of finding *modern-sector* employment. If the present value of the discounted expected real income gain from migration, after taking account of the chances of being unemployed, is positive, then migration is worthwhile. Thus, the rate of rural-urban migration would be a positive function of the individual's *prospective* earnings differential between the urban and the rural sectors. As long as the *expected* urban earnings exceeds the rural one, rural-urban migration would be positive. The formal model is outlined as follows.

The symbols of the model are:

M = level of migration
$M^* = dM/dt$ = rate of migration over time, t
π_u = probability of finding employment in the urban sector, which is a proxy for the urban employment rate
π_r = probability of being employed in the rural sector, a proxy for the rural employment rate
W = urban average wage level
w = rural average wage level
E_u = urban employment level
E_r = rural employment level
U_u = urban unemployment level
U_r = rural unemployment level

where

$$W > w$$

The Harris-Todaro migration equation is

$$M^* = v(\pi_u W - \pi_r w) \tag{8.13}$$

The parameter, v, is a positive constant, and may be referred to as the rural-urban *push-pull factor*. It is a measure of the degree to which the intersectoral earnings differential exerts the push-pull phenomenon upon the individual, toward migrating to the urban sector.

The first term in the bracket is the expected urban earnings, and the second term is the expected rural earnings. Assuming that the probability of finding employment in a sector is, indeed, the sector's employment rate, and furthermore, that the probability of having employment in the rural sector is, in fact, one, then Equation (8.13) can be written as[16]

$$M^* = v(E_u W - w) \tag{8.14}$$

Using Equation (8.14), we demonstrate the relationship between rural-urban migration and unemployment. That is, given, by definition, that

$$E_u = 1-U_u$$

Equation (8.14) becomes

$$M^* = v[W(1-U_u) - w] \tag{8.15}$$

from which

$$\partial M^*/\partial U_u = -vW < 0$$

This indicates that migration is a negative function of the urban unemployment rate: as urban unemployment increases, rural-urban migration decreases, and vice versa. Given this relationship, rural-urban migration needs to be controlled. This raises the following question: Under what circumstances would rural-urban migration cease? That is, could $M^* = 0$? This could be seen by substituting $M^* = 0$ into Equation (8.15), to obtain

$$v[W(1-U_u)] - w = 0 \qquad\qquad (8.16)$$

from which we have

$$U_u^* = 1-(w/vW) > 0 \qquad\qquad (8.17)$$

This gives the *critical level* of urban unemployment, which is the level necessary for rural-urban migration to cease, provided urban wages exceed rural wages. This solution is an equilibrium condition from which any disturbance by way of changes in, say, W, w, or U_u^*, will result in another round of adjustments in the values of these variables.

To see how this model reveals the principal migration problem of a typical LDC, let us consider an LDC having an equilibrium condition such as that given by Equation (8.16), at any given point in time. Assume that the goverment of this LDC undertakes a seemingly successful economic policy initiative that creates more jobs in the urban sector, and assume that this policy action reduces the urban-sector unemployment rate from its equilibrium U_u^* to a level $U_1 < U_u^*$. This situation that disturbs the *migration equilibrium* condition would set adjustments into motion, leading to an increase in the migration rate. This rise in migration rate will again cease ($M^*=0$) after a new higher migration level is reached.

But because the newly created jobs could only go to a fraction of the mix of the existing urban unemployed and the new migrants, the effect will be that the urban unemployment rate will swell. The new equilibrium will be one of a higher M, U_u, and presumably W. This outcome represents what is termed the *urban employment dilemma* in (highly populated) LDCs. The dilemma is that any effort to create jobs in the urban sectors of the LDCs is apt to increase rather than decrease the urban unemployment rate.

The Harris-Todaro model has far-reaching implications that touches on rural-urban migration, intersectoral relative wages, and rural development. One clear policy recommendation that makes itself apparent is that rural wages must be increased to levels that are comparable to their urban counterparts, of course, making allowance for the appropriate *compensating variations* (see Chapter 6).

As discussed above, this policy would be complemented by overall rural development policies aimed at providing rural infrastructure and public utilities.

NOTES

1. Although Jorgenson's (1961, 1967) works, as a dual sector analysis, focused equally on the agricultural and industrial sectors of the economy, it can be generalized to address the economy as a whole. The model is used by Grabowski and Shields (1996) to analyze the concept of the *demographic trap*, and we adapt it here to illustrate the concept of the growth constraint.

2. See Nafziger (1990, p. 238) quoting Simon Kuznets (1965). Several other more recent writers have argued that differences in human resource potentials are responsible for differences in the development levels and potentials of the present-day LDCs and DCs.

3. Other studies include Colclough (1982), Bhagwati (1973), and Simmons (1974).

4. These conclusions were deduced from close scrutiny of the nature of pedagogy, instruction, and curriculum, *vis-a-vis* their suitability within the socioeconomic milieu of particular LDCs. Among these are Bhagwati (1973), Simmons (1974), Islam (1980), and Colclough (1982). A more recent and exhaustive inquiry on the African case can be found in Ezeala-Harrison (1995b).

5. See Mingat and Tan (1985).

6. Hogendorn (1992) gives a report about an American teacher instructing Muslim girls in northern Nigeria 20 years after that country's independence from Britain. According to her syllabus, she was required to teach Dickens *Christmas Carol* to students who knew little about Christmas, had never seen snow or a fir tree, and would have found a pork roast for the holiday completely abhorrent (because to Muslims the pig is an unclean animal). To these girls, *Scrooge, Bob Cratchitt, and Tiny Tim* were equally mysterious and nor did they understand why the book was being studied in the first place.

7. Further details on these and other examples can be found in Middleton *et al.* (1990).

8. Reducing government subsidization of higher education would seem to go directly against the policy recommendations of the model offered earlier. This, however, need not be so. As a merit good, education is to be subsidized only to a certain extent: the individual student has to pay an amount equal to the marginal cost, which would then be supplemented by subsidies to cover the unit cost. This is not the same as the "free education" system that most LDCs provide.

9. More extended analysis on this can be found in Rempel (1994) and Ezeala-Harrison (1994b).

10. The types of PMAs involved are usually scientists, engineers, academics, architects, and physicians. In most cases, their home countries would have incurred considerable expense into their training either directly or indirectly, whereas the benefits of their contributions flow to the further economic growth of the affluent developed countries. However, there could be some "trickle down" flow of benefits to the home countries later as these PMAs remitted some of their earned resources home (see Ezeala-Harrison, 1995b). For more study of this phenomenon, see Glaser (1978). Baldwin (1970) also offers a very insightful analysis. One of the earliest studies of the brain drain

problem can be found in Grubel and Scott (1966).

11. These calculations do not include the financial contributions that the emigrants remit to their home countries. Although the totals of these contributions are very small for LDCs taken together, relative to the magnitude of the "drain," they amount to very substantial sums for some countries. For example, in 1988 a total of about $3.4 billion was remitted to Egypt, amounting to about 10 percent of GDP. In 1990, about 35 percent of North Yemen's GDP was received as remittances from emigrants working mostly in Saudi Arabia and other parts of the developed world.

12. Disguised unemployment, as explained in Chapter 6, exists where the marginal productivity of labor is close to zero such that labor may be withdrawn from production without causing output to fall. Underemployment exists where a worker is employed in an activity in which both the worker's skill and duration of work are underutilized.

13. The informal sector involves activities such as petty trading and hawking, artisanship, roadside mechanics, repairmen, and food retailing. It also includes small-scale subsistence agricultural production.

14. In relation to the African case, see Ezeala-Harrison (1994a).

15. This portion is based on Ezeala-Harrison (1988b).

16. To justify the full-employment assumption in the rural sector, it must be understood that all unemployment in this model is reckoned as *involuntary*. Thus, rural dwellers cannot remain unemployed involuntarily since they always have ample employment opportunities in rural agriculture (commercial or subsistence) and other rural economic activities.

9

Agriculture in the Process of Economic Development

In this chapter we consider the crucial roles of agriculture in economic development. As most LDCs are agrarian economies (see Chapter 1), the attainment of the proper level of agricultural development has always been a persistent development bottleneck for them. The agricultural sector is said to be especially capable of contributing to an LDC's greater economic development because it provides opportunities not only for other sectors to emerge, but also for the economy as a whole to participate in international trade and other international economic flows.[1] In particular, agriculture contributes immensely to economic growth by being a market for the production of other sectors of the economy and being a supplier of food and raw materials to them.

THE LEVELS OF AGRICULTURE IN LDCs

In a broader representation, agriculture encompasses the multifarious economic activities of farming, fishing, hunting, and animal husbandry. Together, these activities are practised at three main levels in most modern LDCs: the subsistence (peasant), commercial, and plantation levels.

The Subsistence Level of Agriculture

Subsistence agriculture, which employs the greater proportion of the rural labor force in most LDCs of Asia, Africa, and Latin America, is characterized by low productivity because of its reliance on ordinary family labor, with virtually no application of capital or any improved (modern) modes of agricultural production. The subsistence level of agriculture is the small-scale self-sufficient agricultural system found in the rural areas of many LDCs today. In this system, the production level is usually geared for the household subsistence and, at times, for local distribution for petty cash required to meet the household's other needs. This is dominated by the production of *food crops* and staples such as grain, root-crop tubers, vegetables, animal trapping, and domestic animal rearing. Its main characteristics are the labor-intensive nature of production and the almost total lack of capital equipment applied to production. Production methodologies involve traditional land-tenure patterns, resulting in very low productivity levels, with an abundance of disguised unemployment and underemployment.

Subsistence production represents more than a mere occupational outlet and source of income to the bulk of the rural dwellers of LDCs, especially in Africa and South Asia; it is the way of life. Current data indicate that whereas less than 28 percent of the population of Europe and less than 27 percent of the population of North America live and work in rural areas, over 68 percent of African and 67 percent of Asian populations are rurally based. Furthermore, over 65 percent of the African labor force engages in rural agriculture for livelihood, compared with under 7 percent in developed countries.[2]

Table 9.1 presents data on population, labor force, and agricultural production for selected regions and continents in both the developed and underdeveloped world. There is a striking difference between the proportionate size of the African subsistence agricultural labor force (75 percent) with a rural labor force of 70 percent, and South Asia (63 percent) with a rural labor force of 75 percent, on the one hand, and the North American agricultural labor force of 5 percent and rural labor force of 26 percent, on the other. For Africa, for example, the table indicates that as 70 percent of the African population are rural dwellers while 75 percent are engaged in subsistence agriculture; this means that up to 5 percent of urban dwellers may be engaged in subsistence activity for their source of living. Thus, the geographical distribution of the population might not necessarily reflect the occupational distribution.

Table 9.1
World Labour Force Distribution by Regional Classification (1988)

Region	Population (millions)	Urban (%)	Rural (%)	% in Subsistence Agriculture
World	5,128	45	55	45
All LDCs	3,931	35	65	62
All DCs	1,198	73	27	7
Africa	623	30	70	75
South Asia	1,570	25	75	63
East Asia	1,302	47	53	51
Latin Amer.	429	68	32	32
Europe	497	75	25	9
North Amer.	272	74	26	5
Japan	123	77	23	11
USSR	286	65	35	20

Key: LDCs: Less Developed Countries; DCs: Developed Countries
Source: World Bank, World Devt. Report, Annex Tables 3 & 31, 1988.

The subsistence family farm is the basic unit of production whose members constitute the main agricultural workforce, but, as already stressed, it is characterized by low productivity because of its reliance on ordinary family labor with virtually no application of capital or modern production methods. To the extent that the subsistence sector is not only the main source of the LDC's labor force but also the sector in which a significant portion of the labor force is employed (or rather underemployed), its level of performance would to a large degree determine the agricultural sector's overall level of performance. Therefore, it is important that greater emphasis be placed on this level of the agricultural sector, with a view to significantly raising productivity and incomes as a means of achieving economic growth and development in the LDC.

The Commercial Level

The commercial level of agriculture is higher than the subsistence level, but involves several small-scale producers engaged in production essentially for market distribution, of *cash crops*, mainly for exports at the national level. This level of production is dominated by the quasi-peasant members of the rural sector, who, in most cases, apply to it the same levels of technology that are applied to subsistence production. Examples of the cash crops produced under this level of agriculture include cocoa, coffee, cotton, rubber, grains, groundnut, and timber.

Productivity may be higher at the commercial than the subsistence level, mainly because far greater acreage is covered by a typical unit, and moreover, more resources are invested. Often the owner is able to hire many workers for the production activity, which is also overwhelmingly labor-intensive involving relatively little capital.

The Plantation Level of Agriculture

This is the large-scale, highly productive, capital-intensive, and mechanized level of agricultural production found in the developed countries. Some LDCs have achieved a degree of this level of agriculture, but for most of them it is still very insignificant compared to the subsistence and commercial levels. At the plantation level, the agricultural sector is able to produce both food crops and cash crops, allowing the economy to become virtually self-sufficient in the supply of food for the population and raw materials for industries and for export. It is generally reckoned that the LDCs must achieve this level of agricultural development if they are to attain economic development. It must be noted, however, that the plantation level of agriculture is capital intensive rather than labor intensive, and must therefore be carefully weighed in the light of the potential *labor-surplus* nature of most LDCs.

POTENTIAL OF AGRICULTURE TOWARD ECONOMIC DEVELOPMENT IN LDCs

There are several ways in which greater agricultural productivity and output can contribute to economic development. In regard to agriculture, the economic development process is viewed as a major structural transformation from an agrarian economy to an economy in which the share of agriculture in the labor force and national output declines with major increases in national income and employment. Japan is often cited as an example of a developed economy whose economic development benefited immensely from the powerful potentials that agriculture could provide, because the development of Japanese agriculture provided this sort of structural transformation. The key developmental role of agriculture is analyzed as follows.

Agriculture as a Source of Food

Higher agricultural output results in increased food supply needed for improvement of the nutritional level. This would reduce the cost of food, thereby freeing resources for savings and investment. Furthermore, providing food needs from domestic sources would result in saving scarce foreign exchange for other needs. As food supplies become adequate to meet the growth of demand from an expanding population, food prices remain stable, quelling discontent and demands for wage increases. The economy benefits greatly from such checks on inflationary tendencies and growth-retarding pressures.

The *food service effect* of agriculture can be illustrated with the following linear relationship expressing the annual rate of food demand as a linear function of the population growth rate, the per capita income, and the income-elasticity of demand for food (agricultural) products:[3]

$$dF/dt = dP/dt + \xi dy/dt \qquad (9.1)$$

where

> F = demand for food and agricultural products
> P = population
> y = per capita income
> ξ = income-elasticity of demand for food and agricultural products
> t = time period

Using this expression, we can deduce a more explicit relationship depicting how the annual growth of demand for food and agricultural products may depend on these other parameters.

Let Y = gross domestic product, then by definition

$$y = Y/P$$

Substituting this into Equation (9.1), gives

$$
\begin{aligned}
dF/dt &= dP/dt + \xi . d(Y/P)/dt \\
&= dP/dt + (\xi/P^2)[P(dY/dt)] - Y[dP/dt] \\
&= dP/dt + (\xi/P)[dY/dt] - (\xi Y/P^2)[dP/dt] \\
&= dP/dt + (\xi/P)[dY/dt] - (\xi y/P)[dP/dt] \\
&= dP/dt\{1-(\xi y/P)\} + (\xi/P)[dY/dt]
\end{aligned}
$$

This can then be written as

$$F^* = P^*\{1-(\xi y/P)\} + (\xi/P)Y^* \qquad\qquad (9.2)$$

where

$F^* = dF/dt$, $P^* = dP/dt$, and $Y^* = dY/dt$, are the time growth rates of the demand for food and agricultural products, population, and gross domestic product, respectively.

Equation (9.2) expresses the food service effect of agriculture. It shows that the growth rate of demand for agricultural products positively depends not only on the population level but also on its growth rate. It also positively depends on the size of the GDP, while it negatively depends on the per capita income. While the relationship with population may be as generally expected, the nature of the relationship between the growth rate of food and agricultural needs and the GDP and per capita income is interesting.

Equation (9.2) indicates that the positive relationship with the GDP enters with a term that we may refer to as the *characteristic distribution of the income-elasticity of demand across the population*, ξ/P. This is not at all surprising given the definition of ξ. However, the negative relationship with per capita income needs to be elaborated on. First, it should be clear that the income-elasticity of demand for food and agricultural products is considerably higher in LDCs than in DCs.[4] Therefore, any given rate of increase in per capita income would have considerably stronger impact on the demand for food and agricultural products in LDCs than it would in high-income countries. But as incomes rise, the situation tends to change.

The above result shows that as per capita income increases, the rate of demand for food and agricultural products decreases by the factor $\xi P^*/P$. This means that as members of the population become more affluent, they tend to spend less of their income on food and agricultural needs, in the magnitude of the income-elasticity of demand for food times the annual growth of the population.

The relationship expressed by Equation (9.2) can be usefully applied to determine the sustainable level of growth for food needs for any country of known population and GDP levels. Conversely, it can be used to estimate an "optimum" level of population that could be effectively sustained by a given level of the growth rate of food and agricultural production. In this connection, it serves as an important policy tool for projecting the pace of agricultural growth that would be compatible with the population and GDP levels of any LDC.

Agriculture as a Source of Raw Materials

The output of the agricultural sector provides needed raw materials for the industrial sector. The benefits of this output for the economy are clear: the country saves on foreign exchange that would have been spent to import industrial raw materials, which it could aptly allocate to the importation of capital equipment. The economy's industrial sector is given significant impetus, for it is able to access its raw material needs more cheaply and within local reach than foreign ones.

As the industrial sector grows and provides employment and income to the population, the agricultural sector receives a boost by way of higher demand for food and raw materials, which could lead to further increases in agricultural productivity. In this way, the agricultural and industrial sectors tend to complement each other's development, promoting economic development.

Agriculture as a Source of Employment and Income

Agriculture is a major avenue for employment and income in LDCs where it is the occupation of about 70 percent of the population of most countries. Higher agricultural output would mean higher income and, therefore, more attractive and worthwhile employment channels. If properly developed, this would not only provide a great deal of relief to the employment problem of an LDC, but it would also serve as an effective means of sustaining economic growth and development. Higher agricultural income would enable the bulk of the population to demand industrial manufactured goods. Such an effective demand for the industrial sector would go a long way in promoting the economy's industrialization effort. As noted above, this is another aspect of the agriculture-industrialization complementarity.

Agriculture as a Source of Investable Resources

Agriculture may provide a significant amount of investable resources for development in various ways. In Chapter 7 we noted that forced saving can be generated by altering the domestic terms of trade against the agricultural sector in favor of the modern sector. As the members of the subsistence agricultural sector tend to save less relative to the modern sector, resources can be appropriated from the agricultural sector by raising the prices of manufactured goods and lowering the prices of agricultural goods. In addition, investable surplus can be generated from agriculture by transferring relatively underemployed labor from it into more productive work in the industrial sector. Such compulsory transfer from agriculture for the benefit of other sectors yields an "invisible surplus" that generates greater taxed revenue for investment.

Agriculture's potential as a source of investable surplus for development is noted to have been very evident in the experiences of Japan and the former Soviet Union.[5] Kuznets stated that in these cases, the "factor contribution" of agriculture was quite large in the early stages of development: for Japan, during the 1880-1900 period, the land tax was over 80 percent of central government taxation, and the income tax rate ranged between 12 and 22 percent in agriculture, compared to 2 to 3 percent in the nonagricultural sectors. For the Soviet Union, forced extraction of surplus from agriculture through a combination of taxation, confiscation, and other measures may have financed the greater part of the rapid industrialization drive of the late nineteenth and early twentieth centuries.

Agriculture as a Source of Foreign Exchange

Agriculture is a very reliable source of foreign exchange needed for the importation of capital stock and equipment. During the early phase of a country's development, it is clear that agricultural exports occupy a dominant position. It does this through both import substitution (foreign exchange saved by replacing imports of food and raw material with domestic production) and export promotion (export of agricultural products). Exports of agricultural raw materials provided over 40 percent of Japan's foreign exchange needs during its nineteenth-century developmental phase.

The foreign exchange saved can be directed toward the importation of capital and investment in human resources development. Through this major contribution, agricultural development can facilitate the structural transformation of the economy.

Despite agriculture's immense potential in fostering economic development in LDCs, there remains the complex problem of developing agriculture to a level at which it could be made to yield this potential. In view of the LDCs' peculiar problems of development, especially as these are heavily related to the development of the agricultural sector—the problems of absolute poverty, unemployment, and severe income inequities—it is necessary that the LDC concentrate on agricultural development as a prelude to its economic development. Most LDCs appear to have recognized this fact and are, in fact, pursuing it. But their efforts in this regard have met with a myriad of problems. The problems of agricultural development in LDCs are extensive—ranging from purely human error related problems to entirely natural phenomena that tend to defy human solutions. We explore these problems by setting them in categories related to the nature of the market for agricultural output.

THE PROBLEMS FACING AGRICULTURE IN LDCs

To reiterate, the problems that retard progress in the improvement and development of agriculture in LDCs are several and varied, and exist on both the supply and demand sides. On the supply side, the main problems emerge from a combination of natural constraints, human deficiencies, and resource limitations. On the demand side, the main problem arises from the nature of the market for agricultural produce and the inability of the producers to adapt to it. We now consider these factors in greater detail.

The Supply-Side Problems of Agricultural Development

While some of the supply-side problems facing agriculture in the LDCs could be overcome through greater endeavors and proper management of resources and opportunity, some are often very difficult and insurmountable, mainly because they touch upon natural factors that are beyond human controls, and against which the LDCs are particularly helpless. The nature of the problems usually governs the degree of success in tackling them. The main problems can be categorized as follows.

Problems of Natural Factors

Most LDCs inhabit the parts of the globe whose weather and climatic conditions are not conducive for agricultural growth. Most occupy the *arid and semiarid* parts, and others inhabit the more tolerable but still very harsh tropical regions. These climatic conditions are largely inimical to the cultivation and growth of agricultural crops, and any attempts to ameliorate these natural conditions (for example, construction of irrigation facilities) are not only extremely expensive, but also apt to meet with failure.

Tropical areas have climates of very high temperatures ranging from lows of 15°C to highs of 40°C all year round. These areas have hard and naturally infertile soils and varied patterns of rainfall. Geographically, they lie within a span of about 2,500 kilometers on either side of the equator, although their tropical effects extend much wider than this range. Three types of tropical climates are generally identified: *the wet equatorial tropical climate*, characterized by high humidity and constant (equatorial) rains of about 190 to 300 centimeters per year; *the monsoon tropical climate*, characterized by a mix of alternate wet and dry seasons; and *the arid tropics*, characterized by little or no rainfalls.

The arid and semi-arid lands of the tropics are desert regions with extremely dry soils that can accommodate little or not vegetation. They receive an annual average rainfall of less than 25 centimeters, while much of the lands are overcome with salt encrustation and sand-dunes formation. United Nations estimates indicate that about 14 percent of the world's population - about 630 million people - live in the arid and semiarid lands of the earth, and most of these are the LDCs of Africa, the Middle East, South America, and parts of Australasia.[6]

Tropical conditions are not favorable to cultivation of agricultural crops. Rainfall is not only inadequate, but also unreliable when abundant, and fluctuates widely. Moreover, the tropical heat, humidity, and absence of frost are conducive to the growth of destructive bacteria, parasites, insects, pests, and several species of tropical diseases that inhibit plant and animal life throughout the year. The sun simply scorches the earth's surface and soil, the crops, as well as animals, plants, and the organic matter and micro organisms that the crops may need. The incessant tropical torrential rains, unpredictable as they are, simply wash away the soil's nutrients, while the ferocious erosions crush and sweep away agricultural crops. These leave behind reddish, baked, and hard laterite soils for most LDCs to use for their agricultural pursuits.

Apart from the volcanic soil of the East African highlands and parts of Asia and the Pacific regions, as well as the clay soil of the alluvial plains of Africa and South America, which are potentially fertile, the soil found in much of the tropics comes from old acid parent rock, and is poor in calcium and plant nutrients. In the forest-covered (rain forest) regions in parts of West and Central Africa, South Asia, and South America, once the forest cover is removed during the process of farming, the proportion of iron and aluminium hydroxides increases, resulting in the formation of laterite soil, which becomes intractably hard and uncultivable.

The severe natural problems facing the tropical areas of the world are not limited to their agriculture. Indeed, these natural problems substantially impair both human and animal health. They cause rapid deterioration of physical structures such as buildings, machines, and infrastructure, and they also negatively affect human productivity in other spheres of economic life. As a result, unfavorable climatic and natural conditions have often been cited as one of the most devastating factors impeding the state and pace of economic and social development in the LDCs.

Problems of Human Inabilities

By problems of human inabilities is meant the behavioral attitudes of members of the LDCs' agrarian societies that have proved to be inimical to the growth of agricultural output and productivity. The most entrenched of these problems is the undue conservatism and resistance to change that agricultural subsistence producers exhibit. Many of these people tend to ignore the applications of modern technology and crop varieties that are often introduced to them. Instead, they adhere to such traditional methods as the *slash-and-burn land tenure, shifting cultivation* (also referred to as the forest fallow cultivation), and *crop rotation* - methods that retard productivity and limit the acreage of cultivation.

In several peasant communities of Africa, say, certain days of the week are declared nonwork days and are set aside for social or religious activities. Often, such observances are based on archaic beliefs respecting the "earth gods" in expectations of more blessings in higher crop yields. These kinds of superstitions only perpetuate the stagnancy and dormancy of the vicious circle of poverty and underdevelopment.

Problems of Resource Constraints

Both financial and physical capital resources are severely lacking in the LDCs' agriculture. Subsistence farmers neither have the collateral securities needed to obtain loans from financial institutions, nor can they afford to meet the usually exorbitant interest rates charged for these loans. Moreover, the industrial sectors are hardly developed enough to supply the needed physical capital equipments such as mowers, tractors, and combine harvesters, which are necessary for raising their level of agriculture. As a result, most LDCs find it very difficult to establish more plantation-level agricultural production, while the small-scale subsistence and commercial levels continue to be predominant in their economies.

The Demand-Side Problems of Agricultural Development

On the demand side, the main problems facing agricultural development in LDCs relate to the marketability of agricultural produce and can be classified as the *inelasticity syndrome* and the *cobweb syndrome*. These terms all refer to the nature of demand in the market for agricultural produce, notably, the unsteadiness and unpredictability of the size of output, and the fact that the nature of these products could spell severe losses for producers in times of bumper yields. We consider these in turn.

The Inelasticity Better-Harvest-Poorer-Farmer Syndrome

In a way, this aspect of the problem of agriculture in LDCs may be considered a natural problem because it arises from the peculiar nature of the elasticities of demand and supply of agricultural products. As food products, agricultural commodities have inelastic demand, for they constitute a major part of the *necessities* of life: food. Furthermore, and for totally different reasons, agricultural products tend to have inelastic supply, especially in LDCs. This situation could be attributed to two factors, both relating to the producer's ability to either increase the quantity supplied in response to higher prices or to reduce quantity supplied in response to falling prices.

Let us first consider a case of rising prices of agricultural products. Unlike the production activities in, say, industrial manufacturing, or mining, whose processes could take a relatively short period of time and could be predictably controlled, and in which, therefore, a producer could easily raise the quantity supplied to take advantage of rising prices, agricultural production involving seeding, planting, harvesting, and marketing must take a considerable length of time to be completed. This has been referred to as the *gestation period* of production, and over this period of time, the producer cannot reasonably respond to price incentives by raising output and supplying more quantities to the market.

In times of falling agricultural prices, the producer cannot easily withhold output from the market, according to the law of supply. To be capable of following the simple law of supply, the producer must be able to maintain an inventory of output onto which any excess supplies would be stored and from which the market could be supplied whenever prices rise again. However, not only would such an inventory be highly costly, but also the construction of its facilities would involve a significant degree of technical expertise. This is because agricultural products are easily perishable, and it would be very costly to build storage and preservative facilities for the inventory, notably, uninterrupted large-scale electrical and refrigerative cold stores. As a result, the supply of agricultural produce in LDCs tends to be highly inelastic.

Given the inelasticities of both supply and demand, any changes in the market conditions of agricultural products result in wide fluctuations of prices and revenues of the producers. In LDCs, the most common situation is that of *bumper harvests* that subsistence- and commercial-level producers often receive due to, say, unpredictably good cropping seasons that may result from favorable weather. The main problem associated with this kind of situation can be illustrated with a simple graphical analysis.

Figure 9.1 is used to analyze the inelasticity better-harvest poorer-farmer syndrome that besets agricultural production in LDCs. Assume the curves S_0 and D_0 represent the initial market supply and demand curves respectively, with market equilibrium at point A, yielding the price p_0 and quantity demanded Q_0. In this situation, a typical producer's total revenue is given by the area p_0AQ_00. A *bumper harvest* would have the effect of shifting the supply curve from S_0 to S_1, resulting in a new market equilibrium at the point B, with market price p_1 and quantity demanded Q_1. This yields a total revenue equivalent to the area p_1BQ_10, which is clearly and significantly lower than the producer's previous revenue. The producer is far more worse off as a result of the bumper harvest that he/she was without the bumper crop.

The Cobweb Syndrome

The *cobweb syndrome* in the LDCs' agriculture is closely associated with the inelasticity better-harvest poorer-farmer problem, but it relates specifically to the problem of instability of agricultural incomes. To analyze the cobweb syndrome, let us assume a situation in which, say, the demand for agricultural products

Figure 9.1
The Inelasticity Better-Harvest Poorer-Farmer Syndrome

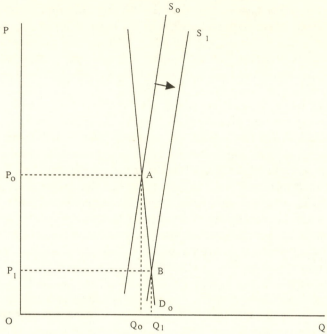

increases significantly due to increasing food needs from the rising population
or rising incomes among the population. The *impact effect* of such a situation
will result in higher prices of agricultural products, and therefore, higher
revenues and incomes for agricultural producers.

As agricultural producers base their next season's investment and production
plans on the going higher prices, while they do not have close control over the
market supply of output (due to the reasons explained above), the ultimate result
would be a relative oversupply, depressing prices and leading to a situation
similar to the inelasticity better-harvest poorer-farmer outcome. This would only
disappoint the producer, prompting a curtailment plan for the following season,
which would then have the opposite effects.

The *cobweb* effects mean that agricultural incomes are not stable; thus,
agricultural producers are not able to properly formulate accurate investment and
production plans. Above all, and most importantly, the message it sends to the
general population is that careers in agricultural employment are highly
unpredictable and unreliable. The effect is to cause agricultural occupation to be
seen as a poor occupation which should only be engaged in by the illiterates and
the uneducated. As a result, the majority of people in LDCs - the youth,
women, and even people with just secondary-school-level education - tend to
desert the agricultural occupation and do not contemplate entering it as a realistic
avenue for employment.

POLICIES TOWARD AGRICULTURAL DEVELOPMENT IN LDCS

An array of key policy issues present themselves for serious and practical consideration in the search for ways to raise the state of agriculture in LDCs. These issues include technological change strategy, agricultural research, extension services, irrigation, education, mechanization, land-tenure reform, and financial credit liberalization. Most of what needs to be done in these various considerations has been implied in the preceding discussions of the problems facing agricultural development in LDCs. In particular, there is the need to effectively tackle the dual problems presented by the inelasticity better-harvest poorer-farmer and cobweb syndromes. In this regard, LDCs must provide adequate storage facilities.

Many LDCs have attempted to address this problem by establishing Marketing Boards. However, in most instances the marketing boards have proven to be merely the means of more effectively taxing rural subsistence- and commercial-level agricultural producers rather than of stabilizing their incomes. Marketing boards are statutory monopsonists of cash-crop exports, with the sole authority to purchase agricultural output from local producers at much lower (fixed) prices, for exports at much higher world market prices. In this way, these producers are virtually guaranteed stable prices for their output. Despite some level of determined efforts shown in many LDCs, the marketing board system has generally failed to solve the problems. In particular, the marketing boards essentially cater only for cash-crop producers, and do not cover food crops and other agricultural output geared for the domestic market. In this way, it fails to benefit the majority of agricultural producers in LDCs.[7]

In this section we focus on an issue that is considered to be most central in the quest for ways to raise the level and productivity of agriculture in modern LDCs. This is the issue of appropriate technology. The general belief is that the technological constraint seems to be the most formidable obstacle in the LDCs' agriculture. Therefore, we consider the subject of *technological variation*, and analyze its policy issues toward agricultural development in LDCs.[8]

Technological Change Strategy for Agricultural Development

A major constraint on productivity growth in the LDCs' agriculture is that the sector is saddled with technology that changes very slowly, if at all. Producers could spend their energies raising the efficiency with which they use that technology but would have limited gains due to the use of stagnant techniques. In LDCs in general, any improvements in agricultural techniques tend to occur over too long an interval of time to have any significant and lasting impact on productivity and income.

Technological variation refers to the application of innovative inventions to traditional ways of accomplishing production tasks, with a view to embodying more efficient and more productive methods into the production process. This variation may be labor-saving, capital-saving, or land-augmenting, but the stress is on efficiency and productivity improvement. In the LDCs, the agricultural sector is still dominated by subsistence-level techniques that have remained the same for centuries because these techniques are bound by archaic customs and observances. These societies are incapable of embracing changes that enhance productivity and efficiency. But the need for higher productivity to meet increasing poverty and economic stagnation in the LDCs underlies a long-overdue necessity to overcome technological redundancy in their agriculture.

The bulk of the studies on agrarian technology and productivity indicate that traditional agriculture can be "efficient" in the standard sense of the term; that is, under existing technology farmers maximize their output from the available set of inputs or obtain a given output level with less input use. However, under virtual technological stagnation, farmers are not able to constantly respond to changing agricultural methods. Rural agricultural producers tend to experiment with alternative techniques over very long periods of time, for decades or even centuries, until they could stumble upon the right method for a given technology. Backed by the appropriate education that instills more progressive attitudes, they may be willing to change if they clearly perceive imminent benefits from a change. This attitude is demonstrated by their observed positive response to changes in prices of their agricultural products.

Before the advent of modern science and its application to farming, fundamental advances were made in all aspects of agricultural technology. The evolution from traditional slash-and-burn tenure methods of shifting cultivation to permanent cultivation in which a crop is grown on a piece of land once every year represents gradual, though masked, technological progress. This evolution was very sluggish; farmers had to discover ways to restore nutrients in the soil by crop rotation and addition of fertilizers, and ploughs had to be developed. The result has been that productivity growth could not match the rapidly growing need for sustenance. This indicates that technology, with little or no variation, lacked the potential for requisite productivity growth, and therefore calls for rapid technological variation to be applied in agrarian societies on an ongoing basis.

A major distinction between the LDCs' agriculture and modern agriculture in developed countries lies in the pace and source of technological change. In the LDCs, technological change is slow and sluggish because it is based mostly on the tinkering of individual farmers or accidents of nature that may, for example, reveal a high-yield seed variety. In contrast, in the developed countries technological change is rapid and varied, and is based on scientific research which produces most of the new techniques used. This crucial difference is technological, and a closer look at it will indicate that the development and modernization of agriculture in LDCs borders mainly on technological issues.

Technological variation deals with such issues as the role of irrigation facilities and chemical fertilizers, and the impact of these on crop yields, crop and plant varieties, and productivity. Clearly, there is no universally best technology for agriculture, as all agricultural techniques must be adjusted to local soil, climatic conditions, and factor endowments. However, a society must clearly innovate in both major aspects of the *mechanical package* and *biological package* of agricultural technology in order to effect a viable technological variation.[9] Thus, the optimal levels of capital-labor substitutability, as well as plant variety-chemical fertilizer complementarity, have to be employed and kept in place. The productivity effects of such technological input in LDC agriculture cannot be overemphasized.

Agrarian production in most LDCs commonly displays certain peculiar and crucial features. The most important of these features with regard to technology, is the seasonal nature of operations: the busy seasons of planting and harvesting when labor needs are high, and the slack gestation periods when the producer would really need none or only a very small workforce for maintenance of the farms.[10] To effect technological variation, there is the need for simultaneous application of mechanical and biological packages. Establishing and using the products of *Agricultural Research Centers*, and creating rural capital such as roads and irrigation systems will enhance varied technology.

LDC governments must adopt more aggressive postures in regard to introducing new inputs and new techniques, and must use *Extension Services* to spread the transfer of these new techniques to the farmers. Rural dwellers in the LDCs learn from their neighbors - and technology travels more rapidly when neighboring agricultural entrepreneurs in a country have equitable assess to varied technological facilities. The key to success in overcoming the major scientific and engineering constraints facing the LDCs' agriculture also involves rural education, which would help increase the channels of contact and encourage people to abandon archaic tenure methods in favor of varied technology.

These are common-sense specifications, but they get at the heart of the failure of the agricultural sector in LDCs. Perhaps it is because such "common sense" is obvious, and not based on any sophisticated computer simulatory modules, that they are not effectively and seriously applied. Implementing these straightforward practical policies will go a long way toward improving agricultural productivity in the LDCs.

NOTES

1. Meier (1976, p. 563) attributes this view to Kuznets (1965).

2. World Bank, *World Development Report*, various issues (1988-1993).

3. This analogy was used by Meier (1976) who credits its formulation to K. Ohkawa, "Economic Growth and Agriculture," *Annals Hitotsubashi Academy*, October (1956), pp. 45-60.

4. As stated by Meier (1976), earlier studies by Johnston and Mellor (1961) indicate that the income-elasticity of demand for agricultural products in LDCs is about 0.6, while

it is in the order of 0.2 to 0.3 in DCs. These researchers further observed that the increase in agricultural output in Japan during the 1880-1920 period seemed to have been of about the same magnitude as the growth of demand during that period, and that this rate of increase corresponded to an annual rate of increase of about 2 percent.

5. While stressing that it would be impractical to measure the contribution of agriculture's investible surplus to economic growth, Kuznets (1965) believed that these contributions were, indeed, very significant in the growth and development of Japan and Soviet Union during the eighteenth and nineteenth centuries.

6. See Kamarck (1976) and Nafziger (1990, p. 166).

7. For more detailed studies on the role of marketing boards in the LDCs' agricultural income stabilization, see Essang (1971), Lewis (1967), or Ezeala-Harrison (1993a).

8. This section is based on Ezeala-Harrison (1993b).

9. Gillis *et al.* (1992) applied the terminologies of mechanical and biological package in their discussions of agricultural development in LDCs. The mechanical package refers to tractors, combines, and other forms of labor-saving machinery which would replace agricultural labor lost to the industrial sector. The biological package refers to improved plant variety such as hybrid corn, seed stock, and the like (termed the Green Revolution).

10. Several studies on this subject abound in the works of Binswanger and Rosenzweig (1984), Bardhan and Rudra (1981), Dreze and Mukherjee (1987), Eswaran and Kotwal (1985), and Osmani (1991). Ezeala-Harrison (1992a), as well as Baffoe-Bonnie and Ezeala-Harrison (1996), offer full analyses of the income and employment implications of these peculiar features of the agricultural sector in LDCs.

10

Industrialization in the Process of Economic Development

Industrialization has always been viewed as a necessary aspect of economic growth and development. The link between industrialization and economic development is so close that an economy's level of development is often measured by the degree to which it is industrialized. The tendency for this close association among scholars and experts in the field of economic development need not be surprising. Ever since Britain achieved the Industrial Revolution and the rest of the developed world *learned* from it and furthered the pace of global economic development through massive industrialization, the main criterion for economic development has been the level of industrial growth and expansion, and its impact on national incomes and per capita incomes.

This chapter examines the concept of industrialization and its various stages of achievement in an economy. The potential of industrialization in the process of development is clearly evident in the development experiences of the DCs. Higher shares of GDP generated by the industrial sector are closely associated with not only rising per capita incomes but also more egalitarian income distribution patterns. Therefore, it is generally believed that the industrialization of an LDC would result in its development.

Industrialization offers substantial dynamic benefits that are important for changing the traditional structure of the LDC, especially where such an LDC is a primary-product exporting economy that is faced with the problems of lagging export demand in the face of rising demand for employment for a rapidly expanding population and labor force. In PART II of this book, dealing with the theories of economic development, we discussed the various postulates of how economic development (and industrialization) may be achieved.

Among other concepts, we examined the notions of balanced and unbalanced growth to industrial development. Also covered was Rosenstein-Rodan's notions concerning the external economies that are realizable through industrialization by the adoption of a "big push" model in the form of a high minimum amount of industrial investment in order to overcome the economic obstacles to development.[1] But how exactly should the term *industrialization* be understood? It is important to provide a precise definition regarding the particular sense in which the term should be understood.

THE SCOPE OF INDUSTRIALIZATION

Industrialization involves a system of production and distribution linkages within an economy. It may be defined as the process of transformation of raw materials, with the application of cooperant human and capital resources, into durable consumer goods, capital goods, and physical infrastructure.[2] It is made up of constituent subsectors, each of which may involve other sets of systems and linkages of production and distribution activities.

There are three main constituent parts which together make up an industrial system. These are the manufacturing activities, tertiary activities, and physical and environmental face-lift.

Manufacturing Activities

In its broad terms, the manufacturing sector of an industrial system includes mining, raw-materials processing, and production of consumer durables. These activities have one thing in common: they involve a certain level of capitalization of production for the transformation of raw materials into finished goods, or extraction of raw materials for further processing. The process creates employment for labor, gives the raw materials higher *value added* enabling them to attract higher prices, and helps their producers gain more effective control over their supply in the market.

The Tertiary Activities

The tertiary sector of industry is composed of the *services* and the *infrastructure or social overhead capital* sectors. The services sector comprise such activities as transport (railways, air transport, shipping, and road transport networks), financial services (banking, stock and capital markets, insurance, etc.), and entertainment and hospitality services. Infrastructure includes health, education, hydroelectric power facilities, water and sewerage systems, roads and highways, post and telecommunications systems, and the like. These are also referred to as *public utilities*, for they are largely *public goods* and involve high *externalities* in consumption.[3]

The Physical and Environmental Face-lift

An often neglected but important aspect of industrialization involves the physical and environmental aspect. Industrialization changes not only the environmental outlook of a country but also the geographical and occupational distribution of its population. Urbanization is the tendency for a significant proportion of the population to reside in urban areas, and it is a necessary side effect of industrialization. The share of a country's urban population relative to its rural population is an important indicator of the country's level of industrialization and economic development.

Urban growth goes with large-scale provision of infrastructure and environmental face-lift, notably, housing and residential facilities, shops and markets, office towers and restaurants, factories, and government developmental facilities. These change the country's facial outlook from rural to urban.[4]

THE ROLE OF INDUSTRIALIZATION IN ECONOMIC DEVELOPMENT

Rather than its general connotation of an avenue for producing a wider variety of products by application of modern technology, industrialization is viewed primarily as a means of improving a poor country's employment conditions and living standards. Pursued in the spirit of this depiction, industrial development in an LDC must be closely interwoven with the development of all other sectors of the economy, especially agriculture. The potential of industrialization in an LDC's economic development is immense. We analyze the most important aspects here.

1. *Employment*: Industrial development would create considerable employment avenues for the bulk of the labor force, skilled and unskilled. This would raise incomes, savings, and demand for goods and services, and would lead to higher economic growth. A high rate of stable industrial employment would enable an LDC to overcome the constraints of the vicious circle of poverty.

2. *Market for primary products*: Industrialization would provide a steady market for agricultural primary products that the industries would require as raw materials. Such a stable market would translate to stable incomes for the greater proportion of the LDC's population that are engaged in agricultural employment. This would enable the LDC to overcome this aspect of some of the problems of its agricultural sector (see Chapter 9).

3. *Foreign exchange*: The export of manufactured goods would earn foreign exchange that is needed for promoting the further economic development of the country.[5] Furthermore, as the economy satisfies its demand for manufactured consumer goods from its local industries, it conserves scarce foreign exchange that would have gone into their importation.

4. *Living standards*: Industrial production is a source of varieties of consumer goods that enable the population to attain improved economic and social well-being.

5. *Greater economic and social stability*: Industrialization promotes a greater sense of confidence and less social tension in society, leading to more stable political systems.

INDUSTRIALIZATION STRATEGIES: THE SEQUENCE AND STAGES OF INDUSTRIALIZATION

Paul Streeten (1975) states that the current disenchantment with industrialization as a strategy of development in LDCs is not well founded because it is a disenchantment with the form that economic growth and development has taken in some LDCs - namely, the lopsided nature of its income distributive effects.[6] Industrialization should be likened to the *servant of economic development*, and for an LDC it must occupy its proper place in the development strategy. Streeten believes that at the onset of the development initiative, industry should produce the simple producer and consumer goods required by the population, the majority of whom live in the rural sectors of the LDC concerned. Materials such as hoes, simple power tillers, and bicycles, as opposed to others like luxurious cars, air conditioners, and other luxury items, may be especially appropriate in meeting the productive and consumption needs of the economy.

Most LDCs have *comparative advantage* in producing relatively simple mass consumption goods that are often better produced in their labor-intensive, capital-saving circumstances. Therefore, it might seem to be a wise strategy for an LDC to opt for a development style that gives priority to satisfying the simple needs of the large number of people. Thus, industries producing food, clothing, furniture, utensils, and other simple household goods, electronics, electric fans, and the like, would thrive greatly, even without the need for heavy protection. The careful planning and choice of the appropriate style of industrialization, according to this prevailing condition of economic life in the LDCs, reflects the issues of *sequential* and *nonsequential* industrialization strategies in the process of economic development. Hence, the industrialization of an economy would ordinarily pass through a series of stages that could be either sequential or *out of sequence*.

In sequence, an economy would thoroughly examine its industrialization potentials with particular reference to the state of the economy's economic indicators and general sociopolitical circumstances, before choosing the specific types of industrial activities to begin with as it embarks on its industrialization drive. In particular, the state of its supply-side and demand-side indicators would be considered. An economy's supply-side indicators include such things as its resource acquisition, state of infrastructural development, relative factor availability, type and skill levels of its labor force, geography, climatic conditions, and environmental disposition. Demand-side factors would include the size of its population, per capita income level, size of the market for industrial manufactures and general consumer goods, as well as its overall state of economic development or underdevelopment. Thus, a relatively unindustrialized LDC that is seeking to follow the sequential pattern of industrialization would typically begin with the establishment of the *light industries* category, then proceed with manufacturing industries, and finally go into heavier industries as the economy matures.

Out of sequence, an economy's industrialization process need not follow any particular pattern in terms of the nature and type of industries being initiated. The economy need not begin with the establishment of, say, light industries. It could initially embark upon heavy industrial projects, or large-scale manufacturing. Nonsequential industrialization is said to have been the model adopted by the Bolshevik regime in the former USSR. We now consider sequential and nonsequential industrialization in greater detail.

Sequential Industrialization

Sequential industrialization typically involves three stages. Ordinarily, these stages could be *evolutionary*; that is, the lower stages could smoothly evolve into the higher one, thereby facilitating a more conducive and supportive path to industrialization.[7]

Stage 1 Sequence

Stage 1 industrialization involves the establishment of industries that are closely allied with the primary sector of the economy. At a relative state of undevelopment (such as Rostow's Preconditions stage), an economy is apt to be more pressed to satisfy the demands for the necessities of life rather than for other needs. As such, the economy's population and market demand would be more suited for the establishment of industries that produce such necessities.

The industries that produce these necessities are likely to be in the class of those referred to as *light industries* (as against standard *manufacturing industries*). These would include such projects as food processing, primary-product processing before export, light textile manufacturing, housing, furniture, and mining and related extractive industries. The establishment of infrastructure and social overhead capital (such as electricity, water and sewerage, transportation networks, and health and educational services) would also fall in this category. Examples of light industrial establishments are flour milling, bakery, brewery, clothing, cocoa butter processing, cotton ginning, palm and vegetable oil milling, and the like.

Stage 2 Sequence

The Stage 2 sequence involves a higher industrial level subsequent to Stage 1. As per capita income rises in an economy that has reasonably progressed with Stage 1 industrialization, the demand for stable *consumer durables* increases. The desire for such durables is initially expressed among the population in terms of rising imports for such them. Examples are radios, sewing machines, bicycles, wares and utensils, plastic products, and leather goods. The economy could then establish industries that produce these consumer durables. At this stage, the economy could be said to have entered the phase of *manufacturing industries* development, and may be associated with Rostow's takeoff stage.

Stage 3 Sequence

Through Stage 2, the economy grows and per capita income rises significantly. More adequate and stable infrastructure is established, light industrial development is expanded, and growth becomes a much more stable feature of the economy. At this stage, government revenues rise substantially as the tax structure becomes more progressive, broad, and extensive across the population. *Heavy industries* whose output would be supportive of the existing industries appear and are supported by the well-developed infrastructural facilities. Moreover, the population's improved income levels could provide effective demand for the heavy industries. This stage of industrialization is associated with industries that produce spare parts for machinery and equipment, industrial machinery, televisions, refrigerators, automobiles, and vehicle assembling. This indicates a highly industrialized and relatively mature economy.

Out-of-Sequence Industrialization

Sequential industrialization is a theoretical format that is deemed to be sequentially feasible under the known general economic conditions prevailing in most LDCs. It does not mean that every economy must necessarily pursue or achieve its industrialization goals by following this sequence. In fact, at times, owing to certain political and ideological considerations, countries pursue their industrialization efforts out of sequence. The general conditions under which an economy may carry out a nonsequential industrialization program are as follows.

1. A country with an abundant mineral endowment (such as crude petroleum reserves) may find it more feasible to establish large-scale petroleum oil refinery industries or mineral smelting plants (such as aluminium smelting). These Stage 3 industries would then be established out of sequence in an LDC, usually involving huge foreign capital and foreign technical assistance inputs.

2. An LDC may adopt an export-oriented strategy of development, under which it goes directly into Stage 2 industrialization for export. This may be done long before the domestic market is large enough, or domestic incomes are high enough, to warrant Stage 2 industries.

3. If a country has a large high-income population that can serve as a supportive domestic *demand threshold*, (usually made up of expatriate residents), it may begin its industrialization program by establishing a significant level of light and standard manufacturing industries, thereby embarking on Stage 2 industrialization that is not preceded by Stage 1.[8]

4. A developed country may achieve Stage 1 industrialization later in its development program if it lacks the necessary materials to produce such light

industry items as furniture and artifacts, goods whose industries are labor-intensive. This will be especially so if labor is relatively scarce in such an economy.

The Import-Substitution Strategy of Industrialization

The import-substitution industrialization (ISI) strategy is a special type of out-of-sequence industrialization. Where it has been adopted in some LDCs, it is deemed to be a way of accelerating the pace of industrialization. Many LDCs vigorously adopted the ISI strategy during the 1960s and 1970s, but unfortunately, the experiences of these countries proved very disappointing, and their ISI strategies failed massively. The question of why the ISI strategy failed in most LDCs has always intrigued economists. We examine the ISI strategy below, and then move to an analysis of its failure to promote industrialization in LDCs.

The initial development plans of most LDCs emphasized programs of deliberate rapid industrialization, although in most cases the role of industrialization is now being increasingly reappraised. The strategy of ISI involves an output mix and choice techniques, many of which tend to conflict with other development objectives. Many of the projects established under ISI strategies in LDCs have tended to be inefficient, high-cost industries operating behind high *tariff walls of protection.*

The industries established under the ISI strategy have largely involved industries and techniques which cater mainly to the high-income group within the highly unequal income distribution setting of the LDC, and usually serve only the needs of entrenched vested interests. Such industrialization strategy is hardly a strategy of industrialization for the greater economic growth and developmental needs of the wider society and its people. As a result, from the time that Paul Streeten clamored for it, the demand is now for a simpler, more appropriate type of industrialization in a general spirit of sequential rather than a nonsequential pattern of industrial development.

The ISI strategy involves the establishment of industries that produce consumer goods in substitution of imports whose *demand threshold* would have been created earlier through the importation of such finished goods. The rationale is simply to "industrialize from the top downward" (Meier, 1976) through the home replacement of the imported manufactured goods (as well as intermediate products and capital goods). The appeal for the popular adoption of this strategy lay in what was observed to have been a favorable experience of the industrialized countries.[9]

Studies such as Chenery's (1960) suggested that the growth of industries based on ISI accounted for a large proportion of total industrialization growth, and further, that the pace of economic development tended to rise with the share of industrial output in the economy. Even Hirschman (1958, p. 112) implied that the achievement of rapid industrial development in some economies that were

seen as relatively *undeveloped* could be attributed to an approach of "industrialization working its way backwards" from the "final touches" stage to domestic production of intermediate goods, and finally that of basic industrial products. Within this scenario, the economy would later establish domestic industries for the production of these final products, the demand for the final products having grown sufficiently large to reach a "domestic
production threshold."

The Route of ISI Strategy

After the country has opened its doors through importation, and thereby created a sufficient level of demand threshold, it then establishes the import-substituting industries for the imported goods and places tariffs on these imports. The case for protection of the domestic industries is supported by the traditional "infant industry argument."[10] The terms of trade problem that usually faces the LDC's exports of primary products is easily contained if the ISI industries are chosen in such a way that they utilize domestic agricultural products as raw materials. Moreover, the economy saves on foreign exchange that was previously spent on the importation of manufactured consumer goods. Employment is created by the ISI, incomes rise, and GDP grows.

Many LDCs in Latin America (for example, Chile and Argentina), Asia (for example, India and Pakistan), and Africa (for example, Nigeria and Ghana) vigorously adopted the ISI during the 1960s and 1970s. Unfortunately, however, the ISI strategy largely failed to lead to industrialization in these LDCs. In most cases, the strategy, at best, succeeded in ushering in industrial growth for a decade or so, while at worst, it can only be seen as a woeful example of winning an industrialization "battle" (temporarily) but losing the economic development "war." What are the major factors that rendered the ISI strategy impotent in LDCs?

Failure of the Import-Substitution Strategy in LDCs

Various technical and logistic factors caused the ISI strategy to fail to promote industrialization in LDCs. The main factors are as follows.

1. *Foreign exchange constraints*: The lack of sufficient foreign exchange required for the importation of goods during the initial phase of creating the demand threshold has tended to present a major bottleneck for an ISI program. As a result, only a partial creation of the demand threshold may be realized, usually within the urban sector of the economy, while the dominant rural sector remains virtually unexposed to the threshold of manufactured consumer goods. Consequently, as the ISI projects are established, they face very limited market demands within the LDC, a problem that ensues even at the very onset of the programs.

2. *Low per capita income constraints*: The prevailing low-income character

of the LDC precludes the creation of a market base sufficiently large to support the newly established industries. This has often presented two-fold problems: first, the scarce foreign exchange that is initially spent on imports creates a balance-of-payments adversity pressure because demand for the imported items is not sufficiently high within a low-income setting; second, the objective of creating a demand threshhold cannot really be achieved in an economy of pervasive low-income population.

3. *Foreign dependence*: In most cases, the choice of specific ISI industries has not been based on the availability of local raw materials. In such situations, the industries are fed by foreign sources of not only raw materials but also management expertise, a skilled labor force, and finance. This results in balance-of-payments difficulties for the economy within a short period of its implementation of the ISI policy.

4. *Economic inefficiency*: The ISI strategy has often imposed an economic inefficiency on the LDC's economy, in the sense of an overall misallocation of resources. In the main instance, the establishment of the industries, usually out of sequence, diverts resources away from economic activities in which the economy possesses comparative advantage, usually agriculture and Stage 1 industrial projects, to activities of weaker comparative advantage. In most cases, the LDC's attention is diverted further away from development of its agriculture, and the agricultural sector is neglected in apparent preference for industry. In other instances, the LDC's savings ability is curtailed as it imports manufactured goods during the demand threshold phase; the LDC may realize lower export earnings from primary products if these products are diverted to feed the ISI industries (often at cheaper prices to their producers); the massive importation of capital goods for the industries, coupled with the importation of manufactured goods required for the creation of the demand threshold, can create severe balance-of-payments problems for the economy.

5. *Technical inefficiency*: As the industries are shielded from competition by tariff protections, on the basis of the infant-industry argument (see note 8), they are not allowed the incentive to innovate, discover, and adopt more cost-saving, efficient, and cheaper production techniques and operation methods. They tend to be monopolies, usually operating under *excess capacity*; and their limited undercapacity output usually suits the prevailing low level of (urban) market demand.

The combination of these problems has helped render the ISI strategy ineffective in most of the LDCs that adopted it. Generally, the tradition of protecting ISI industries by use of tariff rates tends to generate inflationary pressures in the economy. The technically inefficient monopoly firms produce goods of inferior quality for the domestic economy, while using the society's resources most inefficiently under excess capacity operations. The economy suffers a restraint on its agricultural output as well as its generation of exports. Having gone through the disappointing experiences of an *inward-looking* development strategy of industrialization through import substitution, many

LDCs have realized that they need to shift their emphasis toward a policy of sequential industrialization instead.

The Strategy of Export Promotion Industrialization

Attraction to the export promotion industrialization (EPI) strategy as an alternative to the ISI became increasingly pronounced as it became obvious that the ISI strategy was a failure. In a sense, the EPI strategy emphasizes export substitution; that is, the LDC can substitute industrial manufactures, finished and semifinished, for primary-product raw materials in its exported produce. The export orientation would be a slant toward the LDC's nontraditional exports such as processed primary products, semi-finished manufactures, and manufactured light industrial products. The EPI approach simply amounts to a sequential industrialization programme.[11]

NOTES

1. See Chapter 6 (note 10) for an explanation of the slight difference between the balanced growth and unbalanced growth notions, on the one hand, and the big push theory, on the other.

2. A broader definition can be found in Zuvekas (1979).

3. The importance of these infrastructural public utilities is discussed in detail under in Chapter 7.

4. The environmental aspect of industrialization is not always desirable. The creation of urban slums and *ghettos* with their attendant social ills, is usually the result of industrialization. Furthermore, the problems of environmental degradation, acid rain, smog, ozone depletion, and the like, are direct results of industrialization.

5. See the discussion on the strategy of Export Promotion Industrialization below.

6. As stated in Meier (1976, p. 629). See also Hirschman (1958).

7. This may be likened to the Rostow Stage theory (see Chapter 6).

8. This strategy is known as an *import-substitution industrialization* strategy (see below).

9. Studies that focus on the import-substitution strategy can be found in Meier (1976) and Bruton (1970).

10. The infant-industry argument for protection of domestic industries holds that newly established industries, having not yet reached the stage where they can reap scale economies, need to be protected from foreign competition with mature foreign companies who may already be enjoying economies of scale of production. It is important to ensure that the ISI products be made available at prices comparable to those at which the imports sold prior to the tariff imposition. Often, however, this is particularly difficult to realize, and the ISI products might not be competitive enough even under the tariff protection.

11. Meier (1976) provides a vivid account of an industrialization strategy via export promotion in LDCs.

11

Environmental Issues in the Process of Economic Development

The economic progress of a society is based largely on the production and consumption of goods and services involving the overwhelming use of the *environmental* resources that the society has. This is regardless of whether that society operates a free market economy or a socialist or a centralist economic system. Perhaps the most important entity in a society that has direct effect on the quality of human life (or social welfare) is the environment. Economic development cannot be construed without environmental considerations. This is because the majority of the most crucial developmental issues that the society faces, and some of which this book has dealt with in the earlier chapters (issues such as population growth and human resources, agricultural production, and industrialization), all touch heavily on the environmental circumstances of a country. In dealing with the environmental issues in the development process, we must consider the exact sense in which the term *environment* must be understood.

All parts of the world have increasingly continued to interconnect through massive advances in communications technologies, especially in the closing decades of the twentieth century. As a result, the prospects for the twenty-first century are for the world to increasingly shrink (interaction wise), allowing nations to easily relate to each other in ways that were not previously apparent. National and regional environmental issues easily become global issues today: the 1986 Chernobyl nuclear plant accident in the former Soviet Union, the 1988 Exxon-Valdez oil spill off the Alaskan coast of North America, the threatened extinction of the Amazon rain forest and some of its rare species, and the general problems of global environmental degradation. The need for international cooperation to address such issues prompted the Earth Summit of 1992 in Brazil, during which nations sought to determine and adopt more environmentally benign policy approaches.

As far as it concerns economic development, environmental problems and ways to effectively address them are fast becoming uppermost on the agendas of both LDCs and DCs alike. In their struggle to reduce the widening gap between their levels of development and that of the DCs, the LDCs have come to recognize the very close relationship between society's ability to achieve economic development and the quality of that society's environment and its resources. This raises the crucial questions of: (1) What exactly is meant by the environment? (2) In what specific way(s) could a society's ability to achieve or not achieve economic growth and development depend on the nature and quality of its environment? (3) What appropriate policy actions need to be taken in order to promote environmental preservation and sustain continued economic growth and development? The rest of this chapter is devoted to providing answers to these questions.

THE ENVIRONMENT

The society is entirely dependent on the environment and its natural resources to make its living. But what exactly constitutes the environment? In order to encompass the purposes of economic development, the following broad depiction is offered. The environment consists of the following categories:

1. *The habitats*: These include the land surface, earth, forests, waters, atmosphere, and the space.

2. *Renewable natural resources*: These include the wildlife and livestock, the fisheries, trees and plants, and water resources. They are thought to be indefinitely replenishable, although some (for example, land) are location-specific. It is easy for the rate of exploitation of these physical and biological resources to exceed their natural regenerative abilities. Therefore, many renewable resources (for example, fresh water, fertile soil, or clean air) are increasingly scarce, and more damage is being done to the underlying systems that sustain and renew them. This situation threatens the long-term economic growth and development of nations.

3. *Nonrenewable natural resources*: These include various material deposits in the earth (such as oil deposits, gas deposits, and mineral contents. Being nonreplenishable, these are finite and are depletable through high levels of consumption. Although there is currently no evidence that the world is facing the danger of immediate depletion of nonrenewable resources, it is still prudent that conservatory measures be practised.

The Environmental Threat to Development in DCs and LDCs

Initially, the problems of environmental quality were widely regarded as being unique to the industrialized countries. Industrialization brought with it air and water pollution, as well as pollution of the earth surface in areas where industrial solid wastes were discarded. These are problems that LDCs were not thought to have, being relatively unindustrialized, but not for long. The various activities that must be undertaken to initiate and propel economic development would necessarily reduce the quality of the environment. Industrialization, agricultural development, housing, construction and operation of machinery, mining, forestry, and construction and use of infrastructure - all bring about environmental deterioration.

The heavy use of chemicals in the industrial production processes of Europe, North America, and Japan has given rise to the formation of massive industrial byproducts that pollute the atmosphere around these regions, resulting in such environmental hazards as acid rain, ozone layer depletion, and unclean breathing air. Major examples of these areas that are under serious environmental pollution threats include the northeast U.S. corridor, the Windsor-Quebec corridor and the Vancouver-Fraser Valley, in Canada, the Ruhr Valley in Germany, and the Tokyo-Osaka corridor in Japan.

Table 11.1 shows the levels of per capita expenditures on water (treatment) pollution control and the concentration levels of sulphur dioxide (a major air pollutant) across the various developed countries of the world. As these pollution levels and their associated direct abatement costs (as well as their *externalities*: social but unobservable costs) indicate, environmental issues have risen to prominence in the DCs' economic development agenda. Pollution has become a major health threat in these countries. Table 11.1 does not reveal the closely related evidence of the ever huge and rising health costs that these countries incur in combating serious diseases, such as cancer and respiratory diseases—ailments that are highly believed to be closely related to, if not entirely caused by, the high levels of environmental pollution shown in these data. And related to this environmental problems are the health problems resulting from overreliance on highly processed foods in these societies. The high rates of ailments and deaths resulting from heart disease, stroke, cancer, diabetes, and the like, in these industrialized societies relative to the unindustrialized societies are closely

Table 11.1
Pollution Levels (Averages) and Costs (Expenditures) in DCs

Country	Average SO$_2$ Concentration* levels (1975-85)	Per Capita Expenditures** on Water Pollution Control
United States	New York: 39.1	54
France	Paris: 73.6	44
Germany	Berlin: 79.0	71
Britain	London: 64.7	39
Japan	Tokyo: 41.3	60
Canada	Montreal: 28.3	31

  * Annual means, $\mu g/m^3$,
 ** 1980s, in 1980=100 U.S. dollars.
Source: Calculated from data published in Field and Olewiler
        (1994), citing: (1) OECD, *The State of the Environment*,
        Paris, 1991; (2) U.S. Environmental Protection Agency,
        International Comparison of Air Pollution Control,
        Washington D.C., Resources for the Future, 1990; (3)
        Environment Canada.

linked to overdependence on industrial processed foods, as compared to reliance on natural "green" foods in the LDCs.

The major concern of these environmental issues in regard to economic development in the DCs is that, in addition to the direct expenditures on health, there are the costs involved in environmental control - notably, water quality control, hazardous waste disposal, solid waste management, and management of toxic substances from industrial production. Furthermore, huge costs are incurred for materials and equipment towards the promotion and adoption of individual personal physical exercises as part of regular lifestyles, designed to promote the body's ability to tolerate the (overprocessed) unnatural foods that would otherwise cause the body to malfunction and sicknesses. The overwhelming amount of resources, including time and financial resources, that are poured into these lifestyles and related health costs, involve tremendous opportunity costs. These resources would otherwise go a long way toward resolving the substantial and ever present economic problems of inequality and government financial imbalances in these developed societies.

The developed countries are able, however, to invest in rapid environmental clean ups and promotion of environmental quality. Emission standards are imposed on industries and automobiles. Facilities are installed for water purification, and vigorous conservation measures are imposed on natural resources (such as fish stocks, minerals, and trees). All these environmental enhancement measures are carried out in the DCs with minimal economic and social costs because their relatively high level of wealth can easily be used to effect redistributive measures to accommodate the changes. This is not possible in the LDCs where income and wealth levels are dismally low. Figure 11.1 illustrates these differences.

The figure depicts production possibility curves that link levels of economic development and levels of environmental quality for a country. The level of development, measured by the per capita income, is depicted on the vertical axis, while the level of environmental quality, measured by the average level of ambient sulphur dioxide across the country, is depicted on the horizontal axis.

The curves E_1E_1 or E_2E_2 represent the tradeoff curves for typical DCs. As shown, the DC could invest significant resources in environmental control and protection, enabling its tradeoff curve to shift outward, yielding higher economic growth while maintaining its level of environmental quality, or even raising its environmental quality. Unlike a typical LDC, the DC can afford to impose stringent environmental standards on its firms and industries without necessarily jeopardizing the prospects of further growth and development.

The curve E_0E_0 represents the tradeoff curve for a typical LDC: indicating that such a country has a low level of development at a given level of environmental quality.[1]

Given its income constraint, the LDC has to be content with a tradeoff, such as from point B (low development with high environmental quality) to point A

Figure 11.1
Trade-off Between Level of Economic Development and Environmental Quality

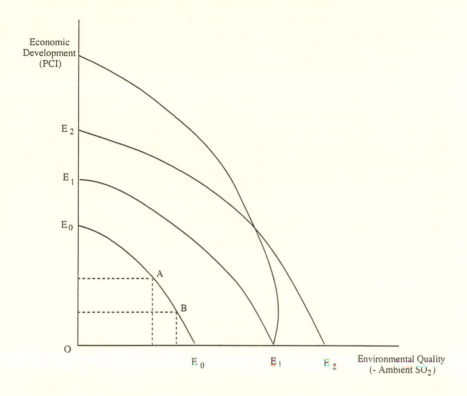

(higher economic growth and development at the expense of lower environmental quality). To achieve economic growth and development without deterioration of environmental quality—that is, cause the curve E_0E_0 either to tilt rightward at the horizontal axis or totally to shift rightward—the LDC requires significant resources to invest in environmental preservation measures.

International Environmental Impacts: The Pollution-Haven Hypothesis

The scenario described above seems unrealistic for a poverty-stricken LDC concerned primarily with economic development and seeking any available means to pursue it, although this LDC fails to see that eventually the resulting environmental deterioration due to economic development would tend to inhibit economic development itself. A major fallout from this scenario reflects what has been termed the *pollution-haven hypothesis* (Field and Olewiler, 1994). This hypothesis simply states that the LDCs are "pollution havens" where industries from DCs could easily relocate their operations, without being compelled to comply with stringent environmental standards and regulations that obtain in their home countries (DCs).

The pollution-haven hypothesis is premised generally on two basic suppositions: (1) tough environmental control measures in the DCs are causing firms and industries to move from the DCs toward relocation in the LDCs where such controls are either lax or nonexistent; and (2) many LDCs, in their desperate bids to attract industries for the creation of jobs and income needed for growth and development, have encouraged, or even tended to lure, such firms and industries with promises of minimal, or outright waiver of any, environmental standards and control measures.

Evidence in support of the hypothesis and its underlying axioms is generally based on opinions formed from observations of the environmental conduct of many multinational corporations (MNCs) that operate in the LDCs. A well-known incident is India's Bhopal pollution disaster in 1985. Given the traditional economic attitudes and behaviors of MNCs (see Chapter 3), what this situation means is that the LDCs would still be worse off. Therefore, the LDCs must not neglect to implement environmental control measures in order to promote and maintain environmental standards, despite their low levels of economic development.

Population and the Environment

The role of population in economic growth and development is fully considered in Chapter 8. Our concern with population here is only insofar as it affects or is affected by environmental quality. The relationship between a country's population and the state of its environment may seem too apparent, especially as the association is often made between the high population density of an industrialized city and the quality of the atmosphere and water around it. Generally, human activity has tremendous effects on the environment; the most noticeable effects are as follows.

Habitat Alteration: Human settlement and expansion have led to massive deforestation for human dwellings, as well as drainage and irrigation of wetlands for agricultural conversion. These phenomena culminate in changes in the environment that are not easily quantifiable.

Soil Degradation: Global agriculture takes heavy toll on soil quality by consuming its organic matter, carbon, and humus. It causes the earth's vegetated land to suffer degradation. The most seriously affected areas are in Asia and Africa.

Pollution: Human activities cause pollution of the environment in many respects, involving both production and consumption. Waste products from production, including toxic material, heavy metals, chemicals, acidic liquids, and gases, degrade forests and other ecosystems, and overwhelm the earth's protective ozone layer. The disposal of human waste directly pollutes the waters and contaminates aquatic species. Water-borne discharges of organic carbon, nitrogen, and phosphorus come mainly from the accumulation of human sewers.

Energy Consumption and Greenhouse Gases: There are various forms of human consumption of energy. As the human population increases, the use of *biomass* energy (firewood and animal dung), as well as *commercial* energy (oil, gas, coal, hydroelectricity, and nuclear power), increases. The extraction of these energy sources degrades the environment. Furthermore, the combustion of the *fossil fuels* (oil, gas, and coal) among these energy sources emit carbon dioxide as a byproduct, which is the largest source of the greenhouse gases. These greenhouse gases tend to trap infrared radiation that would otherwise escape into the atmosphere, resulting in global warming and environmental health hazards.

The total environmental impact of human activity cannot be attributed wholly to population growth. Other facets of human life that are not related to the growth of human population (for example, technological change, changes in lifestyles, and government and national policies) also have major environmental effects.

Environmental impacts on development present themselves very differently to the LDCs than to the DCs. In the DCs, the environmental problems of densely populated urban center are not generally attributable to high population pressures; in these societies, incidences of crowded cities coexist with abundance of living space per head of the population. Moreover, the DCs do not seem to have the problem of overpopulation (see Chapter 8) that most LDCs have. Thus, one major difference between the population impact on the environment in LDCs and the DCs is that whereas the DCs tend to suffer more from the environmental problems that result from urbanization and population density (for example, high waves of urbanization and the growth of urban slums, which are direct results of population pressure), the LDCs also tend to suffer from that *in addition* to those environmental problems that result directly from overpopulation *per se* (such as those discussed in Chapter 8).

Another difference between the DCs and the LDCs is that rapid population growth in the LDCs results in heavy dependence on natural resources (farming, fishing, animal husbandry, and forestry) because economic activity would be mainly agrarian. In most cases, stocks of these natural resources are exploited faster than their rates of natural replenishment. As a result, many LDCs face severe shortages of arable land. Farmers are compelled to overgraze their land or adopt relatively low-yielding cultivation methods such as *crop-rotation* and *shifting cultivation*. Often, this results in the farmlands being abandoned.

The Population-Environmental Impact Model

The preceding effects of a high population level and growth rate on the environment can be analyzed with a simple environmental impact model of population growth. The environmental effect of population is measured by a simple expression of the total impact of that population on their environment and its resources:

$$\Phi = \phi P \tag{11.1}$$

where

Φ = the magnitude of the total environmental impact effect on society
P = population level
$\phi = \Phi/P$ = the magnitude of the environmental impact per head of population

This expression shows that the extent of environmental depletion or deterioration is closely related to population. Thus, population control has positive environmental effect. The environmental impact per capita (ϕ) depends on the degree of conservation and environmental control policies in place. However, such environmental control measures that succeed in lowering the environmental impact per capita may be offset by population increases. Therefore, for environmental control measures to be effective, they must be combined with effective population control measures. In other words, population control policy is part of an overall environmental control policy. These two policies are to be implemented as complements, not as substitutes.

ENVIRONMENTAL ISSUES IN THE DEVELOPMENT PROCESS

Environmental issues in the process of economic development arise from a number of practical angles which every society must unavoidably confront and address. These environmental issues involve direct and serious implications for economic development. The most important of these issues, which we consider here are (1) the problem of sustainability, (2) economic byproduct management, and (3) the problem of development constraints imposed by unsuitable (natural) environmental conditions.

Sustainability and Sustainable Development

One of the most pressing environmental issues of economic development is that of the *sustainability* of the society's (depletable) resources. This implies the problem of how (at what rate) society should use its environmental resources not only to ensure prolonged support of human economic activity for the ongoing generation, but also to ensure that these resources are not extinct through overuse, and thereby jeopardize the economic development and well-being of the society's future generations.

Of course, there is a need to avoid the extinction of natural resources. The LDC must devise ways to adopt the most efficient rate of harvesting (utilization) of, say, the fishes, or trees, or even crude petroleum, to ensure that (1) while the rate of utilization sufficiently meets the economic developmental goals of the current generation, the stock does not get depleted; and (2) the resource use and the processes involved in its harvesting and utilization neither harm the environment nor pose major health risks to present and future generations.

There is currently a great fascination with the principle of *sustainable development* within both DCs and LDCs. Sustainable development is a rule of maintaining an *optimal* rate of resource and environmental exploitation that would neither result in making future generations worse off nor leave the needs of the present generation unsatisfied. Thus, environmental resource allocation rates that either enrich the current generation but might impoverish future generations, or impoverishes the current generation in order to enrich future ones, defeat the sustainable development paradigm. This definition presents some problem with comparisons of intergenerational relative measures of economic welfare.

To overcome the problems that this may pose for economic development policy, we need to adapt the concept of sustainable development to allow for a more comparable measure of intergenerational welfare. In this connection, we may depict sustainable development as the rule of resource use at a rate that ensures that it gives future generations a living level that is at least equal to what it gave to the present generation. In other words, as long as future generations remain at least as well off as the current generation obtained from the use of the environment, the principle of sustainable development is upheld. As a corollary, sustainable development policy is achieved if the rate of exploitation of the environment by the present generation is not such that it renders future generations less well off than the present generation is.

The question here for purposes of economic development policy is how to ensure the equality of intergenerational welfare. This would involve dynamic efficiency models to solve. However, to enable us to deduce the development policy applications, we consider a simplified model of *depletable or exhaustible or nonreplenishable* environmental resource utilization. The following symbols are used in the analysis. Let

W_t = Social welfare level of society at any time, t
U_t = Utility level (a measure of satisfaction) at any time, t
R_t = Resources level at any time, t
U_c = Utility of current generation
U_f = Utility of future generations
R_c = Resources level of current generation
R_{c+1} = Resources level for the next generation
R_f = Resources level of future generation

The society's social welfare level is a function of the level of utility which the society obtains from its use of environmental resources. Utility, in turn, is a function of the amount of environmental resources that the society uses at all times. Therefore, we can write:

$$W_t = W(U_t)$$
$$U_c = U(R_c)$$
$$U_f = U(R_{c+1}) = U(R_f)$$

As the current generation uses its resources, it derives a level of welfare gain which depends on the marginal utility of resource use:

$$\Delta W(\partial U_c/\partial R_c) = \Delta W[U_c'(R_c)] \tag{11.2}$$

Similarly, a future generation's welfare from the environmental resources it inherits is given by

$$\Delta W(\partial U_f/\partial R_{c+1}) = \Delta W[U_f'(R_{c+1})] \tag{11.3}$$

Given that most environmental resources are nonreplenishable, it follows that

$$R_{t+1} < R_t$$

Thus

$$R_{c+1} < R_c$$

Therefore,

$$\Delta W[U_c'(R_c)] > \Delta W[U_f'(R_{c+1})] \tag{11.4}$$

This inequality shows that the future generation will be worse off than the current generation, meaning that the sustainable development objective is not being met by the rate of resource use by the present generation. In fact, by definition, the sustainable development objective could hardly be met inasfar as depletable environmental resources are concerned. This is because every unit of depletable resource used by the current generation is a unit that is unavailable for the use of future generations, indicating that the future generation will probably be worse off than the current generation in this regard.

To sustain the long-term economic development objective, the economy must adopt corrective measures to address its inevitable violation of sustainable development conditions. In this respect, apparently the most important and most effective of such corrective measures would include (1) public-sector investment in education, funded by taxation of the agents (individuals, firms, and industries) and provided freely to the society's youth (members of the future generation); (2) public-sector investment in construction and maintenance of physical infrastructure and social-overhead capital, structures that may be passed on to the use and benefit of the future generation; and (3) *conservation* of environmental resources.

The policy of environmental resource conservation is crucial in the process of economic development. Conservation, is a key principle in an economy's pursuit of the sustainable development objective and deserves a much closer examination.

Environmental Conservation

The stock of environmental resources is the available quantity endowed by nature. Although they may be defined as *free resources* (resources that are superabundant and absolutely nonrivaled in usage), they are also *scarce* (in the economic sense that their supply can only be increased at a positive opportunity cost). As such, the environment and its resources are *public goods*, but their relative scarcity means that their usage at any time affects the stock level that would be available for future generations. For example, the present-day harvesting of wildlife or the fishery will reduce the stock available to breed for the generation of future stock levels for the future. The dumping of liquid and solid waste on the earth's surface will reduce soil fertility in the future. Release of gaseous waste into the atmosphere causes global warming and destroys atmospheric protective ozone layer, posing serious developmental problems in the future.

The amount of resources at any time depends on the initial stock available and the rate at which it was used in the past. Environmental resources may be classified into the following types.

1. **Exhaustible resources**: These are replenishable or renewable resources whose fixed supply at any time can be exhausted, but can be replenished by nature after a necessary period of time. Some in this category, however, are irreplaceable once they are extracted. This class of resources can be further classified into *recyclable* and *nonrecyclable* resources. Recyclable resources are those whose finished products can be reprocessed at some cost for further use. Examples are minerals (exhaustible and nonreplenishable), forestry products (exhaustible and replenishable), and land fertility (replenishable). Nonrecyclable resources are those that either perish upon initial usage, or upon initial usage are transformed into states in which they are no longer usable or valuable. Examples include fuels and oils (exhaustible and nonreplenishable), the fishery (exhaustible and replenishable), and wildlife (exhaustible and replenishable).

2. **Nonexhaustible resources**: These are also referred to as "nature's bounty"; they are those resources whose quantities are abundant in stock. They can be used repeatedly and in perpetuity without being depleted. Examples include land surface, sea, rivers and lakes, the atmosphere, space, and the sun's energy.

The need for conservation of environmental resources concerns exhaustible rather than nonexhaustible resources. The *doomsday theory* of environmental conservation states that appropriate steps should be taken toward conservation of the stock of environmental resources in order for society to avoid reaching their points of exhaustion or "doomsday." However, much as conservationists and environmental activists have based their struggles on this theory, critics have argued against it by arguing that it holds little or no practical validity. Critics of the doomsday theory base their opposition to it on the notion of *choke price*, which may operate within a free market economy to render the doomsday a mere "false alarm." Let us consider this idea of a choke price and how it works.

The choke price of an environmental resource is the price at which substitutes for it would be sought and brought into use as the resource becomes (*chokingly*) costly. The concept of the choke price is based on the studies of Hotelling (1931). Simply stated, Hotelling found that in a free market competitive setting, market equilibrium would only obtain for a stock of natural resources when the rate of increase of its price equals the interest rate in the economy. To analyze the basic tenets of the *Hotelling's Lemma*, let:

r_t = the prevailing rate of interest in the economy at any time t
p_t = the resource price at time t

Then, in equilibrium, the Hotelling principle may be written as

$$\partial p_t / \partial t = r_t \tag{11.5}$$

Equation (11.5) denotes a stable equilibrium. For example, if, say, $r_t > \partial p_t / \partial t$, the supply of resources will fall as entrepreneurs divert their investments into alternative production activities, away from natural resources whose yields are now lower relative to those of other comparable risky ventures. Within an existing market equilibrium setting, this means that the supply curve will shift leftward, resulting in a higher price of resources, until equilibrium is again achieved.

The argument against the doomsday theory is apparently based on the supposition that, under competitive market settings, the choke price is inevitable for every environmental resource. Presumably, as the interest rate represents the rate of yield of all other alternative assets in the economy, rising rates would mean progressively increasing price of resources over time. In this reasoning, not only do interest rates tend to rise over time due to such factors as rising population and the like, but also, over time, increasing amounts of natural resources are brought into use due to the same factors. The demand for the resource rises over time, and its price increases. The choke price is then reached eventually, at which point environmental resources have become so expensive as to prompt the society to adopt substitutes. There is, therefore, no need for any deliberate policy of environmental resource conservation.

It is immediately apparent that the above paradigm suffers from serious flaws as it applies to most LDCs. For one, LDCs are not inherently competitive markets; secondly, the Hotelling principle seems unrealistic in LDCs for reasons surrounding the long-term trends of interest rate and its ability to be the principal determinant of relative profitability of investments. Therefore, the doomsday theory may still be a highly valid consideration in the environmental development of LDCs.

Consequently, environmental conservation appears to be essential in the development process. Environmental conservation is a key element in the policy of sustainable development and must be pursued through various measures in the LDCs. The most attractive and attainable of such measures include *recycling*, as well as the appropriate pricing of natural resources.[2]

Environmental Impact of Economic Byproducts

The LDCs increasingly face the environmental problems of deforestation and global warming, and species extinction. The rapid depletion of forests which act to absorb atmospheric carbon dioxide, means that the increased concentration of carbon dioxide gas in the atmosphere results in elevated temperatures on the earth's atmosphere. This is the so-called global greenhouse effect, which worsens the already unsuitable high temperature problems of the LDCs. In addition, many LDCs also suffer severely from environmental air and water pollution as much as the DCs as discussed earlier. Some Latin American countries, especially Mexico and Brazil, have serious air pollution problems of smog and acid rain arising from the high industrial activities concentrated around the Mexico City and Sao Paulo areas. These areas also have their serious related problems of urban congestion and slums.

The issue of management of the necessary byproducts of economic activities that must be undertaken in the pursuit of economic development represents another important environmental concern in the development process. The production (supply side) and consumption (demand side) economic activities of society each have their necessary by-products, namely, *gaseous, liquid, and solid wastes* generated in the course of these economic activities. These wastes that are discharged into the environment eventually give rise to serious threats to economic development and to human and environmental harmony. The economic development process must involve appropriate ways to minimize the inevitable adverse environmental effects of economic activities that it entails, not only to avoid their direct and immediate welfare consequences for the present generation, but also to prevent their endangerment of the well-being of the future generations.

The byproducts of production, the supply side of economic activities, affect the need to breathe clean air, have clean and uncontaminated water, nonhazardous living space, and unpolluted food supply. The economy should be able to ensure that industries or firms that discharge pollutants into the atmosphere are made to incorporate such *social costs* in the determination of their output levels and pricing, so that their consumers would properly bear such costs. This is because such circumstances have economy-wide effects on the determination of relative rental rates of land and other fixed assets and therefore reflect on the income distribution pattern in the society.

Another problem concerns the management of the more general byproducts of human life on earth: desertification, deforestation, increasingly endangered animal species, toxic contamination of the air, atmosphere, the earth and the waters, acid rain, global warming, ozone layer thinning, and solid waste disposal. Furthermore, there is the "eye sore" effect of environmental use: some members of society derive "psychic" benefits from an *unspoiled* environment.[3]

The byproducts resulting from consumption activities, the demand side of the economy, are much more crucial in the development processes of LDCs, relative to the byproducts from the supply side.[4] This is more so because of the high population levels of the LDCs. Often, the population explosion also brought about high waves of rural-urban migration and their attendant explosive growth of urban communities. Urban slums erupt, where the poor living conditions give rise to congestion, squalor, and unsanitary conditions, with their resulting social problems such as crime and insecurity. Such an environment becomes prone to the spread of diseases and epidemics, all of which are detrimental to economic growth and development.

In many LDCs with significant levels of industrial expansion as well as large-scale applications of chemicals to agricultural production and mining, rivers and lakes have often been used as a means of the disposing toxic waste products and heavy metals. These rivers and other groundwater have been largely contaminated by seepage of hazardous materials from industrial sites and solid waste dumps. This presents serious environmental hazards to the society, translating into the development-environmental quality tradeoff analyzed earlier. The policy approaches to addressing such problems are discussed below.

ENVIRONMENTAL CONSTRAINTS TO ECONOMIC DEVELOPMENT IN LDCs

The LDCs must deal with very serious problems relating to the dilemma of attaining economic development while maintaining environmental quality. To the LDCs, the tradeoff between a country's level of economic development and the quality of its environment is very costly. This is because they lack the resources required for a country to be able to shift its development-environmental quality tradeoff curve outward, thereby simultaneously achieving economic development while promoting environmental quality (by effectively abating environmental pollution, raising natural resource conservation, or tackling unfavorable environmental factors), similar to what the DCs are able to do.

In Chapter 9 we considered the problems that unsuitable (natural) environmental conditions pose for agricultural development in the LDCs. There can be no doubt that the environment is closely linked to the ability to achieve or not achieve economic development in a country. The fact that the less developed regions of the world are those occupying the least environmentally favorable parts of the universe is not merely coincidental. In effect, therefore, the environment is a major force to reckon with in the process of economic development.

As noted earlier, environmental issues in development present themselves very differently to the LDCs and DCs. In addition to those issues already suggested under the population impact, another different respect in which environmental impacts in LDCs differ from those of DCs is that in the DCs, environmental problems are mainly human-made; that is, they result from the pattern of choices of lifestyles of the people in the society. In the LDCs, however, much of the environmental problems are natural; that is, they are imposed by nature. Apart from those arising from the problems of high rates of urbanization and congestion in unhygienic "ghetto" dwellings, as well as some problems of industrial pollution in certain areas of Latin America, most of the LDCs' environmental problems arise from natural causes (see below). In water pollution, for example, parts of Africa and South Asia suffer from water contamination due to pollution from the natural sources rather than by industrial waste products. Some of these waters are contaminated with *guinea worms* and other water-borne parasites that infect humans and animals.

The regions of Africa, Asia, and Latin America and the Caribbean are all tropical and semi-tropical, with unconducive weather and climatic conditions for human, animal, and plant growth and development. Most of these areas have arid or semi-arid climates, associated with very harsh environmental living conditions. The climates of these tropical areas range in extreme temperatures from lows of 15°C to highs of 40°C all year round, with very infertile soils and very little or no rainfall.

Geographically, the bulk of the areas occupied by the underdeveloped continents lie within a span of about 2,500 kilometers on either side of the equator, with their tropical effects extending much wider than this range. The *wet equatorial tropical climate*, characterized by high humidity and constant (equatorial) rains of about 190 to 300 centimeters per year; *the monsoon tropical climate*, characterized by a mix of alternate wet and dry seasons; and *the arid tropics*, characterized by little or no rainfall, are the three types of tropical climates found in these regions.[5] In recent years, the effects of the types of severe drought that are characteristic of these areas have been seen in the world by the famines of Ethiopia (1985 and beyond), Somalia (1993 and beyond), Mozambique, and Sudan, in Africa. They have also been evident in the Philippines and Bangladesh, in Asia.

The environmental adversities presented by the tropical conditions of the LDCs have tended to grossly impede economic production and general developmental activities ranging from education and human resource development to agriculture, infrastructural construction, and industrial activities. The severe dehydrating effects of the tropical heat is restrictive of the application of human mental and physical efforts in production. It necessitates the constant needs for food and nourishment during the course of every production activity involving labor, thereby tending to not only raise the labor costs of production, but also to render labor relatively less productive than capital (resulting in the desire for employers to prefer capital to labor, that is, unemployment).

The tropical environment, with its attendant extreme heat, high humidity, and absence of frost, are conducive to the growth of destructive bacteria, parasites, insects, pests, and several species of tropical diseases that constantly inhibit plant and animal life. Tropical storms are incessant and can be extremely destructive. The unpredictable torrential rains simply wash away the soil with its ferocious erosions, often sweeping away agricultural crops and leaving behind lands that are largely unsuitable for habitation.

Arguably, some potentially fertile areas exist in the tropics. Much has been written of the volcanic soil of the East African highlands and parts of Asia and the Pacific regions, as well as the clay soil of the alluvial plains of Africa and South America. These are all areas of the tropical zones that may be particularly suitable for agricultural development. Other than these, however, the bulk of the soil found in much of the tropics are formed from old acid parent rock, poor in calcium and other plant nutrients. Most parts of West and Central Africa, South Asia, and South America, are rain forest regions. Agricultural land tenure in these areas must involve the removal of the forest, and as this is done, the proportion of iron and aluminium hydroxides in the soil tends to increase, resulting in the formation of laterite soil which becomes intractably hard and uncultivable. Agricultural output is, therefore, always very limited relative to the amount of investment made; this is a major constraining factor in economic development.

As already noted, the harsh, unsuitable environmental conditions that most LDCs must deal with are not limited to their agriculture. Indeed, the environmental hazards also substantially impair human as well as animal health. They cause rapid deterioration of physical structures such as buildings, machines, and infrastructure, and they impair human productivity in almost all spheres of economic activity. The problem is now widely recognized as central in the perpetually dismal economic and social development of the LDCs.

Development-Oriented Environmental Policies in LDCs

Although the development-environmental quality tradeoff model suggests that economic growth and development tends to be accompanied by negative environmental outcomes, it should also be understood that there are clear positive links between economic development and environmental quality. These links reflect cause and effect relationships. On the one hand, high environmental quality enables economic development to proceed much more quickly and smoothly; on the other hand, higher levels of economic development can help alleviate environmental problems as the country can afford to invest in environmental enhancement programs. However, these cause and effect relationships are far from automatic; appropriate policy directions are required to initiate and attain them.

Being relatively undeveloped, environmental problems would be more detrimental to economic development in the LDCs than in the DCs. In the LDCs, environmental problems impair labor productivity through adverse effects on human health, soil fertility, and the quality of assets and property. Therefore, there is a critical need for determined environmental public policy in the

Clearly, as already stated, the implication of the pollution-haven hypothesis is not only that the LDCs would eventually be severely devastated environmentally, but also that their economic development prospects would further be set back many decades. For one, as the LDC brings in the pollution-prone industries without requiring strict environmental standards, eventually the resulting environmental deterioration would inhibit economic growth. Secondly, these foreign industries can only perform as much as they always have done in the LDCs, namely, as MNCs whose primary objectives are usually far from operating in such a way as to prioritize the economic development of the host LDC. Thus, the LDC must always promote environmental preservation by maintaining strict but reasonable environmental controls and standards. They must not yield themselves as pollution-havens.

Apart from the pollution side of the environmental problem in LDCs, there also is the more serious aspect relating to unsuitable environmental conditions that the LDCs inhabit. To the LDC, this presents the most challenging environmental constraint to economic development. The development process must involve programs designed to improve environmental conditions. Of central importance is the need to encourage the choice of rural dwelling among the population through aggressive programs of rural development and agricultural development. These programs are to be combined with programs of education, urban planning, and infrastructural construction. With the improved level of development that these policy actions would give, the LDC could easily be capable of shifting its development-environmental quality tradeoff curve outward.

The environment is often concerned with the issues of externalities and property rights. Much of the forests and lands are not owned by individuals or groups; rather, they are essentially open-access or common-property resources. Therefore, users of these resources, basing their economic decisions on the cost-benefit outcomes to themselves, are likely to disregard the (negative) externalities their actions inflict upon the environment, often resulting in the overexploitation of the (environment) resource. Thus, inappropriate property-rights allocation is recognized as the major problem that results in the uneconomic use of the environment. Hence, an important environmental preservation policy would be the creation and effective functioning of property-rights institutions.

Instituting a system of individual or group property rights over forests and lands would create incentives for the owners to invest in environmental rehabilitation (such as fighting erosion and constructing irrigation facilities for farming), conservation (through appropriately priced and guarded exploitation of natural resources), and preservation (such as enforcement of environmental standards). This system could be accompanied by governmentally legislated standards for industrial emissions.[6]

Poverty in LDCs most affects the degree of use and abuse of the environment. Conservation measures, or sustainability measures, designed to promote environmental preservation would have little importance in a society where there are food shortages. Increasing wealth and economic well-being is the ultimate solution to this environmental problem, for, as people get better off economically, there is a reduced tendency to exploit natural resources more ruthlessly. But people are not getting better off in the LDCs. Thus, the forests are depleted by slash-and-burn farmers, and the trees are depleted by loggers who ignore environmental costs as they pursue their immediate means of sustenance.

As it is, the benefits of environmental conservation extend not only to the LDCs but also to the entire world. For example, rain forests (in LDCs) support much of the world's species which possess overwhelming ecological, biological, and medical values for the entire world. As stressed earlier, rain forests also absorb the carbon dioxide that is released as a byproduct in human and animal respiration, the buildup of which is responsible for global warming. As such, these forests are global *public goods*: they extend significant benefits to every society in this world.

This means that the LDC should not be expected to solely bear the costs of preserving these environmental resources, although they exist within their jurisdictions. An LDC should be compensated and given greater incentive to promote conservation of these resources. The rest of the world has an important stake in this preservation. The rich countries, in particular, should extend much greater compensation to the poor LDCs in this regard.

NOTES

1. The LDC's level of environmental quality is also low mainly because, as discussed later in this chapter, it is usually faced with an overwhelming amount of natural environmental hazards that severely reduce its environmental quality and inhibit economic growth and development, unlike a typical DC.

2. Ezeala-Harrison (1995c) contains a study that offers a practical model detailing how this may be pursued in a free market economy.

3. This is known as the *existence value*, or *nonuse value*, of environmental resources. It measures the satisfaction (utility) derived from knowing that some good exists in its unspoiled or natural state. The existence value is found by asking people how much they

would wish to pay or contribute to ensure that some natural scene or *common property* resource, such as a game-reserve, natures park, rare scenery, and the like, is preserved.

4. This is because of the LDCs' relatively low levels of industrialization. The byproducts of the supply side, such as those cited here, are a more serious threat to the industrialized economies of the developed countries.

5. See Chapter 9 for details on these and their impact on agricultural (under)development in these regions.

6. We must understand that the policy approaches outlined here are not expected to be the panacea for all the environmental problems of LDCs. In fact, some policy actions may not be suitable for certain LDCs. For example, establishing property rights in LDCs with serious population pressures might deprive a significant bulk of the population of their means of sustenance. It might also result in more unequal distribution of wealth. Therefore, an LDC simply has to adopt environmental policies that better suit its own peculiar socioeconomic conditions.

12

Development Planning and Policy Issues

This chapter deals with the involvement and role of central government in economic development, and focuses on two aspects of government activities in the development process: (1) the leverage of using economic policy instruments, at both micro and macro levels, to promote, direct, and stabilize the key economic indicators; and (2) the long-term planning and programming of key predetermined objectives of long-run economic development. The need for these planning and policy measures in LDCs is important first, because of the inherent inadequacies of an unrestricted free market system in ensuring the attainment of the broad goals of economic development, and second, because the requirements of a fully "competitive" economic system may result in declining economic growth and worsening inequity and poverty.

Economic stabilization policy involves the use of traditional micro- and macroeconomic policy instruments such as money supply, interest rates, government spending, taxation, labor market counseling and placement programs, human resources planning and development, and population controls to influence key economic variables with a view to directing them toward some desired target levels. These key economic variables include the national income (GDP), employment (or unemployment), the rate of inflation, the balance-of-payments account, and the international exchange rate of the country's currency.

Economic planning, unlike stabilization policy, is a more fundamental aspect of economic policy aimed at overcoming the limits that resource constraints, and their methods of allocation over time, impose on the rate of economic growth and the pace of economic development. Planning is designed to choose and coordinate investment projects in order to channel scarce factors into their most optimally productive uses. As such, development planning also encompasses the use of micro- and macroeconomic policy instruments toward achievement of their longer term objectives. These two aspects of government activism in the development process deserve special attention in the development policies of LDCs.

ECONOMIC POLICIES AND INSTRUMENTS IN THE DEVELOPMENT PROCESS

An LDC can use several policy instruments to guide the direction and pace of its development process; namely, the traditional instruments of monetary and fiscal policies, and legislative controls of prices and quantities (wages, rental rates, labor, land reform, immigration, and industrial organization). Often, however, most LDCs attempt to stabilize their economies by focusing on their fiscal and financial systems. It is very difficult for most LDC governments to pursue traditional monetary and fiscal policies, for while their financial systems are ill prepared to operate effective monetary policies, their taxation and public expenditure structures are inadequate for restoring fiscal balance. The problem is compounded by malfunctioning public administration systems amidst political ineptitudes or instabilities.

Monetary Policy

Monetary policy is the manipulation of the money supply by the Central Bank to influence the interest rate in the desired direction so as to remove a recession or reduce inflation. In the *monetarist* doctrine of macroeconomic policy, an economy should formulate and maintain a steady rate of growth of the money supply at all times as a way of smoothing out any fluctuations in the economy that may be imminent due to the *business cycle*. This is because controlling the money supply is thought to be a means of regulating economic activity and controlling inflation. Higher interest rates lead to higher savings in the economy, while low rates lead to increased investment, employment, and income. In this way, a freely functioning money market enables scarce resources to be allocated most efficiently and productively.

Prescribed for a developed economy, the use of monetary policy could prove to be an effective means of "fine-tuning maintenance" of the economy over its course of growth and development. For an LDC, however, the effectiveness of monetary policy as a stabilization policy instrument may be limited. This is because their markets and financial institutions may not be as properly developed, organized, and functional as they are in the DCs. Because of the predominant low level of education and inflexible information flow channels in LDCs, the interest rate seldom has the ability to transmit the needed signals and elicit the appropriate responses from economic agents as required.

Moreover, even where interest rate changes can impact the market, the financial markets are often weak on the demand side. This is because of the pervasive low levels of income and poor credit-worthiness of potential borrowers. The dominance of small-scale producers and consumers who operate in the informal sectors of the LDC's economy means that they will largely remain outside the mainstream of the money market. Most importantly, the financial markets and financial institutions in most LDCs are controlled by foreign interests, for most commercial banks are subsidiaries of major private companies in the DCs. Therefore, their operations, like most other multinational corporations in LDCs, are often geared solely toward short-term profit making rather than the financial and general economic development of their hosts.

The problem of "currency substitution" prevails in the LDCs. This problem arises from the population's long-term lack of confidence in their local economy. They usually resort to "substituting" foreign currencies (such as the U.S. dollar or the British pound sterling) in place of the local currency to serve the "store of value" function of money. Thus, the money supply in the LDC is virtually impossible to measure accurately, and the monetary authorities are often rendered powerless to significantly control economic variables through monetary policy.

The cumulative effect of these conditions is, again, the problem of *dualism* in the money and financial markets of LDCs: a formal sector and an informal sector. The formal sector is the organized and foreign-controlled money market, which often has controlled interest rate levels and mainly caters to the *modern sector* of the economy, satisfying the needs of the upper- and middle-class local and foreign businesses. The informal sector is the unorganized and unregistered money-lender-dominated financial arrangements that serve the needs of the informal and *traditional* (rural) sectors of the economy. It is in these sectors that the greater bulk of the population participates, given the dominant position of the (low income) traditional and rural sectors.

Alternative Monetary Policy Options for LDCs

How then can monetary policy be made effective in an LDC? A few practical alternative policy options are immediately evident. Given the peculiar conditions existing in the LDC, the dualistic financial market is unlikely to channel credit to the small-scale entrepreneurs and investors whose operations determine the extent of economic progress in LDCs. Therefore, the following alternative options are envisaged.

1. **More direct initiatives:** It may be necessary for the central bank authorities to opt for direct selective and sectoral credit controls in order to extend credit opportunities to the dominant informal sectors of the economy. Such options are being tried in Bangladesh under the *Gramliean Credit System* initiative, with reported records of success.

2. **The role of the central bank:** The central bank of the LDC can become involved more directly and actively in promoting economic progress. It should be able to step in to finance the various productive ventures that the foreign-controlled commercial banks would not finance, especially offering education and advice, with a view to instilling commercial knowledge and business skills into local, but enterprising and resourceful entrepreneurs. Such educational and informative programs are a rare facility that is in severely short supply in the

LDC, but which the dualistic financial markets cannot provide.

3. Use of development banks: *Development banks* are financial institutions established specifically to cater for the financial needs of selected sectoral economic activities. An *Agricultural Development Bank* or a *National Housing and Mortgage Bank,* for example, could be established to serve the needs of small-scale farmers in the rural sector or extend housing loans to low- and middle-income members of the workforce, respectively. As these categories of the population are often regarded as "unsafe borrowers" under the dualistic financial system, the development banks may prove to be the only effective way of extending needed finances for the development of an LDC economy's dominant traditional sector.

Fiscal Policy

Fiscal policy involves the use of taxation and government expenditure to influence economic variables. Under conditions of ill-organized financial markets, most LDCs have to rely heavily on fiscal measures not only to stabilize their economies but also to effectively mobilize their domestic resources for economic growth. The two sides of fiscal management are taxation and government spending.

The LDC government needs to generate and mobilize resources to finance its public expenditures in administration, law and order, and national security, and infrastructural development (including public utilities, social overhead capital, education, health services, and the like). The pace of economic and social progress depends largely on the government's ability to generate sufficient revenues to provide these nonrevenue-yielding public facilities. In addition, given the low level of development of private-sector capital, there may be the need for the government to engage in direct economic activities of ownership and control of public corporations.

Public Revenue: Direct Taxation, Indirect Taxation, and Sales and Royalties

The prevailing low-income levels in most LDCs tend to preclude the use of such direct and progressive taxes as income taxation and property taxation as a means of raising government revenue. Moreover, as a means of stimulating private investment among local entrepreneurs, or attracting foreign investment, huge tax concessions are given to firms and corporations. Therefore, corporate taxes or profit taxes are virtually nonexistent. As a result of the weakness of the direct tax base, the LDC has to rely heavily on indirect taxation - taxes that do not fall directly on personal income - as a source of public revenue. The most important of these taxes are custom duties (import taxes levied as tariffs, and export taxes levied on goods bound for the export market) and excise duties (taxes placed on domestically produced goods). Indirect taxes are clearly more attractive to LDCs as they are far cheaper and relatively easier to collect.

Generally, most LDCs face ever increasing problems of fiscal deficits. That is, the amount of public revenues they collect usually falls far short of their public expenditures. The reason for such a situation in an LDC is obvious: coupled with the weak direct taxation base, the low level of industrialization also means that the indirect tax base will be weak. Moreover, the agricultural sector, as the sector that employs the largest proportion of the population, is often taxed to its limit. Nonetheless, the amount of revenue generated from the agricultural sector is generally inadequate.

Over time, especially since the late 1970s, the accumulation of these annual deficits has given rise to serious problems of huge public debts, both internal and external debts, in these countries. The effects of such debts have included severe balance-of-payments adversities, capital flight, weakening of the international exchange rate of the country's currency, and undermining of international confidence in the LDC's economy.

The general weakness of the tax base in most LDCs has led to a situation where most LDC governments take direct ownership of all royalties and sales of their countries' resources, especially mineral resources such as crude petroleum oil, gold, diamond, bauxite, manganese, and coal. This is a legitimate means of state funding that substitutes for revenue sources in the absence of adequate public revenue sources. In many LDCs, the revenues from the sales of these resources outweigh not only what they could collect in taxes, but also revenues that many developed countries collect in taxes in their own countries. Yet, these LDCs often combine revenues from these resources with a level of direct and indirect taxation revenues collected in their countries.

Relative to their developmental needs, most LDCs seem to have had a significant level of revenue to reasonably finance their expenditures. Unfortunately, however, far from experiencing prosperity under growth and development, most of them have instead been saddled with huge external debts and massive poverty. The problem is apparently not that of the availability of revenue. Recent studies indicate that the problem is due to corruption, mismanagement, lack of responsible and effective leadership, and a general *human factor decay* (see Chapter 3).[1]

Government Spending and Deficit Financing

The public sector in the LDC is often the largest economic sector, probably because of the peculiar state of the economy as underdeveloped as explained above. Above all, however, given its low-income situation, an LDC must rely on its government to provide the momentum and direction for its economic development. The LDC's government must play a central role analogous to that of an entrepreneur with a business development, namely, decision making, coordination, risk bearing, and administration of the economic development initiative and agenda. Such is the central role that the public sector must play in the process of an LDC's economic development.

Where an LDC does not possess a rich natural resource endowment (such as crude petroleum oil), it most likely relies on *budget deficits* to raise the needed financing required to, not only initiate and carry out the developmental programs, especially the construction of infrastructure (*capital expenditures*), but also stabilize the economy and finance its *recurrent expenditures*. Under such circumstances, many LDCs have accumulated huge and crippling public debts. The weights of servicing and accommodating these debts, especially the external debts, have tended to impoverish many LDCs. Many of them have even resorted to incurring more debt to service the existing debt, leading to yet heavier indebtedness.

The *debt crisis*, as this cycle of the indebtedness syndrome came to be known during the 1980s and 1990s, led most LDCs to adopt the so-called *Structural Adjustment Programs*, usually at the instance of their creditors through the World Bank and IMF, with a view to better addressing the debt problem. Unfortunately, however, among the major "structural adjustments" that these LDCs are asked to undertake is the drastic cutting of the public sector, including massive privatizations of state enterprises (including public utilities), deregulation of most economic activities in all sectors of the economy, and removal of all government subsidies on "merit goods" (see Chapter 7). These "adjustments" are apparently designed to enable the government to balance its budgets and better manage its debt (mainly to the benefit of its creditors who are in the DCs and are the ones who pressure, or even force, these LDCs through the World Bank and the IMF, to undertake the "structural adjustments").

It is important also to stress the blatant inconsistencies whereby most of the LDCs with the most abject poverty-stricken populations are the ones that devote the overwhelming sizes of their budgets to military spending. One may sympathize with some of those LDCs where ethnic conflicts, political turmoil, and civil wars have led to high "defense" expenditures. However, in many others, massive military spending has been undertaken solely to maintain despotic, autocratic, and mainly military regimes in power. Most of these poor countries have failed to formulate and adopt the most appropriate political systems that would suit their peculiar circumstances. Many blindly adopted the Western political systems of their colonizers, in most cases of which it simply became unworkable, alienated their populace, and have stagnated or broken down. In others, the problem of *human factor decay* simply meant that their political leaders were so corrupt, irresponsible, and inept that they just plunged the economy into massive disrepair.[2]

Deficit financing is the act of using an expanded money supply (that is, by increasing the quantity of money in circulation) to finance a government budget deficit. Many LDCs, such as Brazil or Argentina, have in the past vigorously resorted to this method of fiscal expansion to finance many development projects. This is also referred to as inflationary financing because it almost always increases the rate of inflation in the economy. However, in addition to their expanded spending ability, such inflationary financing may have some other positive side effects, which the authorities may wish to see take place.

In Chapter 6, we considered how inflation may be deliberately used as a means of forced saving in raising the needed finances for investment. Rising inflation would raise relative prices in favor of producers and firms, increasing profits and subsequently encouraging more investment. Moreover, a higher inflation rate, especially where it is not immediately built into the going nominal interest rate, confers cheaper funding to borrowers, who then might borrow more for investment and consumption, boosting aggregate demand. In addition, rising inflation would cause resource transfers from nonsavers to savers, leading to greater investment capacity and growth.

The inflationary consequences of deficit financing, however, could prove to be far more destructive than constructive to the economy. Hyperinflation is often the actual result of unguarded deficit financing, and could set the economy into severe recession and stagflation. As hyperinflation erodes all confidence in the country's currency and the economy as a whole, savings for long-term investment and growth suffers, capital flights occur, and serious balance-of-payments problems arise, while severe economic hardships descend on the economy, together with their social and political repercussions.

Most LDCs should not adopt deficit financing except as a very short-run measure designed to quickly enable the government to implement a key infrastructural development initiative. And even then, it must serve as a very last resort. The experiences of many LDCs have shown that once deficit financing is embarked upon as a means of raising government spending, it tends to be overdone, with severe consequences in the interim. Irresponsible political leaders (especially military dictators) in many LDCs (particularly in Africa) have tended to use deficit financing as a personal source of free-spending cash (for example, Ghana, during the 1970s; and Zaire, during the 1970s to 1990s). Such situations have resulted in the economic destruction of these LDCs.

Unlike the DC, the role of public-sector spending is central to the LDC's economic development. However, under the prevailing conditions of "human factor decay" in most LDCs, it seems that an increasing role of the public sector would retard rather than promote the development process. The policy implication, therefore, is that as long as an LDC fails to produce more responsible, accountable, honest, and dedicated leaders who would champion its economic development agenda, it should continue to operate the policies of structural adjustment programs as a way of minimizing the damages that increased public-sector spending could cause under irresponsible political leadership. But if an LDC is able to solve its "human factor problem," especially as it relates to responsible political leadership, then a large public sector and higher government spending would be highly important in propelling and accelerating the pace of development.

Microeconomic Policies in Development

So far we have dwelt on *macroeconomic policy* issues, which are mainly short-run policies used to fine-tune and stabilize the economy on its growth and development paths. Microeconomic policies are policies that are centered on specific and particular (micro) sectors of the economy. Where *macro* policies provide short-term "dressing" of the economy as it progresses along the desired directions, *micro* policies are long-term policy frames that shape and expand the growth and development paths themselves along those directions.

The potentials of microeconomic policy and planning in the economic development of LDCs are analyzed in a recent study by Ezeala-Harrison and Baffoe-Bonnie (1994). Upon testing for the relative importance of micro parameters on the one hand, and macro variables on the other, in long-term perspectives of GDP growth in selected LDCs, the study reveals that micro policy parameters would be more effective in planning for long-term GDP growth, while demand management (macro) policies would be less than effective.[3]

Many planning initiatives in LDCs have emphasized inappropriate policy parameters in the past. An example is the high priorities placed on the acquisition of sophisticated (foreign) technologies in LDCs, although all that is needed for effective planning in these countries is the proper mobilization of resources and the adoption of an appropriate mix of resource prices in allocating resources. Micro policy and planning are designed for determining and avoiding such policy flaws.

The major parameters of micro policy planning include employment and human resource development, such as education and training (see Chapter 8), infrastructural development, productivity of resources (such as agricultural sector development and land redistribution), and income redistribution and equity measures. In particular, micro policies are able to address the important issue of unequal income redistribution: antipoverty measures, *safety nets*, social welfare programs, and tax reforms. These measures are vital to the long-term economic and social development of the LDCs.[4] The rest of this chapter deals with the broader aspect of micro policy and planning, generally known as *economic development planning*.

ECONOMIC DEVELOPMENT PLANNING

Economic planning is a deliberate attempt to coordinate economic decision making over the long run in order to influence, direct, and even control the growth of an economy's major economic variables, namely, national output, employment, consumption, and the pattern of income distribution. In effect, an economic development plan represents a specific set of quantitative economic targets projected for a given period of time, over which some specific policy actions are initiated toward the achievement of clear-cut and identifiable targeted projections, the overall aim being to achieve a predetermined set of development objectives.[5]

Development plans may be *comprehensive* (where they are made to cover aspects of the broad range of the national economy), or they may be *partial* (where they cover only specific sectors of the economy, such as agriculture, industrialization, or export promotion). Todaro (1994) describes the planning process as an exercise in which the government chooses social and economic objectives, sets various targets for them, and finally organizes a framework for implementing, coordinating, and monitoring their achievement.

Within the expansive existing literature on economic development planning, five key planning objectives are generally documented: (1) to raise the economy's rate of growth, (2) to increase the GDP, (3) to achieve a significantly augmented level of national consumption over time, (4) to reduce the level of unemployment, and (5) to achieve greater equity in national income distribution across the population.[6] Achieving increased rates of economic growth requires astute government policy to guide the movement and direction of the appropriate parameters of the economic system. Development planning models are also designed to assess the long-run consequences of policies affecting the allocation of resources, particularly the division of investment among sectors (Todaro, 1971).

They draw on the results of theoretical growth models, but differ from them in the sense that they contain empirical estimates and can be solved with numerical methods. Moreover, they are usually disaggregated sectorally and involve more complete specifications of development processes and specific policy constraints. Hence, whereas planning models are useful for studying more complex and disaggregated systems like the economies of most less developed countries (LDCs), the theoretical growth models are useful for studying the general character of growth in abstract settings (Taylor, 1981).

The ideal planning process, as envisaged in neoclassical theory, is broadly conceived as consisting of various basic stages, each of which is associated with a particular type of planning model. Although the formulation of a comprehensive plan is the goal of these models, it is sometimes necessary to base this on a more partial sectoral analysis, for in most poor LDCs, with limited data and limited industrial diversification, partial plans may be the most that can be accomplished. Most development plans are based initially on some formalized macroeconomic model, and complemented by a detailed selection of specific investment needs within each sector through the technique of project appraisal and social cost-benefit analysis.

The usefulness of planning and programming development is recognized, especially for LDCs, where the ability to put available resources to adequate use has been a long-term hindrance to economic growth and development. However, although many LDCs have vigorously embarked upon development planning in the course of their economic histories, many of these have met with very disappointing failures. Failure of a development plan is normally judged in terms of the plan's inability to attain its major objectives. Unfortunately, such have been the experiences of most LDCs that have attempted the course of development planning.

The Rationale for Planning

The theme for every planning initiative involves the attainment of a set of quantitative economic targets over a specified time span. The process ordinarily involves choosing the set of economic objectives, setting the targets for them, and then organizing the implementation, coordination, and supervision of their programs of achievement.

The basis for economic planning in any economy rests on the so-called *market failure* phenomenon. That is, the free market economic system (of *laissez faire*), left on its own, inherently fails to allocate the society's scarce resources efficiently. This is to say that, the free market system not only fails to yield the most desirable economic outcomes for society (such as full employment and high rate of growth), but also fails to prevent such common economic problems as gross inequality in income distribution, unemployment, inflation, and recessions. It is this failure that warrants the need for economic planning, especially for an LDC.

Planning Models and Methodologies

The operational methodologies of economic planning are often based on some planning models used to set the strategies (the macro dynamic model), set the sectoral targets (the multisectoral input-output matrix), and assess the efficiencies of the plan's individual projects (the cost-benefit project appraisals).[7] As for using the macro dynamic models, the problem with their projections is that they are only first approximations of the general directions that an economy might take. They lack not only operational guidelines, they also lack pertinent specifications as to the relevant sectoral (micro) policy parameters that the planner might target.

The Input-Output Matrix

Perhaps the most important aspect of a plan program is its quantitative input-output (I/O) table that relates how the output of each industry is allocated across other industries and sectors of the economy, on the one hand, and how the inputs used by each industry are drawn from other industries and sectors, on the other. Within the I/O matrix, it is observed that the total production in any sector of the economy is due not only to the primary inputs (land, labor, and capital) employed in that sector, but also to the intermediate goods and services produced by the other sectors of the economy, and employed in that particular sector as inputs.

The I/O table provides the planner with (1) important insights into the structure of the economy, especially in regard to relative sectoral shares in national output; (2) knowledge of how interdependent the sectors are in terms of how much each sector contributes to each other's performance; and (3) an understanding of which sectors are the key sectors of the economy (in terms of which sector has the lion share of total output). This may be illustrated with a hypothetical I/O flow matrix as follows.

We assume that the economy is made up of three sectors, agriculture, industry, and services, whose total output and inputs are represented in Table 12.1.

Rows: The data of the rows of Table 12.1 show the distribution of each sector's total output, as inputs across all the other sectors, of the economy. This measures the total supply of the sector's output to the economy. Consider the first row, for example. The data in this row indicate that the agricultural sector produced a total output of 200, out of which 40 is used by the sector itself (say, as seed or feed-grains), 50 goes into the industrial sector as inputs (raw materials), nothing of the agricultural output is required as inputs for the services sector, while 110 is sold as consumer demand for final agricultural output (including domestic food consumption and exports). These give the total contribution of the agricultural sector as 200, of which 90 constitutes total usage as inputs.

Columns: The columns show the role of each sector as a purchaser of inputs from the other sectors. This measures the total demand of the sector's output in the economy. The second column, for example, shows that the industrial sector is a user of inputs from agriculture (50), itself (10), and services (10). It also shows that total input demand by industry from the whole economy is 70.

We also note that total supply by each sector (rows) equals total demand by each sector (columns) - that is, 200 for agriculture, 100 for industry, and 50 for services. As mentioned earlier, this I/O table enables the planner to peruse the structure of the economy from the standpoint of the mutual interdependence of

Table 12.1
Hypothetical Input-Output Table

Output			Input			
	Agric	Industry	Services	Market demand	Total Int.	Total used
Agric.	40	50	0	110	90	200
Indust.	10	10	0	80	20	100
Serv.	15	10	10	15	35	50
Total used	65	70	10	–	145	–
Primary inputs	135	30	40	–	–	205
Grand total	200	100	50	–	–	–

the various sectors as well as determining the "leading sectors" in terms of their relative importance in the economy's GDP.

To enable the planner to determine the various levels of "projected" sectoral outputs for the plan program, the input-output coefficients may be constructed from Table 12.1. Let us denote the agricultural, industrial, and services sectors as sectors 1, 2, and 3, respectively. Then, the ratio of the amount of sector 1 output needed as inputs per unit of the sector's total output is: $40/200 = 0.2$. Letting the letter, a, stand for an element in a matrix, this may be denoted in the traditional matrix notation as: a_{11}. Similarly, the amount of sector 2 output needed as inputs per unit of sector 1's total output is: $10/200 = 0.05$, and may be denoted in matrix notation as a_{21}. And the amount of sector 3 output needed as inputs per unit of sector 1's total output is $15/200 = 0.075$, which may be denoted as a_{31}. Hence, the input-output coefficient matrix of the I/O table is:

$$A = \begin{bmatrix} a_{11} & a_{12} & a_{13} \\ a_{21} & a_{22} & a_{23} \\ a_{31} & a_{32} & a_{33} \end{bmatrix} = \begin{bmatrix} 0.2 & 0.5 & 0 \\ 0.05 & 0.1 & 0 \\ 0.075 & 0.1 & 0.2 \end{bmatrix}$$

This I/O matrix, A, is known as the matrix of technical coefficients. It shows how much or the proportion of each sector's total output (or contribution) that is required as inputs by each of the other sectors of the economy. For example, the element $a_{12} = 0.5$, shows that, for every unit of sector 2 (industry) output, 0.5 units of sector 1 (agriculture) output is required as inputs, of course, under *ceteris paribus* (all things remaining constant). Thus, the matrix, A, summarizes the production process. It gives a complete picture of the amount of flows of inputs and outputs into and out of each sector of the economy.

The planner can then use A to determine the required (planned) levels of production of each sector according to the plan objectives. The planning task, therefore, simply reduces to the need to determine the sectoral levels of production projected in line with the desired level of final demand of goods in each sector. This task may be accomplished as follows.

Let

q_1, q_2, q_3 = the outputs of sectors 1, 2, and 3, respectively
Q_1, Q_2, Q_3 = the projected final demand levels in sectors 1 2, and 3, respectively

Then, by definition, for each sector, total output equals total contributions that the sector makes to all the other sectors as inputs, and it also equals total intermediate use plus final market demand. Therefore, the following system of simultaneous equations obtains for the hypothetical economy represented by the above model:

$$q_1 = 0.2q_1 + 0.5q_2 + [0q_3] + Q_1 \qquad (12.1)$$
$$q_2 = 0.05q_1 + 0.1q_2 + [0q_3] + Q_2 \qquad (12.2)$$
$$q_3 = 0.075q_1 + 0.1q_2 + 0.2q_3 + Q_3 \qquad (12.3)$$

This system is written in the compatible matrix form:

$$\begin{bmatrix} 0.8 & -0.5 & 0 \\ -0.05 & 0.9 & 0 \\ -0.075 & -0.1 & 0.8 \end{bmatrix} \begin{bmatrix} q_1 \\ q_2 \\ q_3 \end{bmatrix} = \begin{bmatrix} Q_1 \\ Q_2 \\ Q_3 \end{bmatrix} \qquad (12.4)$$

Assuming the planner's desired and projected final demand levels expected from sectors 1, 2, and 3 are Q_1, Q_2, and Q_3, respectively, then, using (12.4), the planner is now able to determine the plan's target levels required to yield these projected levels of final demand in each sector. This is easily obtained by solving (12.4) using *Crammer's Rule*.[8]

Project Appraisal and Cost-Benefit Model

The day-to-day operational decisions regarding the allocation of limited public funds into various competing public projects must be guided with consistent evaluations of the projects on which the resources are spent. This is the essence of the project evaluations technique. It is a microeconomic comparative study of any project in terms of its total costs (private monetary costs plus social costs) and its total benefits (private monetary benefits plus social benefits) to society.

The basic idea of the cost-benefit (CB) model is that, in order to decide on the general economic viability of a plan project involving public funds, it is necessary to weigh the project's total potential benefits against its total potential costs to society. The need for this recourse arises because the normal yardstick of commercial profitability which guides the investment decisions of private-sector investors would not be appropriate for public-sector decisions. This is because, whereas private investors are generally guided by profitability motives, public-sector investments are often guided by social welfare maximization (especially in an LDC), and these two motives often conflict. In particular, where social costs and social benefits diverge from private costs and benefits, the decision to maximize social welfare cannot be based on the criterion of commercial profitability.

The social viability of a public project involves a number of factors:

1. *Objective-based assessment*: A set of the key objectives of the national economic planning program may be used to weigh the social worth of a plan project. This approach is handy especially where difficulties exist in attaching numerical values to certain socioeconomic goals and targets, such as self-reliance, modernization, political stability, national unity, and the like.

2. *Use of shadow prices*: The *shadow price* is the measure of the actual value of a commodity (input or output) in terms of its real social worth. The shadow price differs from the market price of the commodity according to the extent to which the market price has been affected by factors such as input price distortions (resulting in, say, wages exceeding the social opportunity cost of labor and undervaluing the social opportunity cost of capital), inflation, taxes (including tariffs), currency overvaluation or undervaluation, subsidies, artificial scarcity, an so on. In the cost-benefit calculations of alternative public projects, if market prices of commodities are used under circumstances of input price distortions such as explained above, the result would be that the real cost of capital-intensive projects would be grossly underestimated, thereby promoting such projects and rejecting socially less costly labor-intensive projects. The use of shadow prices is essential for LDCs especially, given their proneness to input price distortions and to have significant divergence between the market prices and the shadow prices.

After the necessary adjustments are made to reduce market prices to shadow prices, then the selection criterion of projects on the grounds of their relative viabilities, would require having to reduce the stream of a project's benefit flows and costs over a given relevant time span, to an index whose value could then be used to rank projects for selection. This involves a dynamic dimension known as the *net present value* (NPV) of a project. We now turn to an example of how to construct a simple cost-benefit model.

Let

C_t = money cost of project at time t
c_t = unobservable social costs (negative externalities) at time t
B_t = monetary benefits at time t
b_t = unobservable social benefits (positive externalities) at time t
m = life span of project (expected) in years
V_m = the project's scrap value at time $t=m$

Then, the total cost of the project is given as

$$\Sigma_0^m (C_t + c_t)$$

and the total benefit is

$$\Sigma_0^m (B_t + b_t) + V_m$$

Hence, the *net benefit* (NB) of the project to the society is

$$NB = [\Sigma_0^m (B_t + b_t) + V_m] - \Sigma_0^m (C_t + c_t)$$

Before discussing the application of the CB model, we must extend the concept to cover its net present value aspect. For practical purposes, the use of NPV becomes apparent because of the obvious difficulties associated with determining the future values of costs and benefits. The present value gives us the discounted present worth of the entire aggregate future value of each item. This is formulated as follows.

Deriving a Project's Net Present Value

Assuming the current value of the total benefits of a project, B_0, is a good proxy for the project's present value (PV), then we can write:

$$PV = B_0$$

Let ρ = the project's annual rate of return (expected), that is, the project's rate of yield as a percentage of its value. The total benefits from the project at year 1 $(t=1)$ is given as

$$B_1 = B_0 + \rho B_0 = B_0(1+\rho)$$

Similarly, the total benefits from the project at each of the subsequent years until the end of its life span: $t=2$, $t=3$,...,t, are given as

$$B_2 = B_1 + \rho B_1 = B_1(1+\rho) = B_0(1+\rho)(1+\rho)$$
$$= B_0(1+\rho)^2$$
$$B_3 = B_0(1+\rho)^3$$
.

.
$$B_t = B_0(1+\rho)^t \tag{12.6}$$

Using Equation (12.6), the PV of the project is obtained as

$$PV = B_0 = \frac{R_t}{(1+\rho)^t} \tag{12.7}$$

Using this result, the PV of the above model may be written as:
and the NPV would be given as

The decision rule: The selection criteria for projects is then based on a

$$\Sigma_0^m [\frac{B_t+b_t}{(1+\rho)^t}]$$

$$NPV = \Sigma_0^m \frac{B_t+b_t}{(1+\rho)^t} + V_m - \Sigma_0^m \frac{C_t+c_t}{(1+\rho)^t} \qquad (12.8)$$

decision rule that depends on the sign of Equation (12.8):

   (a) If NPV > 0, the project is a viable one, and should be established.
   (b) If NPV $\leq$ 0, the project is not viable, and is rejected.

Using this approach, alternative competing projects of a plan program are ranked in the order of their NPVs, and the one(s) with the highest positive NPVs are selected as resources would permit.

The rate return, ρ, is a measure of the planner's social rate of discount. This rate may differ from the market *rate of interest (r)*, which is the rate normally used by private-sector investors in calculating the profitability of investments. The planner's rate of discount, ρ, may be selected according to the planner's subjective evaluation placed on future and subsequent benefit flows: the higher these future flows are valued in the government's planning scheme, the lower will be the social rate of discount.

The internal rate of return: Given that an economy may wish to allocate its scarce resources into the sectors and projects that yield the highest flow of returns (benefits), it is sometimes easier for the planner to determine a project's *internal rate of return* (IRR) from the NPV, and then use the comparison between the IRR and the market rate of interest (a measure of the average yield in all other alternative projects). Selection would then be made of a project if its IRR exceeds the market rate of interest.

To determine a project's IRR, the planner simply sets the NPV equal to zero; that is, the planner seeks for the level of ρ that would allow the project to break even. Under break-even conditions, the PV of total costs equals the PV of total benefits, such that NPV = 0. That is:

$$\Sigma_0^m \frac{B_t+b_t}{(1+\rho*)^t} + V_m = \Sigma_0^m \frac{C_t+c_t}{(1+\rho*)^t} \qquad (12.9)$$

From this, the planner may solve for the *critical rate of return*, $\rho*$.
The decision rule in this case becomes:

   (a) If $\rho* \geq r$, the project is a viable one, and should be established.
   (b) If $\rho* < r$, the project is not viable, and is rejected, because the

resources to be invested in it could be placed elsewhere in the economy to earn a higher market rate of return (r) than the project would yield.

Again, various competing projects of a plan program could be ranked in the order of the extent to which their IRRs exceed the economy's market interest rate, and the highest ranking projects would be selected as resources would permit.

NOTES

1. The problem of corruption and irresponsible leadership is the subject of a number of recent research studies that have centered on the issue of chronic underdevelopment in some LDCs, especially those of Sub-Saharan Africa. See: Adjibolosoo (1994a, 1994b), and Ezeala-Harrison (1994a, 1995a).

2. The role of political leadership in the LDCs' economic development and underdevelopment has generally been recognized as a crucial issue. More recently, this subject is attracting increasing research attention under the topic of *Human Factor Issues in Development*; Adjibolosoo (1994a), addresses the problem with particular focus on the problem of Sub-Saharan Africa's perpetual state of underdevelopment; the topic is addressed to cover the LDCs in general in Ezeala-Harrison (1995d). See also Ezeala-Harrison (1995b) for a study that explains Africa's educational inappropriateness as a major consequence of the overall "human factor" problem.

3. However, the study also showed that the relative effects of the micro policy parameters would differ according to the level of development of the country concerned. For instance, a low-income agrarian economy (such as that of a typical Sub-Saharan African country) needs more emphasis on resource management than infusion of high technology, while a relatively high-income economy (such as those of East Asia) requires more technologically biased planning.

4. For a model that addresses how to determine the pertinent policy actions needed to initiate and promote these micro policies in LDCs, see Ezeala-Harrison and Baffoe-Bonnie (1994).

5. See Killick (1976), Dasgupta (1974), or Waterston (1965).

6. Among the major studies are Dasgupta (1974), Killick (1976), Chakravarty (1966), Lefeber (1968), Eckaus and Bhagwati (1972), Waterston (1965), and Lewis (1966).

7. The plan's macro model could be based on one of the major macroeconomic growth models such as the Harrod-Domar or Solow growth model, which is then used to work out the key policy parameters that would guide the plan. These models are fully expounded in Part II of this book, and so we do not replicate them here.

8. Let the solutions be represented by q_1^*, q_2^*, and q_3^*. Assuming the hypothetical figures: $Q_1 = 432$, $Q_2 = 568$, and $Q_3 = 320$, solve for the values of q_1^*, q_2^*, and q_3^*, using (12.4).

Part IV

THE PROCESS OF ECONOMIC DEVELOPMENT: THE EXTERNAL DIMENSIONS

13

International Trade and Economic Development

This chapter deals with the influences and potentials of international trade in economic development: pertinent issues such as the effect of international trade on the structure and character of the development process in LDCs, how it may have affected and promoted international inequality, and what may be done to reshape international trade to enhance, or rather to not retard, the pace of economic development in today's LDCs.

Although the topic of international trade in economic development has not hitherto been formally taken up in this book, the role of international trade in the development process has featured repeatedly throughout the preceding chapters. International trade is one of the most central aspects of a country's development, and more so if that country is an underdeveloped one. In Chapter 1, the degree of *foreign dependence* that is, the extent to which an economy depends on the foreign trade sector for not only markets for sale and purchases, but also as a source of resources for development in the form of aid, grants, loans, and the like-is explained as one of the major characteristics of underdevelopment. This places international trade within the centre stage of the development process for most LDCs.

In Chapter 6 in particular, the role of international trade is reviewed thoroughly under the structuralist line of thought. Trade is posited to be a most important, if not the most important, single factor that has shaped the development achievements and the underdevelopment situations of countries during the twentieth century. Over this period, primary exports have traditionally accounted for the bulk of the GDPs of almost all LDCs of Africa, Asia, the Middle East, and Latin America and the Caribbean. This trend has remained unchanged today. Many recent works, including Bliss (1989), Bruton (1989), and Lewis (1989), have focused on the important issues of trade and economic development.

International trade permeates every facet of a country's economic life in ways over and beyond ordinary imports and exports of goods and services. It involves international transactions as well as administrative rules of conduct in short- and long-term international payments, banking services, currency exchanges, capital movements, technological transfers, and even sociopolitical transactions such as sports and cultural exchanges.

THE PLACE OF INTERNATIONAL TRADE IN DEVELOPMENT

The importance of international trade in economic development may have been recognized as early as the *mercantilist* era of economic thought.[1] Even before this period, Adam Smith had argued that only the size of the market could limit the level of economic growth that a society could achieve. In this tradition, classical and neoclassical economics vigorously supports free and unrestricted trade among nations in asserting that trade opens up opportunities for people in all countries to improve their welfare.

The "trade as engine of growth" paradigm is expounded in Chapter 6. A brief review of its key tenets may be useful here as a prelude to highlighting the potentials of genuine trade in fostering development. Historical evidence indicates that indeed international trade was a powerful engine of economic growth and development for most present-day developed countries. This is because, as nations are inherently self-insufficient, (free) trade offers the following immense advantages to a country.

1. Market for mass exports: Mass export of primary agricultural produce, as well as industrial manufactured products, create foreign exchange for the purchase of vital capital resources for industrialization and infrastructural development.[2] International trade simply removes the constraints that limited market demand might place on a country's pace of development.

2. Capital acquisition through trade: International trade opens up opportunities for a country to acquire much needed capital equipment to apply to its industrial and infrastructural needs. This enables an economy to be able to apply diversified machinery, tools, equipments, and semifinished products in its everyday economic activities without being restricted to only those equipments that it alone could produce domestically.

3. Capital acquisition through borrowing: A country is able to receive loans, grants, trade credits, aid, and the like, from its richer international trading partners. Such resources are crucial to a country's development as it could apply them toward importation of capital or other development needs. Moreover, a country could access borrowing and aid facilities available in international financial institutions such as the International Bank for Reconstruction and Development (IBRD) or the World Bank, the International Monetary Fund (IMF), and the United Nations Development Program (UNDP).

4. Technological transfer: A country could easily apply foreign technologies that it encounters through international trade, in order to enhance its own production systems and methods. Such ready-made technology that is available through the constant interaction that only international trade allows would otherwise be unavailable or very slow and expensive to develop and apply.

5. International friendship and sociocultural exchanges: Through the constant and frequent interaction among countries in the course of international trade, international good-will and friendly relations develop among them. They learn each other's consumption patterns, other institutional and organizational arrangements, values, ideas, and lifestyles. International cultural exchanges through sports and the arts flourish. This promotes world peace and harmony, enabling development to occur.

The classical theory of international trade and its role in economic development is based on the *comparative advantage paradigm*. It states that a country performs better by concentrating on the production of those goods and services for which it possesses a comparative advantage over others, and then trade those goods for those of other countries. By so doing, each country, with its comparative cost advantage, can produce its products more cheaply than others, so that through trade all countries would benefit immensely by way of obtaining goods more cheaply than they would have if they produced all goods themselves.

In determining the degree of comparative advantage, the costs of production are measured in terms of opportunity costs. To illustrate, let us assume that the DCs have a comparative advantage relative to LDCs in the production of manufactured goods, because the DCs can produce manufactured goods at lower costs in terms of agricultural products foregone, as against the LDCs. Following this situation, the DCs should specialize in the production of manufactured goods and trade it for agricultural produce with the LDCs, who also specialize in the production of agricultural produce in which they have comparative advantage. In this way, not only do the total of goods exchanged increase massively, but also the costs of acquiring these goods are much lower through trade, for both DCs and LDCs.

The comparative advantage phenomenon has provided a major impetus for global free-trade policies. Through such free trade and exchange, over time international income redistributions take place as free product and factor mobilities equalize prices and incomes across countries. This implies a more equitable distribution of the benefits of international progress, and therefore a more even spread of economic development across the world. International trade is thus an *engine of growth* and development. This has been the conclusion of at least classical and neoclassical economics, for whom trade is a *vent for surplus*, for it is trade that enables a country to overcome the limits set by the extent of the market against specialization and the division of labour.[3]

The Failure of Trade in the Development of LDCs

As seen in Chapter 6, the massive development potential of international trade appears to have been lost in present-day LDCs.[4] Instead, international trade has become one of the factors that have contributed to their ongoing impoverishment. The main reasons for this situation, as propounded in structuralist theory, are analyzed in Chapter 6. We highlight the key issues here.

After the Great Depression and the two World Wars, confidence in the stability of the international economic order was severely shaken, and many economists began to question whether the international economy could be the engine of economic growth for developing countries in the twentieth century in the same way that it had been in the nineteenth century. The main question was whether the international economy could continue to provide expanding opportunities for trade in such a way that developing countries could not only benefit from it but also use it as a major instrument for sustained economic growth and development.

In the nineteenth century, for instance, the policies of the *gold standard* and international free trade created a world economic order within which international trade expanded much faster than world output, as the rapidly advancing economies of Europe provided growing markets for the expansion of primary products and manufactured goods produced by the then developing countries. However, during the 1930s, the gold standard was abandoned, devaluation of currencies occurred, and countries embarked upon rampant protectionist trade policies. As a result, the pace of international trade and international capital flows seriously slowed down. And so did the benefits and opportunities that accrued to nations through international trade.

The pace of world trade came to be dominated by the developed countries to the increasing disadvantage of the developing countries. The prospects for expansion of trade by the developing countries in a world economy that was largely dominated by the developed countries seeking to maximize their individual advantages from trade were very dim indeed. In particular, the developed countries resorted to aggressive trade protectionism in response to the combined advents of productivity slowdowns and nationalism. Generally, empirical evidence supports the view that international trade has lost its engine of growth (Reidel, 1984).

The engine of economic growth that trade was in the nineteenth century has been totally lost to the twentieth-century LDCs. During the nineteenth century, rapid growth in Western Europe, particularly in England, was transmitted to other countries through international exchange. But the rapid growth of the DCs of the twentieth century has not been, and is not being, transmitted to the LDCs of the world. This failure is due mainly to the deliberate actions of the DCs through their attitudes, conduct, and designs, adopted in order to remain ahead in what they apparently have perceived to be a highly "competitive" world economic order in which "only the strong survive."

BALANCE OF NATIONAL AND INTERNATIONAL TRADE

Trade patterns are governed by the various policies, attitudes, and strategies adopted by the various countries, regions, and trading blocs of the world. Before we consider these issues, we must understand the following terms and definitions.

The Terms of Trade

The terms of trade (TOT) facing a country is the relationship between the average price of the country's exports and the average price of its imports. If the average price of exports is higher that the average price of imports, the country is said to have a favorable terms of trade; if otherwise, it has an unfavourable (or adverse) terms of trade. This depiction of the TOT is used to formulate an explicit formula for the TOT, termed the *net barter terms of trade* and defined simply as the ratio of the average price of a country's exports to the average price of its imports.

Let the average price of exports and imports, respectively, be: P_X and P_M; then the TOT is given by

$$\text{TOT} = P_X/P_M \qquad (13.1)$$

From this expression it is clear that as P_X rises relative to P_M, the country's TOT improves, and as P_M rises relative to P_X, the country's TOT deteriorates.

Much of the evidence based on many recent empirical studies (such as Cuddington and Urzua, 1989) as well as evidence from World Bank data (1991), indicate that the TOT of manufactured goods have been much more favorable relative to that of primary products, thereby lending support to the structuralist position.

The Balance of Trade

Trade balance relates to volumes. The balance of trade facing a country is the relationship between the volume of the country's exports and the volume of its imports over a specified time period. If the volume of exports is greater than the volume of imports over the given time period, the country is said to have a favorable trade balance; otherwise, it has an adverse trade balance.

The Balance of Payments

A country's balance-of-payments (BOP) account at some point in time (say, at the end of one yearly period) is the relationship between the total receipts (inflows) that it procures and the total payments (outflows) that it incurs in the course of its international trading transactions with the rest of the world over that period. The BOP, as a typical statement of account, is made up of two sides: the credit side (of all receipts entries) and the debit side (of all payments entries). Furthermore, each of these two sides is composed of three sections: the current account section, the capital account section, and the net reserves section.

Current Account covers entries of all *visible* and *invisible* items of trade. Visible items of trade are merchandise exports (in the credit section) and merchandise imports (in the debit section). The invisible items include services in both sections (such as banking, shipping, insurance, tourism, etc.). The *capital account* includes all money lent or invested from abroad. It also includes all monetary and financial transfers involving such things as profit, interest payments, and dividends repatriated across borders. A prominent example is the cash remittances that foreign workers send to their home countries.

By definition, the BOP must balance annually. A country with, say, a $2 billion deficit on its current account (due to a huge deficit balance of trade) may get $2 billion in the form of a short-term (or long-term) grant or loan from another country or external financial institution to finance this deficit and thus balance its BOP. This means that the country balances its BOP by running a surplus on its capital account in the amount of $2 billion. Alternatively, most countries have official reserves of foreign currency and gold that they can draw from and use to cover any current account deficits that might arise.[5] Ultimately, however, whether or not a country's official reserve changes depends on its exchange rate policy. Therefore, we need to fully understand how the exchange rate of currencies are determined and maintained.

Exchange Rates and Exchange Rate Policies

The exchange rate of a country's currency is the rate at which that currency exchanges for the currencies of other countries. Its value at any time depends on the exchange rate policy that is being pursued by the country concerned. A country may pursue a *fixed* exchange rate policy (in which case the exchange rate is pegged at some level); a *flexible* exchange rate policy (in which case its level is determined by the currency's supply and demand in the free international money market); or a *quasi-fixed* exchange rate policy (in which case the currency is allowed to float, but the rate is not allowed to rise above or fall below certain levels).

Devaluation is a special type of fixed exchange rate policy whereby the rate is fixed and maintained below its current level, or below the level which the free market (supply and demand) would yield. A country's currency may also be *overvalued* if the exchange rate is fixed and maintained above its market value. Devaluation of a country's currency effectively raises the domestic prices of imports in the country and lowers the prices of the country's exports in foreign markets. Apparently, the purpose of devaluation is to encourage higher export sales and discourage imports, probably in an effort to correct a balance of trade deficit. This may succeed, however, only if the country's exports have *elastic demand* in foreign markets, while its imports also have *elastic demand* in the domestic market.[6]

Under the *Bretton Woods* system of fixed exchange rates, the central banks of various countries frequently intervene in the international currency market to "regulate" the value of their currencies.[7] For example, if their exchange rate goes under pressure to depreciate, they sell foreign exchange from their reserves to buy (and thereby effectively raise the demand for) their own currency. This action provides support for the currency and stabilizes its exchange rate around the current level. If, on the other hand, a country's exchange rate gets too high, its central bank may buy foreign exchange to increase its reserve, thereby increasing the supply of its currency and reducing its price, the exchange rate, in the international money market. A country might occasionally allow its currency to depreciate because it might be lacking sufficient reserves of foreign exchange to support it. This is a usual situation that most LDCs face.

As a country's exchange rate is assumed to be the price at which it bought imports and sold exports, changes in its exchange rate policies amount to adjusting this price and altering the volume of export and import transactions. Capital flows are also affected by exchange rate policies because the amount of foreign capital inflow and outflow depends on the relative strength or weakness of the domestic currency. Thus, the exchange rate is a central parameter in the degree of international trade, and therefore in the degree to which development is transmitted through trade.

In a free trade world with floating exchange rates, a state of relative parity would be established among the currencies of all the trading partners. This situation has been explained by a theory known as the *Purchasing Power Parity* (PPP) theorem. It states that exchange rates tend toward equality in international purchasing power with each other. This is because free adjustments in their exchange rates allow each currency to achieve relative parity in line with the relative strengths of their economies. To illustrate the PPP concept, let us consider one major economic factor that easily affects a country's exchange rate, namely, inflation.

Inflation erodes a currency's purchasing power. The difference between inflation rates in different countries determines the relative strengths of their respective currencies, and the extent to which one country's currency erodes in terms of the others. For example, if, say, a country's inflation rate grows faster than its trading partner's inflation rate, the country's currency depreciates (or devalues, presumably by the amount of the difference between the inflation rates); and if its inflation is slower, it revalues its currency. In this way, this country brings its costs back into line with the international norm and thus would not be trading at an unfair disadvantage (under higher inflation) or advantage (under lower inflation). This may be expressed by the statement that "real exchange rates are constant", the real exchange rate being the exchange rate adjusted for differential inflation rate.[8]

THE PATTERNS OF REGIONAL WORLD TRADE

World Bank data (1991) indicate that since the post-World War II period, whereas the rate of growth of exports of the LDCs taken together has been less than one-half of that of the DCs taken together, the LDCs' rate of growth of imports far exceeds that of the DCs. Associated with this pattern of trade is the fact that the LDCs, in their trade with the DCs, tend to have unfavorable terms of trade as well as deficits in their balance of trade. The balance of trade adversity, however, was offset by net capital flows from the DCs to the LDCs. The data further reveal that this pattern has long changed.

Over the decade of the 1980s, the rate of growth of exports of the LDCs rose sharply and exceeded that of the DCs, as the pattern of imports was also reversed. At the same time, capital flows from the DCs to the LDCs declined significantly. This recent trade and capital flows pattern reflects the problems of instability especially introduced in the international economic order by the debt crises that erupted during this time.

The debt crises of the 1980s spelt a major shift in the patterns of trade of the LDCs. Prior to this period, import expanded far more rapidly than exports, and trade deficits were offset by capital flows inflows. The reverse became the case after the 1980s, a shift that was especially very prominent in Latin America and the Caribbean, the Middle East, and North Africa; the major debtor nations of the world.

Sub-Saharan Africa, whose trade is dominated by primary produce, experienced very high rates of export growth that exceeded import growth during the pre-1980s period. During the 1980s, however, they had absolute declines in both export and import growth. This region has been particularly hurt by international trade imbalances: persistent adverse terms of trade has perhaps retarded economic growth and development far more in Sub-Saharan Africa that anywhere else in the world.

Asia's trade performance has been the most impressive among the developing regions of the world. Except for the two big economies of China and India, both of which pursued major trade-restrictionist policies during the post-World War II era, it could be safely inferred for this region that international trade has played the "engine of growth" role that it did for the nineteenth-century developing countries. The most rapid expansion of trade occurred in the Newly Industrializing Countries (NICs) of East Asia, notably Singapore, South Korea, Taiwan, Thailand, and, to a lesser extent, Malaysia and Indonesia. In these countries, export expansion far exceeded import expansion, yielding consistent balance of trade surpluses throughout much of the post-World War II period. This trend has basically continued to date; even the two South Asian "sleeping giants," China and India, witnessed a rapid opening up of their economies to international trade in the 1980s and 1990s.

The relative successes of the Asian NICs is attributable to their abilities to diversify their structure of trade. Unlike the other LDCs, the NICs were able to reduce the primary-produce composition of their exports. World Bank (1991) data indicate that exports of primary produce declined to less than 20 percent of the NICs' exports. Instead, these NICs diversified their manufacturing exports from their labor-intensive, light manufacturing character (of the post-war period) to broader range manufacturing composition such as chemicals, steel, machinery, and myriad of heavy-industrial goods. Most of these were exported to the DCs, while the NICs imported mainly primary produce from the LDCs.

It is important that we observe why the Asian countries succeeded in maximizing the gains from international trade, and were able to use it as the engine of growth during the twentieth century, while the other LDCs, especially Sub-Saharan Africa, failed to do so. In the immediate post-war period, most East Asian NICs, especially Indonesia, Malaysia, and Thailand, were prototypes of the LDCs: agricultural, primary-product exporting, and low-income economies. Over the years, however, each of these countries was able to rapidly expand its primary-product-dominated exports through aggressive pursuit of competitive production methods in them. At the same time they established complementary manufacturing industries across a broad range of export products, thereby diversifying their economic bases. They then simply reaped the benefits of complementarity between industrialization and agricultural development, enabling them to easily succeed in the increasingly competitive world market.

A few countries in Latin America have also attained the NIC label through their abilities to achieve a relative degree of success in growth through international trade. These include Mexico, Argentina, and Brazil. The debt crisis, however, severely hit these countries very hard, and their performances have suffered significantly as a result.

Trade Protectionism

Protectionism arises as countries adopt various trade restrictionist measures to protect their domestic markets on behalf of domestic producers, against foreign competitors. These measures include:

Trade embargo: Through this policy, a country simply bans the products of a potential trading partner within its markets. This is usually adopted as a punitive measure (referred to as *trade sanctions*) against a country, normally in response to a political situation. Examples are the trade sanctions that several countries imposed against South Africa because of its *apartheid* policy up until 1994, or against Iraq after the 1991 Gulf War.

Trade quotas: This is the policy of restricting the quantity of traded goods and services. It may be used as a means of observing a bilateral or multilateral previous agreement, such as when some countries agree to limit their competitions in certain products in the markets of partners to enable the partners' producers maintain a certain level of the share of their domestic markets. Trade quotas are also used for political reasons.

Trade tariff: This tariff is the most commonly used protectionist measure. It is the tax, import duty, that is imposed on goods imported into the country. Imposition of the tariff would result in increases in the prices of imports, and reduction in their quantities demanded. This effectively gives a competitive edge to domestic producers of similar goods.

Subsidies: This takes the form of grants or tax concessions extended to domestic producers to enable them achieve overall lower unit costs of production, which effectively makes them more competitive relative to foreign producers.

Countervailing duties: A country would place special tariffs on incoming foreign products whose production were subsidized by their home governments. This is designed to protect the importing country's domestic producers from the supposedly "unfair competition" posed by the foreign producers.

There are several other forms of trade barriers known as *nontariff barriers*. These include different forms of import restrictions, product standard and quality regulations, environmental regulations, and health and safety standards.

The application of these protectionist measures goes totally against the free-trade principles expounded in the comparative advantage doctrine. Several arguments have been advanced to support trade protectionist actions. The major ones include the so-called *optimum tariff agreement*, which argues that a country suffering from an unfavourable terms of trade could improve its terms of trade by imposing a tariff in order to restrict the volume of imports.

Another argument for protectionism is the *infant-industry argument*. It advocates for measures to "protect" supposedly newly established (infant) industries which are not able to compete with well-established and mature foreign industries. These infant industries have not reached their maturity stages where they could reap scale economies and compete effectively.[9] There also is the most-used *anti-dumping* argument, advocated as a legitimate means of preventing low-cost producers of inferior quality products from "dumping" these products in the markets of their trading partners.

Overall, today's international economy is far from anything resembling that of the nineteenth century in which most of the present-day DCs operated as developing economies. The LDCs have no chance of achieving much growth through trade, unless attitudes change, especially in the DCs, which is highly unlikely. The recognition of this fact has led to a call for the emergence of a *New International Economic Order*, in which the LDCs would basically be "freed" from the choking effects on their development that the present world order of trade is inflicting on them.[10]

NOTES

1. Mercantilism is the economic doctrine that appeared between the Middle Ages and

the period of the universal dominance of *laissez faire*. It emphasizes the importance of international trade, and pioneered the accounting notion of the balance of payments between a nation and the rest of the world. (For more details on this school of economic thought, see Brue, 1994). However, the mercantilist notion of international trade was based on the idea that a country might have *absolute advantage* (in terms of lower production costs) over another in production of an item, so that this country would export its more competitive products and take advantage of the markets of its trading partner. The Ricardian comparative advantage paradigm (see below), on the other hand, advocates that this country should rather *specialize* in production of the output in which it has greatest comparative advantage, while its partner specializes in the other.

2. See Chapter 6 for concrete examples and experiences of some current developed countries in this regard.

3. The leading figure in classical economics, Adam Smith, in his *Inquiry into the Causes of the Wealth of Nations*, stressed the idea that trade would enable a country to reap full benefits from the advantages of economies of scale. Putting this in modern microeconomic terms, we state that trade enables the country to utilize its productive resources more efficiently, and thus move onto a point on its production possibility frontier. For Ricardo, however, the long-run *stationary state* equilibrium of the economy (see Chapter 4) must still obtain eventually despite trade, although in the short run, international trade would still be an engine of growth.

4. Lewis (1980) offers a candid examination of the trend in the "slowing down of the engine of growth." Reidel (1984) also gives an empirical study of the relationship between trade and economic growth in LDCs.

5. A country's BOP is analogous to an individual's monthly or yearly statement of personal account. The individual can spend more than she earns (a current account deficit) as long as she can either borrow (to create a capital account surplus) or draw from her savings (reserves) to finance the spending deficit.

6. This is because if either the country's imports or exports, or both, have inelastic demand, reduction in their prices (due to devaluation) would not result in any significant changes in the amounts traded, resulting simply in heavy revenue losses (for the country's exports) and heavier expenditures (on imports). Such a situation would only worsen any existing balance of trade deficits.

7. The Bretton Woods Conference of 1944 (in Britain) was organized to find ways to better organize the international monetary system. It established a system of fixed exchange rates for a country as long as such a country was not in "fundamental" BOP disequilibrium. A country in fundamental or chronic BOP disequilibrium should allow its exchange rate to depreciate.

8. A practical example that is very close to the experiences of most LDCs will illuminate this explanation. Suppose two countries A and B have equal purchasing power (their exchange rates are at par) at a point in time, year 1, with zero inflation rate in either country. Assuming that by the end of year 2, an inflation rate of 5 percent arises in country A. According to the PPP model, country A's exchange rate would, over time, depreciate by 5 percent in order for country A to maintain stability in the volume of trade that it transacts with country B.

9. This is considered thoroughly in Chapter 10 under the topic of Import Substitution Industrialization; see that section for analysis of the major flaws of this policy.

10. For more on this, see Poulson (1994, p. 425).

14

Role of Free Trade and Regional Integrationism

The focus of this chapter is on the onset of the so-called free-trade areas and regional trading blocs in the order of world trade among nations. As countries realized their economies' dependence on trade, they also realized that trade brought with it certain dangers that go with opening their economies up to the influence of the rest of the world.

The virtues of free and unrestricted trade were so highly promoted in the world that it found its way into the economic development planning and policymaking of every country that saw itself as a free-market-based economy. Nations based their trade policies on the driving force provided by the *comparative advantage* paradigm, namely, that each country's welfare would be greatest when each country specializes in the production and export of products in which it has comparative advantage over others, while importing from its partners those products whose comparative advantage are lower abroad.

Over the decades, however, countries gradually came to realize that totally uncontrolled international trade had certain problems associated with it, problems such as dumping, unequal factor prices, varieties of product qualities and standards across countries, health and environmental concerns, and the like. Therefore, most countries instituted various forms of trade restrictionist measures, on the one hand, to regulate and correct for these problems, and on the other hand, to protect their domestic economies from foreign competition. At the same time, certain world bodies and international institutions began to be formed to address the problems that are bound to arise with greater world trade. Further, countries began to realize the need to form free-trade alliances with their neighbors so as to take full advantage of their proximities to each other, by forming regional trading blocs (or free-trade areas).

As the developed countries vigorously embarked on trade protectionism, LDCs began to be increasingly frustrated as they realized that such attitudes severely threatened their capabilities of achieving growth and development through trade. The protectionist actions of the DCs simply set the clock back for world trade; it led to poor terms of trade for trading partners (especially LDCs), and resulted in slow growth of industrial specialization and exports for partners.

As a result, countries advocated *economic integration* among regional neighbors. Through integration, countries reduce or abolish all trade barriers among them. This could range from the loosest form of integration (such as a mere preferential trade agreement), to a deeper form (such as a completely free-trade area), or a customs union, a common market, an economic union, and a much complete form of total economic and monetary union.[1]

Due to the frustrating and disappointing experiences that the LDCs encountered in international trade, it was increasingly felt that the LDCs should pursue expansion of trade among themselves as a means of overcoming some of the major denials that they have suffered in trading with the DCs (see Lewis, 1980). This is the so-called South-South trade (see Chapter 2), and it could best be accomplished through increased regional integration among the LDCs. Essentially, this entails groups of LDCs attempting to stimulate development among themselves by extending preferential access to each other's exports, thereby making a major shift away from reliance on the markets of the DCs.

Regional integration in the LDCs has been seriously pursued since the 1960s period, and through it, South-South trade did flourish. However, over time, it was discovered that the extent of intraregional expansion of trade among the LDCs has been limited, and has fallen short of the extent needed to foster rapid economic growth and development among the participants. For various reasons, attempts at regional integration simply faltered. We now turn to examine the prelude to the onset of the various aspects of regional integration, and their historical trends in the world economic order.

THE TIDE AGAINST GLOBAL FREE TRADE

The formation of regional economic blocs is widely regarded as a potential threat to further expansion and development of multilateral and liberalized world trade. This is more so as the global economy increasingly polarizes around regional economic interests built mainly around the European Union (EU), the United States, and Japan (see below).

Regional integrationism is on the rise worldwide, especially among the DCs. It is fueled by the rise of concentrated (narrow) interests of groups who perceive that they would lose out if free trade were allowed to run its course. Such groups include owners and workers of various industries such as textiles, steel mills, automobiles, chemicals, or even agricultural produce. These *pressure groups* lobby their political leaders to enact strict protectionist laws to guard their respective industries against foreign competition.

World Trade Agreements: The GATT

Such were the strengths of the forces against global free trade that world leaders realized that there was need to negotiate and safeguard mutual interests in world trade. The *General Agreement on Tariffs and Trade* (GATT) was established as a negotiating body that monitored and supervised global multilateral trade agreements. As the wave of protectionism raged during the 1930 (which may or may not have played a significant role in the Great Depression), international trade simply collapsed. The post-depression era, therefore, brought increasing efforts in the developed countries to seek for ways to forestall any such trade slumps in the future. Through a series of meetings and conferences arranged to discuss the need to lessen trade restrictionist policies among countries, the GATT evolved.

GATT rules were enacted to govern tariffs and act as supervisory mechanism among the world's trading partners.[2] A very prominent GATT provision is the *most favored nation (MFN)* status that is accorded to a GATT member. MFN grants that every member of GATT automatically receive tariff reductions as long as such reductions have been extended to any member. Also, under the auspices of GATT, various global trade negotiations aimed at promoting more global trade liberalization are frequently pursued. One such attempt is referred to as the Uruguay Round of trade agreements, in which various countries sought to reach agreement toward simultaneous tariff reductions and lowering other forms of trade barriers.

From its inception, GATT has generally resulted in significant tariff reductions through multilateral agreements. It is agreed that the level of tariffs facing member countries of GATT are much lower today than they have ever been. For LDCs, joining GATT has enabled them to participate in its various multilateral negotiations, thereby giving them the opportunity to present their multifarious cases to the DCs. It seems that GATT has generally been in the interest of the LDCs by enabling them to suffer lesser trade barriers than they would have suffered without such a multilateral agreement.

Nonetheless, much of the benefits of GATT's provisions, such as the MFN, have accrued solely to the DCs, for many of its provisions are designed to be more favorable to the DCs than the LDCs. For example, tariff reductions on goods exported by the DCs - industrial manufactured goods - far outweigh tariff reductions on goods exported by the LDCs, that is, primary products.

Although there exists a GATT principle of preferential treatment of the exports of LDCs, known as the *generalized system of preferences* (GSP), which provides for reduced tariffs on *selected* manufactured goods exported by the LDCs, the countries have not really benefited much from it. This is because many key industrial manufactured products exported from LDCs are exempted from benefits of the GSP: textiles and apparel, processed raw materials, and a wide range of industrial and labor-intensive products. It appears that the range of goods favored by the GSP are those that are exported by the Asian NICs; it is generally true that the benefits provided by this situation played a significant role in the relative successes of these Asian NICs.

The increasing emergence of trading blocs is rapidly changing the world international economic order. These blocs are apt to usurp the global multilateral trading arrangements (governed within the GATT) which have always guided global trade and the world economy since the immediate post-World War II period. These changes will certainly affect the LDCs, positively or negatively. For those among them who are able to enter into the formation of these trading blocs with some developed countries with large markets, the outcome might be beneficial, whereas for others who currently receive some favored treatment from some DCs, the outcome seems bleak.

Forms of Regional Integration

Several forms of trade agreements among nations exist. While some involve very mild trading arrangements, others extend to wider economic and even political cooperation. The various forms are as follows.

1. *Preferential Trade Agreement* (PTA) is an arrangement among countries, whereby members adopt reduced tariff rates and extend preferential treatments to the imports of each other. This seems to be the loosest form of integration.

2. *Free-Trade Area* (FTA) is the form of agreement that removes trade protectionist barriers among the member countries, while allowing each country to retain these barriers against nonmembers.

3. *Customs Union*: In addition to all the provisions of the FTA, the Customs Union stipulates that member countries retain common trade barriers against nonmembers.

4. A *Common Market* provides for a much more involved form of integration. In addition to the provisions of the Customs Union, a Common Market involves the free movement of productive resources (such as capital and labor) between each other's economies.

5. The *Economic Union* is a much more complete and extensive form of economic integration: it provides for all the above conditions, but goes further in integrating the monetary systems of member countries. The Economic Union, basically, unites member countries toward the formation of a political union.[3]

One of the most effective and modern regional integrations is the European Union (EU). It began in 1957 as the European Economic Community (EEC), a Customs Union. It then converted to a Common Market in 1970, and now is becoming a complete Economic and Monetary Union. Among the LDCs, Latin America entered a Free Trade Association in 1960, while the Caribbean countries formed their Free Trade Area (CARIFTA) in 1968. In Africa, the East African Community (EAC) was formed in 1967, while the Economic Community of West African States (ECOWAS) was formed in 1975. A Preferential Trade Area (PTA) agreement was reached in 1984 among some Eastern and Southern African countries.

In Asia, the Association of South East Asian Nations (ASEAN) was formed since 1967. Generally, despite the widely recognized common interest in it, the history of regional economic integration among the LDCs is marked by failure. Since the 1950s, a number of regional agreements have been concluded. Many of these achieved successes initially, but have now either disintegrated or become paralyzed, for reasons ranging from internal squabbles and hostilities (for example, the Central American Common Market), to lack of sufficient drive needed to sustain the agreement (for example, the East African Community), or outright internal opposition among member states (for example, ECOWAS).

As a result of these experiences, regional integration has neither helped to promote rapid growth in intraregional trade nor led to rapid economic growth and development in the LDCs in the ways expected.[4] Currently, the DCs have renewed their interests in regional integration, and many have pursued it vigorously and concluded major agreements. A major example is the North American Free Trade Agreement (NAFTA) between the two developed economies of North America (U.S. and Canada) and their developing neighbor, Mexico.

The renewed efforts at regional integration among the DCs since the 1980s is not unconnected to the relative successes of the NICs of Asia and Latin America, as well as the Japanese export dynamism, especially as these deeply penetrate and threaten to overwhelm the markets of the DCs. This happens as the DCs increasingly encounter the decline of their aging industries whose productivities now face aggressive competition in world markets.[5]

NOTES

1. See Nafziger (1990).

2. Many countries, especially the DCs, tend to disregard the GATT rules and simply carry out any trade practises that they presume will suit their economic interests and circumstances at any time. For a good account of this and other GATT operations, see Gillis *et al.* (1992, pp. 473-480).

3. The United States of America is an example of a political union that formed out of the formation of a strong Economic Union. The 1789 Constitution of the U.S. provided for a *complete economic and monetary union* among the initial 13 states that formed it (see Nafziger, 1990).

4. The main reasons why regional integration failed to be effective and beneficial among many LDCs have been discussed in some recent studies such as Asante (1986). Shiells (1995) discusses the rapid proliferation of regional trade blocs, with implications for why very little of the trade among LDCs are intraregional despite the efforts to integrate.

5. Traditional European- and North American-dominated industries such as textiles, footwear, steel, automobiles, and chemicals now face increasing competition from cheaper, high-quality products of Asia and Latin America, whose lower wages allow their products to be more competitive.

15

International Finance and Economic Development

This chapter examines the role of international finance and monetary issues in economic development, including the acquisition and accumulation of financial resources, and the international debt crisis. Countries ordinarily acquire financial resources through sales of exported goods and services, or through transfers from others sources in the form of loans, grants, credits, or other forms of diverse payments. International debt is incurred through borrowing, as countries obtain credits from lenders in order to finance (balance-of-payments) deficits that they occur over the course of their development programs.

In the course of economic development of every country, international financial flows occupy a central position. As a country engages in international trade and trades its exports in the international market, it receives foreign exchange payments which it may then either spend immediately to acquire additional resources (capital, raw materials, or finished consumer goods), or save as foreign exchange reserves for future use. At any given time period, a country that spends more than it earns in terms of foreign exchange will have to finance such a deficit by borrowing from foreign sources or generating more goods and services in exports. Where this recourse becomes impossible, the country ends up taking foreign loans, thereby entering into foreign debt.

The nature of international capital flows and its role in economic development changed drastically during the twentieth century. As Nurkse (1953) stated, quite unlike the preceding period of the nineteenth century, the twentieth century witnessed a situation in which international capital flows did not contribute to economic growth in the LDCs. This represents a radical departure from the situation that neoclassical thinkers had presumed - namely, an international economic order in which openness and free trade characterized world trade, allowing capital to flow freely into areas of highest yield. Indeed, the evidence appears to generally support the structuralist view that capital flows have rather been vehicles for exploitation of the (periphery) LDCs by the (core) industrialized developed countries.

The controversy over whether international financial flows constitute a boost or a hindrance to economic growth for present-day LDCs has raged on even more vigorously with the onset of the international debt crisis in the early 1980s. Many LDCs have suffered major economic setbacks and have continued to do so. Many have been compelled to adopt what has been termed as "structural adjustment programs" designed to balance the government budgets, cut public spending, and introduce some wide-ranging free market and deregulatory reforms that largely limit the size of government involvement in the economy, and apparently save money to service debt. In most cases this has resulted in a series of negative economic consequences such as high unemployment, declining wages, massive spending cuts, and subsidy removals from social services and economic infrastructure. The situation has brought serious social and economic instability to the LDCs, while not really leading to any perceptible economic gains other than to ensure that money constantly flows to the DCs to service debt.

NATURE OF INTERNATIONAL FINANCIAL MOVEMENTS

International capital flows could be in the form of *private capital* or *official government capital*. Government capital comes in the forms of foreign government lending or payments, and loans from international financial institutions, or financial aid and assistance (*bilateral loans and grants*) from foreign governments and other agencies. Private capital is in several different forms, such as direct capital investment made by private foreign investors, stocks and bonds purchases by foreign investors, cash loans or export credits from foreign financial institutions, and grants and other forms of aid from private sources.[1]

The two main international financial institutions are the World Bank and the International Monetary Fund (IMF), both located in the United States. These bodies extend finances solely through official capital flows in form of multilateral loans and grants. When these institutions or foreign governments extend official financial flows to a country on *concessional terms*, it implies that such finances are either gifts, grants, or loans with liberal terms (*soft loans*), as compared to those available in the private international capital markets. Loans that are granted in this category for the express purpose of promoting the recipient's economic development program are ordinarily termed *foreign aid*, or technically referred to as *official development assistance*. This contrasts with loans extended on terms similar to those that obtain in the private international capital markets on *nonconcessional* (or commercial) terms.

Following the precedent set by the nineteenth-century and early twentieth-century experiences of the "European offshoots," namely, the United States, Canada, Australia, and New Zealand, which relied heavily on foreign capital for their economic growth and development efforts, many LDCs contracted significant private capital flows that grew very rapidly after the post-World War II period. Those of Latin America especially (Brazil, Argentina, Mexico) as well as India, received heavy capital flows. The trend of heavy indebtedness in LDCs continued into the 1980s, with the main creditors being the international financial institutions, the United States, Britain, France, and Germany.

THE DEBT CRISES

The debt crisis was a global phenomenon involving both the DCs and LDCs. To the DCs, it qualified the risks of loss to which their banks and lenders were exposed if the LDCs failed to repay their debts. To the LDCs, however, the debt crisis had much more serious ramifications. It implied the range of economic, social, and political consequences of being caught not only in a situation of heavy indebtedness, but also of honoring the debt-servicing commitments of constantly generating substantial amounts of resources to make foreign payments. The debt crisis that arose during the early 1980s was precipitated by the nature of indebtedness itself: the interest compounding and continuous need for servicing could only be sustained through further indebtedness.

Most LDCs have incurred huge foreign debts.[2] Many of these were incurred helplessly in the desperate attempt to raise sufficient investment resources for economic development. Usually, the debts were incurred after the country's accumulated foreign exchange reserves were depleted. Most started as short- and medium-term trade debts that would soon pile up. Others were procured as long-term debts. The creditors are usually private financial institutions and the international financial institutions such as the World Bank and the IMF, all based in the developed countries.

Typically, an LDC would seek a quick way and means to achieve economic growth and expansion. This often led to its contracting of all kinds of commercial loans and supplier credits from Western creditors. Such credits were quite easy to obtain because most LDCs used to have good credit ratings due to their promising stable revenue sources from primary-product exports. However, as they received these funds, in most cases a significant proportion of them were spent on capital-intensive public projects and military hardware. Large parts were also used to finance recurrent government budget deficits, while others were used to finance the consumption of foreign conspicuous consumer good imports; others were placed in the foreign personal bank accounts of corrupt political leaders, government ministers, and other officials.

The results of the huge accumulation of external debt for most LDCs have ranged from severe economic destabilization in some (such as those of Sub-Saharan Africa and Latin America) to mild initial economic setbacks and later economic progress in others (such as some of the Newly Industrializing Countries (NICs) of Asia and Latin America: South Korea, Mexico, and Argentina).

Since the effects of indebtedness on a country are determined by the uses to which the incurred debt resources had been put, foreign indebtedness has had different results in the development profiles of different LDCs, depending, of course, on how the borrowed funds had been used. Ostensibly, most LDCs entered into debt with an intention of eventually paying it off, within the premise that the borrowed resources would be invested in viable productive projects: investments that would augment overall productive capacity, creating jobs, raising incomes and economic growth, and ultimately generating potential for higher revenue required for the servicing and amortization of the debt.

Thus, while high debt-servicing ratios have been consistent with rapid economic expansion and development in some LDCs, they have been very devastating for others. For example, in some of the NICs (Malaysia and South Korea, for instance), debt servicing in 1986 were between 9 and 13 percent, while between 1980 and 1986, total output in these countries grew at annual averages of between 4 and 9 percent. Therefore, heavy indebtedness need not be particularly inimical to the development effort, although it has almost always been so for many other LDCs in Africa and Latin America. For these, it has meant that they are currently compelled to allocate close to 30 percent, on the average, of their individual total foreign exchange earnings for servicing external debt. Thus, the very resources needed for economic development are diverted to debt servicing. Underdevelopment is therefore perpetuated in these countries.

The Burden of Debt on Economic Development

Indebted LDCs tend to enter into various arrangements that enable them to service (manage) their debts while basically maintaining some level of economic life. During the 1980s, most of these countries negotiated their debt obligations through multilateral arrangements with their creditor groups.[3] Such arrangements enabled them to reduce their servicing burdens and to lengthen their repayment terms (this implies that their debts are *rescheduled*). However, its effects have still been detrimental to economic growth.

Debt and Structural Adjustment Programs

As the international institutions that often act to help reschedule the debt of the LDCs, the World Bank and the IMF often imposes certain economic conditions to which the debtor country must submit if it is to receive the rescheduling assistance. The assistance would normally be for the World Bank/IMF to extend credit (through official capital flows) to the LDC over a given duration, say, three years, and reschedule the country's debt, with interest and principal rolled over onto the new debt.

For most LDCs, the conditionalities that the World Bank/IMF attaches to this offer is that the country implements a Structural Adjustment Program (SAP): a series of wide-ranging economic reform packages. These typically range from monetary and fiscal restraints to currency devaluation and trade liberalization. Generally, the SAP would require the debtor LDC to reduce or eliminate its budget deficits (mainly through drastic and massive spending cuts on social services), limit credit creation, dismantle price controls and allow for more market-oriented price determination, massively reduce the size of the public sector through privatizations, and reduce public-sector wage rates.

These SAP measures would often bring overwhelming economic hardships to the country's citizens, which in turn give rise to economic and social instability; all the while there are no guarantees that the program would succeed in bringing about growth and development, let alone repaying the debt.[4]

As already indicated, a huge international debt hanging over a country need not necessarily be inimical to the country's development. The Asian NICs have been able to use their borrowed funds to generate sufficient economic progress in such a way that export growth could provide the means to effectively meet their debt obligations. In this way, these countries receive high and reputable international credit ratings among their creditors.

For other LDCs, however, especially those of Sub-Saharan Africa and South Asia, the borrowed resources were irresponsibly squandered, mostly through corrupt dealings and transactions. As a result, these countries have continued to reel under the pressure of the debt burden. They have very poor credit ratings internationally due to their track records of economic mismanagement coupled with poor economic performance.

Clearly, an indebted LDC can still perform reasonably well if it has the determination to do so. Even with the adoption of structural adjustment programs, a country with effective and dedicated political leadership can achieve economic success. The NICs are good examples. The main factors that are perpetuating underdevelopment in most LDCs are not necessarily debt-related. They are *human factor* problems (see Chapters 3 and 8), and the LDCs simply have to address these if they are to achieve economic growth and development.

NOTES

1. The degree to which a country could benefit from international capital inflows depends on its *absorptive capacity* for foreign resources (see Chapter 5). The limited levels of absorptive capacity of some LDCs may have hindered the usefulness of international finance for them, resulting in such finances being lavished on noneconomic ventures.

2. The major debtor nations of the world are evenly spread across the underdeveloped continents (the Southern economic hemisphere). These are, in Latin America: Mexico, Brazil, Argentina, Venezuela, Peru, Colombia, Chile, and Nicaragua; in Asia: South Korea, Indonesia, Philippines, India, Pakistan, Malaysia, Taiwan, and Thailand; in Africa: Nigeria, Egypt, Zambia, Zaire, Algeria, Congo, Madagascar, Morocco, and Ivory Coast.

3. These creditor groups include such groups as the *London Club*, the *Paris Club*,

private commercial banks, or official (government) creditors, all in the DCs.

4. This is the finding of Loxley (1986b) in the case of African LDCs. He found little evidence that IMF programs led to growth and balance-of-payments equilibrium, although different countries were able to achieve different isolated inflation, growth, and trade objectives. See also, Loxley (1986a, 1994).

Selected Bibliography

Adedeji, A. 1989a. *Toward a Dynamic African Economy: Selected Speeches and Lectures 1975-1986.* in J. C. Senghor (ed.). London: Frank-Cass.

Adedeji, A. 1989b. *African Alternative Framework to Structural Adjustment Programmes for Socio-Economic Recovery and Transformation.* New York: UN Economic Commission for Africa.

Adjibolosoo, S. 1994a. "The Human Factor and the Failure of Economic Development and Policies in Africa." In F. Ezeala-Harrison and S. Adjibolosoo (eds.), *Perspectives on Economic Develpment in Africa.* Westport, Conn.: Praeger.

Adjibolosoo, S. 1994b. "Corruption and Economic Development in Africa: A Comparative Analysis." In F. Ezeala-Harrison and S. Adjibolosoo (eds.), *Perspectives on Economic Develpment in Africa.* Westport, Conn.: Praeger.

Amin, S. 1973. *Neo-Colonialism in West Africa.* New York: Monthly Review Press.

Amin, S. 1981. "Underdevelopment and Dependence in Black Africa - Origins and Contemporary Forms," In D. L. Cohen and J. Daniel (eds.), *Political Economy of Africa.* London: Longman.

Arrighi, G. 1973. "International Corporations, Labour Aristocracies and Economic Development in Tropical Africa." In G. Arrighi and J. S. Saul (eds.), *Essays on the Political Economy of Africa,* New York: Monthly Review Press.

Austen, R. 1987. *African Economic History: Internal Development and External Dependence.* London: Heinemann.

Assante, S. K. B. 1986. *The Political Economy of Regionalism in Africa: A Decade of ECOWAS.* New York: Praeger.

Baffoe-Bonnie, J. and Ezeala-Harrison, F. 1996. "Wage Determination in Agricultural Labour Markets Under Monopsonist Labour Tying Arrangements." *Applied Economics,* 28 (3): 163-173.

Balassa, B. 1976. "The Impact of Industrial Countries' Tariff Structure on their Imports of Manufactures from LDCs." *Economica,* 34: 372-383.

Baldwin, G. B. 1970. "Brain Drain or Overflow." *Foreign Affairs,* 48: 358-372.

Balogh, T. 1962. "Misconceived Educational Programmes in Africa." *Universities Quarterly:* 243-249.

Bardhan, P. K., and Rudra, A. 1981. "Terms and Conditions of Labour Contracts in Agriculture: Results of a Survey in West Bengal 1979." *Oxford Bulletin of Economics and Statistics,* 43 (1): 89-111.

Barnum, H. N. and R. H. Sabot. 1975. "Migration, Education and Urban Surplus Labor in Tanzania." *OECD Development Center Employment Series* (Monograph), October.

Basu, K. 1984. *The Less Developed Economy: A Critique of Contemporary Theory.* New York: Basil Blackwell Inc.

Basu, K. 1980. "Optimal Policies in Dual Economies." *Quarterly Journal of Economics*, 95.

Bauer, P. T. 1982. "Foreign Aid: What is at Stake?" *Public Interest* (Summer). Cited in Todaro (1994, p. 554).

Bauer, P. T. 1985. "Foreign Aid: Rewarding Impoverishment?" *Swiss Review of World Affairs* (October). Cited in Todaro (1994, p. 554).

Behrman, J. 1987. "Commodity Price Instability and Economic Goal Attainment in Developing Countries." *World Development*, 15 (5): 559-573.

Bhagwati, J. N. 1973. "Education, Class structure, and Income Equality." *World Development*, 1.

Bhagwati, J. N. (ed.). 1977. *The New International Economic Order: The North-South Debate.* Cambridge: Cambridge Press.

Bhagwati, J. N. 1985. "Trade in Services and the Multilateral Trade Negotiations." *The World Bank Economic Review*, 1 (4): 549-569.

Bhagwati, J. N. 1987. "GATT and Trade-In Services: How Can we Resolve the North-South Debate." *Financial Times*, (November 27).

Binswanger, H. P. and Rosenzweig, M. R. (eds.). 1984. *Contractual Arrangements, Employment and Wages in Rural Labor Markets in Asia.* New Haven: Yale University Press.

Blaug, M. *et al.* 1967. *Causes of Graduate Unemployment in India.* Harmondsworth, England: Penguin.

Blaug, M. 1973. *Education and the Employment Problem in Developing Countries.* Geneva: ILO.

Bliss, C. 1989. "Trade and Development." In H. Chenery and T. N. Srinivasan (eds.), *Handbook of Development Economics, Volume 2.* Amsterdam: North Holland, Elsevier Science Publishers.

Blomqvist, A. G. 1978. "Urban job Creation and Urban Unemployment in LDCs: Todaro vrs. Harris-Todaro." *Journal of Development Economics*, 5: 3-18.

Boltho, A. 1988. "Is there a Future for Resource Transfers to the LDCs?" *World Development*, 16 (10): 1159-1166.

Brue, S. L. 1994. *The Evolution of Economic Thought*, 5th ed., New York: Dryden Press, Chapter 21.

Bruton, H. 1970. "The Import Substitution Industrialization Strategy for Economic Developmet: A Survey." *Pakistan Development Review*, 10 (2): 123-146.

Bruton, H. 1989. "Import Substitution.", In H. Chenery and T. N. Srinivasan (eds.), *Handbook of Development Economics, Volume 2*, Amsterdam: North Holland, Elsevier Science Publishers.

Cassen, R. H. *et al.* 1986. *Does Aid Work?* New York: Oxford University Press.

Chakravarty, S. 1966. *Capital and Development Planning.* Cambridge, Mass.: MIT Press.

Chakravarty, S., and Eckaus, R. S. 1964. "An Approach to Multi-Sectoral Model." In P.N. Rosenstein-Rodan, ed. *Capital Formation and Economic Development.* Cambridge, Mass.: MIT Press.

Chakravarty, S., and Lefeber, L. 1965. "An Optimizing Planning Model." *Economic Weekly*, 12 (2).

Chenery, H. B. 1960. "Patterns of Industrial Growth." *American Economic Review* (September): 639-641.

Chenery, H. B., and N. G. Carter. 1973. "Foreign Assistance and Development Performance." *American Economic Review*, 63: 459-468.

Chichilnisky, G. 1981. "Terms of Trade and Domestic Distribution: Export-led Growth with Abundant Labour." *Journal of Development Economics*, 8 (2).

Cline, W. R. 1975. "Distribution and Development: A Survey Literature." *Journal of Development Economics*, 1: 359-400.

Cline, W. R. 1982. "Can the Asian Experience be Generalized." *World Development*, 10: 81-90.

Colclough, C. 1982. "The Impact of Primary Schooling on Economic Development: A Review of the Evidence.", *World Development*, 10.

Coombs, P. H., and M. Ahmed. 1974. *Attacking Rural Poverty: How Nonformal Education Can Help.* Baltimore, Md.: Johns Hopkins University Press.

Corden, W. M., and Neary, S. P. 1982. "Booming Sector and Deindustrialization in a Small Open Economy." *Economic Journal*, 92: 825-848.

Cuddington, J. T., and Urzua, C. M. 1989. "Trends and Cycles and the Net Barter Terms of Trade: A New Approach.", *Economic Journal*, 99 (396): 426-442.

Darity, W. Jr. 1982. "Mercantilism, Slavery and the Industrial Revolution." *Research in Political Economy*, 5: 1-21.

Darity, W. Jr. 1990. "British Industry and the West Indies Plantations." *Social Science History*, 14: 117-149.

Darity, W. Jr. 1992. "A Model of 'Original Sin': Rise of the West and Lag of the Rest." *American Economic Review Papers and Proceedings*, 82 (2): 162-167.

Dasgupta, A. K. 1974. *Economic Theory and Developing Countries.* London: Macmillan.

Davidson, B. 1964. *The African Past: Chronicles from Antiquity to Modern Times.* Boston: Atlantic Monthly Press Books.

Davidson, B. 1972. *Africa: History of a Continent.* New York: Macmillan.

DeLancey, V. 1992. "The Economies of Africa." In A. A. Gordon and D. L. Gordon (eds.), *Understanding Contemporary Africa*, Boulder and London: Lynne Rienner Publishers.

Dore, R. 1976. *The Diploma Disease, Education, Qualification and Development.* Berkeley: University of California Press.

Dreze, J. and Mukherjee, A. 1987. "Labour Contracts in Rural Asia: Theories and Evidence." *Development Research*, London School of Economics.

Dreze, J., and Sen, A. 1990. *Hunger and Public Action.* Oxford: Oxford University Press.

Dutt, A. K. 1992. "The Origin of Uneven Development: The Indian Subcontinent." *American Economic Review Papers and Proceedings*, 82 (2): 146-150.

Eckaus, R. S., and Bhagwati, J. 1972. *Development and Planning: Essays in Honour of Paul Rosenstein-Rodan.* London: Allen and Irwin.

Eckaus, R. S., and Parikh, K. S. 1968. *Planning for Growth: Multi-Sectoral, Intertemporal Models Applied to India.* Cambridge, Mass.: MIT Press.

Edwards, E. O., and Todaro, M. P. 1973. "Education Demand and Supply in the Context of Growing Unemployment in LDCs." *World Development*, March/April.

Ellsworth, P. T. 1961. "The Terms of Trade Between Primary-Producing and Industrial Countries." *Inter-American Economic Affairs*, 10 (1). Reprinted in I. Livingstone (ed.), 1981.

Essang, S. M. 1971. "The Impact of the Marketing Board on the Distribution of Cocoa Earnings in Western Nigeria." *Seminal Paper*, (NISER/University of Ibadan).

Eswaran, M., and Kotwal, A. 1985. "A Theory of Two-Tier Labour Markets in Agrarian Economies.", *American Economic Review*, 75, (March): 162-177.

Ezeala-Harrison, F. 1988a. "An Application of the Efficiency Wage Hypothesis to Modelling LDC Labour Problems." *Journal of Economic Development*, 13 (1): 71-94.

Ezeala-Harrison, F. 1988b. "A Stability Analysis of the Harris-Todaro Model of Rural-Urban Migration and Urban Unemployment in LDCs." *Nigerian Journal of Economic and Social Studies*, 30 (3): 299-311.

Ezeala-Harrison, F. 1992a. "Efficiency Wages in Agriculture: Analysis of Monopsony Wage and Employment with Effort-Augmented Production Functions for LDCs." *Journal of Economic Development*, 17 (2): 159-180.

Ezeala-Harrison, F. 1992b. "An Empirical Framework for the Efficiency Wage Model: Use of Micro Data." *Journal of Economic Studies*, 19 (3): 18-35.

Ezeala-Harrison, F. 1993a. "Structural Re-Adjustment in Nigeria: Diagnosis of a Severe Dutch Disease Syndrome." *American Journal of Economics and Sociology*, 52 (2): 193-208.

Ezeala-Harrison, F. 1993b. "Varied Technology and Agricultural Productivity in Developing Countries." *Productivity and Quality Management Frontiers*, 4 (2): 834-843.

Ezeala-Harrison, F. 1994a. "What Ails African Economies: Lessons from Over-Stretched Underdevelopment." In F. Ezeala-Harrison and S. Adjibolosoo (eds.), *Perspectives on Economic Development in Africa*, Westport, Conn.: Praeger.

Ezeala-Harrison, F. 1994b. "African Subsistence Labour Allocation: A Model with Implications for Rural Development and Urban Unemployment." In F. Ezeala-Harrison and S. Adjibolosoo (eds.), *Perspectives on Economic Development in Africa*, Westport, Conn.: Praeger.

Ezeala-Harrison, F. 1995a. "Over-Stretched Economic Underdevelopment in Sub-Saharan Africa." *Briefing Notes in Economics*, 14 (January).

Ezeala-Harrison, F. 1995b. "Africa's Diploma Disease: Diagnosis of the Nonsequential Agenda of Education." Paper presented at the Conference of the *Canadian Association for the Study of International Development*, Montreal, (June).

Ezeala-Harrison, F. 1995c. "Analysis of Optimal Recycling Policy in a Market Economy." *The Natural Resources Forum*, 19 (1): 31-38.

Ezeala-Harrison, F. 1995d. "Human Factor Issues in the History of Economic Underdevelopment." *Review of Human Factor Studies*, 1 (1): 1-25.

Ezeala-Harrison, F., and Adjibolosoo, S. (eds.), *Perspectives on Economic Development in Africa*, Westport, Conn.: Praeger.

Ezeala-Harrison, F., and Baffoe-Bonnie, J. 1994. "Theoretical and Empirical Issues in National Income and Consumption Planning in LDCs." *Journal of Economic Development*, 19 (2): 117-137.

Field, B. C., and Olewiler, N. D. 1994. *Environmental Economics* (1st Canadian Edition). Toronto: McGraw-Hill Ryerson.

Fieldhouse, D. K. 1986. *Black Africa: Decolonization and Arrested Development 1948-1980*. London: Allen & Unwin.

Fields, G. S. 1980. *Poverty, Inequality, and Development*. Cambridge: Cambridge University Press.

Flanders, M. J. 1964. "Prebisch on Protectionism: An Evaluation." *Economic Journal*, 74.

Fleming, M. 1955. "External Economies and the Doctrine of Balanced Growth." *Economic Journal*, 65: 241-256.

Frank, A. G. 1967. *Capitalism and Underdevelopment in Latin America*. New York: Monthly Review Press.

Frank, A. G. 1969. *Latin America: Underdevelopment or Revolution?* New York: Monthly Review Press.

Frank, A. G. 1992. "The Development of Underdevelopment, (1966). Reprinted in Wilber, C. K., and Jameson, K. P. *The Political Economy of Development and Underdevelopment*. New York: McGraw-Hill.

Gelb, A. (ed.). 1988. *Oil Windfalls: Blessing or Curse?* New York: Oxford University Press (for World Bank).

Ghai, D. 1987. "Success and Failures in Growth in Sub-Saharan Africa." Geneva: *ILO Working paper*.

Gillis, M., Perkins, D. H., Roemer, M., and Snodgrass, D. R. 1992. *Economics of Development*. New York: W. W. Norton.

Glaser, W. 1978. *The Brain Drain*. London: Allen and Unwin.

Glassburner, B. 1988. "Indonesia: Windfalls in a Poor Rural Economy." In A. Gelb (ed.): *Oil Windfalls: Blessing or Curse?* New York: Oxford University Press (for World Bank).

Godfrey, M. 1979. "Rural-Urban Migration in a Lewis-Model Context." *The Manchester School*, 47.

Grabowski, R., and Shields, M. P. 1996. *Development Economics*. Cambridge, Mass.: Blackwell Publishers, Chap. 4.

Green, R. H. 1967. "Four African Development Plans: Ghana, Kenya, Nigeria and Tanzania)." *Readings in Applied Economics of Africa*, 2: 21-32.

Griffin, K. R. 1970. "Foreign Capital, Domestic Savings, and Economic Development." *Oxford Bulletin of Economics and Statistics*, 32.

Griffin, K. R., and J. L. Enos. 1970. "Foreign Assistance: Objectives and Consequences." *Economic Development and Cultural Change*, (April): 313-327.

Grubel, H. B., and A. D. Scott. 1966. "The International Flow of Human Capital." *American Economic Review*, 56: 268-274.

Gulhati, R. 1987. *Recent Economic Progress in Africa: A Preliminary Political Economy Perspective*. Washington, D.C.: Economic Development Institute, World Bank.

Gulhati, R., and Nallari, R. 1988. "Reform of Foreign Aid Policies: The Issue of Inter-Country Allocation in Africa." *World Development*, 16 (10): 1167-1184.

Haddad, W. *et al.* 1990. "Education and Development: Evidence for New Priorities." *World Bank Discussion Paper No. 95* (Washington, D.C.).

Hagen, E. E. 1980. *The Economics of Development*. Homeword Ill.: Irwin.

Hamada, K. 1977. "Taxing the Brain Drain: A Global Point of View." In J. Bhagwati (ed.), *The New International Economic Order: The North-South Debate*. Cambridge: Cambridge Press.

Hall, P. 1983. *Growth and Development: An Economic Analysis*. Oxford: M. Robertson Press.

Harris J. R., and Todaro, M. P. 1970. "Migration, Unemployment and Development: A Two-Sector Analysis." *American Economic Review*, 60 (March).

Higgins, B. 1968. *Economic Development: Problems, Principles, and Policies.* New York: W. W. Norton.

Higgins, B., and Higgins, J. D. 1979. *Economic Development of a Small Planet.* New York: W. W. Norton.

Hirschman, A. O. 1958. *The Strategy of Economic development.* New Haven, Conn.: Yale University Press.

Hirschman, A. O. (ed.) 1961. *Latin American Issues: Essays and Comments.* New York: Twentieth Century Fund.

Hirschman, A. O. 1961. "Ideologies of Economic Development in Latin America." In A. O. Hirschman (ed.), *Latin American Issues: Essays and Comments.* New York: Twentieth Century Fund.

Hirschman, A. O. 1971. *A Bias for Hope: Essays on Development in Latin America*, New Haven, Conn.: Yale University Press.

Hirschman, A. O. 1987. "The Political Economy of Latin American Development: Seven Exercises in Retrospection." *Latin American Research Review*, 22 (3).

Hodd, M. 1992. *The Economies of Africa*, London: G. K. Hall and Company.

Hogendorn, J. 1992. *Economic Development* (second edition). New York: Harper Collins.

Hotelling, H. 1931. "Economics of Exhaustible Resources.", *Journal of Political Economy*, 39: 137-175.

House, W. J., and Rempel, H. 1978. "Labour Market Segmentation in Kenya." *Eastern Africa Economic Review*, 8: 35-54.

House, W. J., and Rempel, H. 1980. "The Determinants of Interregional Migration in Kenya." *World Development*, 8: 25-36.

Illich, I. 1970. *Deschooling Society*, New York: Harper and Row.

IMF. 1987-1994. *International Financial Statistics* (Various Issues and Supplements on Trade Statistics). Washington, D.C.

Inikori, J. E. 1977. "The Import of Firearms into West Africa 1750-1807: A Quantitative Analysis." *Journal of African History*, 18 (3): 339-368.

Inikori, J. E. 1989. "Slavery and the Revolution of Cotton Textile Production in England." *Social Science History*, 13: 343-379.

Inikori, J. E. 1992. "Slavery and Atlantic Commerce, 1650-1800." *American Economic Review Papers and Proceedings*, 82 (2): 151-161.

Islam, R. 1980. "Graduate unemployment in Bangladesh: A Preliminary Analysis." *Bangladesh Development Studies*: 47-74.

Johnson, H. G. 1967. "Analysis of Prebisch's Views on the Terms of Trade." In H. G. Johnson (ed.), *Economic Policies Towards Less Developed Countries.* London: Allen and Unwin.

Johnston, B. F., and Mellor, J. W. 1961. "The Role of Agriculture in Economic Development." *American Economic Review*, September: 571-581.

Jones, C., and Kiguel, M. A. 1994. "Africa's Quest for Prosperity: Has Adjustment Helped?" *Finance and Development*, 31 (2): 2-5.

Jorgenson, D. W. 1961. "The Development of a Dual Economy." *Economic Journal*, June: 309-334.

Jorgenson, D. W. 1967. "Surplus Agricultural Labour and the Development of a Dual Economy." *Oxford Economic Papers*, (November): 288-312.

Kamarck, A. 1971. *The Economics of African Development*. New York: Praeger.

Kamarck, A. 1976. *The Tropics and Economic Development: A Provocative Inquiry into The Poverty of Nations*. Baltimore: Johns Hopkins University Press.

Kay, C. 1989. *Latin American Theories of Development and Underdevelopment*, London: Routledge.

Kea, R. A. 1971. "Firearms and Warfare on the Gold and Slave Coasts from the Sixteenth to the Nineteenth Centuries." *Journal of African History*, 12 (2): 185-213.

Kenderick, D., and Taylor, L. 1970. *Numerical Methods and Non-Linear Optimization Models for Economic Planning*. New York: Prentice-Hall: 220-244.

Killick, T. 1976. "The Possibilities of Development Planning." *Oxford Economic Papers*, (July).

Killick, T. 1991. *The Developmental Effectiveness of Aid to Africa*. Washington, D.C.: World Bank Working Paper No. 646.

Kuznets, S. 1963. "Notes on the Take-Off." In W. W. Rostow (ed.), *The Economics of Take-Off into Sustained Growth*. Proceedings of Conference of International Economic Association (London and New York).

Kuznets, S. 1965. *Economic Growth and Structure*. New York: Oxford University Press.

Leeson, P. F. 1979. "The Lewis Model and Development Theory." *The Manchester School*, 47.

Lefeber, L. 1968. "Planning in a Surplus Labor economy." *American Economic Review*, (June): 345-349.

Lewis, S. R. Jr. 1989. "Primary Exporting Countries." In H. Chenery and T. N. Srinivasan (eds.), *Handbook of Development Economics, Volume 2*. Amsterdam: North Holland, Elsevier Science Publishers.

Lewis, W. A. 1954. "Economic Development with Unlimited Supplies of Labour." *The Manchester School Journal of Economic and Social Studies*, 22 (2): 139-192.

Lewis, W. A. 1955. *The Theory of Economic Growth*. London: Allen and Unwin.

Lewis, W. A. 1966. *Development Planning*. New York: Harper & Row.

Lewis, W. A. 1967. *Reflections on Nigerian Economic Growth*. Paris: OECD Publication.

Lewis, W. A. 1972. "Education and Economic Development." *International Social Science Journal*, 14 (4): 685-699.

Lewis, W. A. 1979. "The Dual Economy Revisited." *The Manchester School Journal of Economic and Social Studies*, 47: 211-229.

Lewis, W. A. 1980. "The Slowing Down of the Engine of Growth." *American Economic Review*, 70 (4): 555-564.

Lewis, W. A. 1984. "The State of Development Theory." *American Economic Review*, 74 (1).

Livingstone, I. (ed.). 1981. *Development Economics and Policy: Readings*. London: Allen and Unwin.

Loxley, J. 1986a. *Debt and Disorder: External Financing for Development*. Boulder, Colo.: Westview Press.

Loxley, J. 1986b. "The IMF and World Bank Conditionality and Sub-Saharan Africa." In P. Lawrence (ed.) *World Recession and the Food Crisis in Africa*. London: James Currey.

Loxley, J. 1994. "Africa's Debt Crisis: The African Position Toward the Solution." In F. Ezeala-Harrison and S. Adjibolosoo (eds.), *Perspectives on Economic Development in Africa*, Westport, Conn.: Praeger.

Maizels, A., and Nissanke, M. K. 1984. "Motivations for Aid to Developing Countries." *World Development*, 12 (9): 879-900.

Mazumdar, D. 1976. "Migration and Urban Labour in LDCs." *Oxford Economic Papers*, 28: 406.

Meier, G. M. 1976. *Leading Issues in Economic Development* (3rd ed.). New York: Oxford University Press.

Metcalf, G. 1987. "A Microcosm of Why Africans Sold Slaves: Akan Consumption Patterns in the 1770s." *Journal of African History*, 28 (3): 377-394.

Middleton, J., Ziderman, A., and Adams, A. 1990. "Making Vocational Training Effective.", *Finance and Development*, 27 (1).

Mingat, M., and Tan, J. P. 1985. "On equity in Education again: An International Comparison." *Journal of Human Resources*, 20.

Morawetz, D. 1974. "Employment Implications of Industrialization in Developing Countries: A Survey." *Economic Journal*, (September).

Myrdal, G. 1957. *Economic Theory and Underdeveloped Regions*. London: Duckworth.

Nafziger, E. W. 1990. *The Economics of Developing Countries* (2nd ed.). Englewood Cliffs, N. J.: Prentice Hall.

Neumark, S. D. 1977. "Trans-Saharan Trade in the Middle Ages." In Z. A. Konczacki and J. M. Konczacki (eds.), *An Economic History of Tropical Africa*. London: Frank Cass.

Nurkse, Ragnar. 1953. *Problems of Capital Formation in LDCs*. New York: Oxford University Press.

O'Brien, P. K. 1982. "European Economic Development: The Contribution of the Periphery." *Economic History Review*, 35: 1-18.

O'Brien, P. K., and Engerman, S. L. 1991. "Exports and the Growth of the British Economy from the Glorious Revolution to the Peace of Amiens." In B. L. Solow (ed.), *Slavery and the Rise of the Atlantic System*. Cambridge: Cambridge University Press.

Oliver, R., and Fage, J. D. 1988. *A Short History of Africa* (6th ed.). London: Penguin Books.

Osmani, S. R. 1991. "Wage Determination in Rural Labour Markets: The Theory of Implicit Cooperation." *Journal of Development Economics*, 34: 3-23.

Pickett, J. 1990. *The Low-Income Economies of Sub-Saharan Africa: Problems and Prospects*. Abidjan: African Development Bank, Economic Research Papers, 12.

Poulson, B. W. 1994. *Economic Development: Private and Public Choice*. St. Paul, Minn.: West Publishing.

Powelson, J. P. 1977. "The Strange Persistence of the Terms of Trade." *Inter-American Economic Affairs*, 30 (4).

Prebisch, R. 1959. "Commercial Policy in the Underdeveloped Countries." *American Economic Review Papers and Proceedings*, 49 (2).

Prebisch, R. 1961. "Economic Development or Monetary Stability: The False Dilemma." *Economic Bulletin for Latin America*, 6 (1).

Prebisch, R. 1962. "Economic Development of Latin America and its Principal Problems." *Economic Bulletin for Latin America*, 7.

Prebisch, R. 1963. *Toward a Dynamic Development Policy for Latin America.* New York: United Nations.

Prebisch, R. 1964. *Toward a New Trade Policy for Development.* Report of the Secretary-Gerneral of UNCTAD. New York: United Nations.

Prebisch, R. 1984. "Five Stages in my Thinking on Development." In G. M. Meier and D. Seers (eds.), *Pioneers of Development.* New York: Oxford University Press for the World Bank.

Psacharopoulos, G. 1988. "Education and Development: A Review." *World Bank Research Observer,* 3, (January): 99-116.

Psacharopoulos, G., and M. Woodhall. 1985. *Education for Development: An Analysis of Investment Choices,* New York: Oxford University Press.

Ranis, G., and Fei, J. C. H. 1964. *Development of the Labour Surplus Economy: Theory and Policy.* Homewood, Ill.: Irwin.

Reidel, J. 1984. "Trade as the Engine of Economic Growth in Developing Countries Revisited." *The Economic Journal,* 94 (March): 56-63.

Rempel, H. 1994. "The Role of Urban Informal Activity in the Rural-to-Urban Transition in Africa." in F. Ezeala-Harrison and S. Adjibolosoo (eds.), *Perspectives on Economic Development in Africa,* Westport, Conn.: Praeger.

Riddell, R. C. 1992. "The Contribution of Foreign Aid to Development and the Role of the Private Sector." *Development:* 7-15.

Rodney, W. 1972. *How Europe Underdeveloped Africa.* London: Bogle-L'Ouverture Publications.

Rosenstein-Rodan, P. N. 1957. "Notes on the Theory of the Big Push." In H. S. Ellis (ed.), *Economic Development for Latin America,* London: Macmillan.

Rosovsky, H. 1965. "The Take-off into Sustained Controversy." *Journal of Economic History,* March: 271-275.

Rostow, W. W. 1961. *The Stages of Economic Growth: A Non-Communist Manifesto,* Cambridge: Cambridge University Press.

Rostow, W. W. (ed.) 1963. *The Economics of Take-Off into Sustained Growth.* Proceedings of Conference of International Economic Association, London and New York.

Sapir, A. 1985. "North-South Issues in Trade-In Services." *The World Economy,* 8 (1): 27-41.

Sapir, A. 1986. "Trade in Investment-Related Technological Services." *World Development,* 14 (5): 605-622.

Schultz, T. P. 1971. "Rural-Urban Migration in Columbia." *Review of Economics and Statistics,* 53: 157-163.

Schultz, T. P. 1981. *Economics of Population.* Reading, Mass.: Addison-Wesley Publishers.

Schultz, T. W. 1981. *Investing in People: The Economics of Population Quality.* Berkeley: University of California Press.

Schumacher, D. 1988. "Determinants of the Major Industrialized Countries Exports to Developing Countries." *World Development,* 10: 1317-1328.

Sen, A. K. 1987. *The Standard of Living.* Cambridge: Cambridge University Press.

Serpell, R. 1993. *The Significance of Schooling: Life-journeys in an African Society,* New York: Cambridge University Press.

Sheridan, R. 1973. *Sugar and Slavery: An Economic History of the West Indies.* Baltimore, Md.: Johns Hopkins University Press.

Shiells, C. 1995. "Regional Trade Blocs: Trade Creating or Diverting? *Finance and Development*, 32 (1): 30-32.

Simmons, J. 1974. "Education, Poverty and Development." *World Bank Staff Working Papers*, 188, Washington, D.C.

Simmons, J. 1979. "Education for Development Reconsidered." *World Development*, 7: 1005-1016.

Singer, H. 1950. "The Distribution of Trade between Borrowing and Investing Nations." *American Economic Review*, 40: 473-485.

Singer, H. 1958. "The Concept of Balanced Growth and Economic Development." University of Texas Conference on Economic Development, (April).

Singer, H. 1970. "Dualism Revisited: A New Approach to the Problems of Dual Societies in Developing Countries." *Journal of Developing Areas*, 7.

Singer, H. 1975. "Science and technology for Poor Countries." In *The Strategy of International Development*. London: Macmillan. (Reprinted in Meier, 1976).

Solow, B. 1985. "Caribbean Slavery and British Growth: The Eric Williams Hypothesis." *Journal of Development Economics*, 17: 99-115.

Streeten, P. 1975. "Industrialization in Unified Development Strategy." *World Development*, (January).

Streeten, P. 1981. "World Trade in Agricultural Commodities and the Terms of Trade with Industrial Goods." In P. Streeten (ed.), *Development Perspectives*, London: Macmillan.

Streeten, P. 1983. "Development Dichotomies." *World Development*, 11 (10).

Strick, J. C. 1994. *The Economics of Government Regulation* (2nd ed.). Toronto: Thompson Educational Publishing.

Summers, R., and Heston, A. 1990. *State of the World Report*. Washington, D.C: Worldwatch Institute.

Sunkel, O. 1973. "Transnational Capitalism and National Disintegration in Latin America." *Social and Economic Studies*, 22 (1): 135-140. (Reprinted in Meier, 1976).

Taylor, L. 1979. *Macro Models for Developing Countries*. New York: McGraw-Hill.

Taylor, L. 1981. "IS-LM in the Tropics: Diagrammatics of the New Structuralist Critique." In W.R. Cline and S. Weintraub (eds.), *Economic Stabilization in Developing Countries*. Washington, D.C: Brookings Institution.

Tinbergen, J. 1967. *Development Planning*. London: Weidenfield and Nicolson.

Todaro, M. P. 1971. *Development Planning: Models and Methods*. Nairobi: Oxford University Press.

Todaro, M. P. 1973. "Education, Migration, and Fertility." *IBRD Conference Paper* (Washington, D.C.), October.

Todaro, M. P. 1994. *Economic Development* (5th. ed.). New York: Longman.

United Nations Development Programme. 1992. *Human Development Index*. New York: Oxford University Press.

Viner, J. 1953. *International Trade and Economic Development*. Oxford: Clarendon Press.

Waterston, A. 1965. *Development Planning: Lessons of Experience*. Baltimore, Md.: The Johns Hopkins Press.

Williams, E. 1966. *Capitalism and Slavery*, New York: Capricorn Publishers.

World Bank. 1980-1983. *World Development Report* (Various Issues). New York: Oxford University Press.

World Bank. 1985-1993. *World Development Report* (Various Issues). New York: Oxford University Press.

World Bank, 1986. "*The Financing of Education in Developing Countries: An Exploration of Policy Options.*" Washington, D.C.

Zuvekas, C. Jr. 1979. *Economic Development: An Introduction.* New York: St. Martin's Press.

Index

Ability to save, 63-67, 87, 96, 142, 145, 146, 149

Afghanistan, 57

African, 35-38, 41-46, 50, 51, 53, 54, 57, 58n.1, 124, 135, 140, 157, 167, 167, 168, 170, 177, 210, 231, 250, 251, 258

African development, 13, 14, 32n.1, 45, 105, 112, 124n.2, 169, 172, 177, 182, 183, 201, 231

Agricultural development, 44, 45, 48, 112, 169, 171, 175, 176, 178, 181, 184n.1, 197, 209-211, 218, 243

Agricultural labor, 11, 45, 47-53, 57, 100n.1, 103, 158-160, 164, 167-184, 187, 208-211, 213n.2, 218, 219, 222

Agricultural production, 22, 168-171, 174, 178, 179, 195, 208

Agricultural productivity, 8, 13, 22, 31, 35, 36, 41, 43, 45, 47-50, 67, 69, 103, 106, 112, 125, 130, 132, 139, 143, 157-160, 163, 164, 168-179, 181-184, 187, 193, 200, 210, 223, 225, 226

Agricultural sector, 13, 36, 45, 48, 104, 132, 169, 171, 174, 175, 182-184, 187, 193, 219, 222, 225

Agriculture, 8, 13, 22, 31, 35, 36, 41, 43, 45, 47-50, 67, 69, 103, 106, 112, 125, 130, 132, 139, 143, 157-160, 163, 164, 168-179, 181-184, 187, 193, 200, 210, 223, 225, 226

Anti-dumping, 244

Argentina, 38-40, 54, 108, 192, 220, 243, 254, 255, 257

ASEAN, 250

Asia, 18, 21, 22, 26-35, 37, 38, 40, 41, 48, 51, 52, 57, 106, 116, 121, 134, 169, 170, 177, 192, 200, 209, 209, 210, 231, 235, 242, 250, 251, 255, 257

Australasia, 18, 22, 30, 34, 143, 177

Australia, 22, 32, 37, 106, 141, 254

Autonomous investment, 86, 87, 91, 92, 132, 133

Backward linkages, 38, 111, 112

Balance of payments, 52, 239, 245

Balance of trade, 7, 239, 240, 242, 245

Balanced growth, 100, 105, 109-111, 124, 185, 194

Bangladesh, 30, 40, 209, 217

Banking, 12, 34, 107, 134, 186, 235, 240

Bentham, Jeremy, 61

Bhagwati, J., 24, 162, 167, 231

Big push theory, 109-112, 124, 185, 194
Birth rate, 92, 142, 147
Bourgeoisie, 72, 81
Brain drain, 6, 139, 140, 161, 162, 167
Brazil, 39, 54, 158, 195, 207, 220, 243, 254, 257
Britain, 24, 35, 36, 40-42, 57, 106-108, 113, 124, 137, 157, 161, 162, 167, 185, 245, 255
Budget deficits, 22, 32, 51, 54, 58, 122, 135, 157, 183, 220, 236, 239, 242, 243, 254-257
Burma, 27, 52
Burundi, 46, 57, 157
Business cycle, 7, 8, 13, 44, 45, 62, 63, 72, 79, 82, 90, 133, 138, 140, 164, 216, 217, 219

Cambodia, 40, 52, 57
Cameroon, 30, 56, 157
Canada, 19, 22, 24, 30, 32, 36, 106-108, 113, 157, 161, 162, 197, 251, 254
Capital availability in LDCs, 3-6, 13, 23, 25, 28, 29, 32, 35, 36, 40, 44, 45, 47, 49, 54, 62-64, 67-70, 72, 75-83, 86-90, 93-98, 100, 102-104, 129-142, 146, 238-242, 245, 250, 253-257; accumulation, 62, 63, 67, 69, 72, 76, 77, 81, 90, 96, 100, 129, 130, 137, 141, 146, 150
Capital-labor ratio, 95, 96, 129
Capitalism, 62, 72, 76, 79, 80, 83
Capitalist, 36-39, 44, 70, 72-74, 76-83, 117, 120, 123
Caribbean, 22, 27, 31, 33, 38, 116, 121, 123, 209, 235, 242, 250
CARIFTA, 250
Center-Periphery paradigm, 36, 38, 39, 42, 43, 101-105, 114-116, 121, 123, 124, 162, 163, 201
Chad, 30, 46
China, 22, 25, 26, 30, 34, 38, 40, 44, 81, 242

Circular deterioration hypothesis, 13, 105, 114, 122
Classical theories, 24, 34, 61-67, 69, 70, 72, 82, 85, 87, 89, 94, 96, 99, 100, 102, 113, 115, 124, 142, 157, 236, 237, 245
Cocoa, 42, 46, 53, 115, 116, 171, 189
Coffee, 42, 46, 116, 171
Colonial, 25, 35, 38, 40, 42-47, 50, 56, 58, 78, 116, 122, 157, 163
Colonialism, 37, 38, 43, 58, 105, 116, 121, 122
Colony, 42, 43, 116
Commercialization point, 119, 120
Common market, 248, 250, 251
Communism, 72, 80
Communist, 71, 72, 79, 83
Comparative advantage, 35, 51, 103, 112, 113, 188, 193, 237, 244, 245, 247
Competition, 35, 53, 58, 66, 72, 93, 102, 104, 123, 193, 194, 244, 247, 248, 251
Competitive model, 49, 51, 53, 62, 66, 73, 85, 111, 120, 133, 159, 161, 194, 206, 207, 215, 238, 243-245, 251
Conditionality (of IMF loans), 55, 135
Congo, 46, 56, 257
Constant capital (Marxian), 67, 71, 75-78, 80, 82, 88, 90, 96-100, 113, 117, 120, 143, 145, 146, 149, 165, 176, 209, 210, 226, 236, 237, 241
Consumption, 7, 9, 11, 16, 17, 23, 35, 43, 49, 51, 54, 63, 69, 71, 72, 87, 90, 92, 98, 100, 105, 107, 108, 116, 121, 122, 129-132, 152, 158, 186, 188, 195, 196, 200, 201, 207, 208, 221-223, 225
Contradiction (Marxian), 76, 78
Corporations (multinational in LDCs), 58, 104, 122, 134, 200, 217, 218
Currency, 52, 53, 215, 217, 219, 221, 228, 235, 240, 241, 257
Customs union, 248, 250

David Livingstone, 58
Debt crisis, 24, 135, 220, 243, 253-255
Deficit financing, 131, 219-221
Demand threshold, 190-193
Demographic (projections for LDCs),
   142, 148, 167
Dependency, 45, 58, 105, 112,
   121-123, 145, 146, 149, 150
Dependency burden, 145, 146, 149,
   150
Dependency ratio, 146
Dependency theory, 105, 112, 121-123
Deregulation, 58, 220
Devaluation, 55, 238, 240, 245, 257;
   of national currencies, 55, 238, 240,
   245, 257
Developing countries, 48, 51, 69,
   79-81, 115, 155, 160-162, 238, 242
Development, 3, 6, 10-15, 17-19,
   21-48, 50, 51; economic, 53-59,
   61-63, 65, 69, 70, 71, 79-81, 83, 85,
   88, 89, 92-94, 96, 101-116, 120,
   121, 122-124, 127, 129-131,
   133-146, 148, 150-152, 155, 156,
   157-164, 166, 167, 169, 171, 172,
   174-178, 181-183, 184-188, 190-193,
   195-205, 207-213, 215-224, 231,
   233, 235, 236-238, 241-244, 247,
   248, 251, 253-257
Development bank, 218
Development of agriculture, 130, 176
Development planning, 79, 215,
   222-224, 247; policies in LDCs, 158,
   167, 215
Diminishing returns, 35, 62, 64-67, 69,
   72, 76, 82, 143, 145
Diploma disease, 48, 125, 155-158,
   161, 162
Disguised unemployment, 117, 119,
   120, 125, 132, 163, 168, 170
Domar's model, 98
Doomsday theory (of environmental
   resources), 206, 207
Dual sector model, 146, 167
Dualism (in economic development),
   14, 18, 19, 49, 50, 108, 120, 158,
   217

Dualistic development, 14, 102, 116,
   117, 123, 217, 218
Dutch disease, 52, 53

EAC, 250
East Africa, 42, 58
East Asia, 26, 28, 30, 38, 40, 51, 231,
   242
Economic policies (in LDCs), 3-15,
   17-19, 21-26, 28-48, 79-83, 85,
   87-89, 93, 94, 96, 99-117, 119-121,
   122-124, 160-164, 166-168, 169,
   171, 251, 253-257
ECOWAS, 250, 251
Education, 6, 12, 40, 47-50, 139, 140,
   150-161, 163, 167, 180-183, 186,
   204, 210, 211, 216-218, 222; formal
   (in LDCs), 161, 164
Efficiency, 19, 28, 29, 32, 51, 77, 79,
   80, 83, 130, 181, 182, 203; in
   production, 19, 28, 29, 32, 51, 77,
   79, 80, 83, 130, 181, 182, 203
Efficiency wages, 42, 49, 53, 55, 63,
   65-68, 70, 73, 75, 78-80, 83, 103,
   118, 120, 123, 133, 157-159, 162,
   164, 166, 216, 228, 251, 254
Efficiency wage model, 833
Egypt, 108, 168, 257
Elastic demand, 240
Elasticity, 5, 18, 100, 103, 114, 147,
   149, 172, 173, 183
Emigration, 139, 142, 161, 162
Employment policies, 11, 13, 17, 26,
   48-50, 53, 61, 62, 73, 85, 87, 100,
   115, 117, 118, 120, 122, 125, 132,
   150-152, 155-166, 168, 172, 174,
   180, 184-187, 192, 215, 216, 222,
   224
Engine of growth, 24, 34, 37, 113,
   114, 236-238, 242, 243, 245
England, 34-37, 238
Environment (in development), 11, 24,
   34, 55, 101, 122, 139, 160, 162,
   195-197, 200-203, 205, 207-212
Environmental development, 9, 15, 21,
   28, 33, 42, 109, 116, 186-188,

194-213, 244, 247
Environmental impact, 201, 202, 207
Equity, 15, 18, 44, 222, 223
Ethiopia, 44, 57, 81, 137, 209
Europe, 18, 21, 22, 28-30, 32, 34-39,
    43, 44, 57, 58, 81, 106, 108, 112,
    116, 122, 137, 140, 143, 170, 197,
    238
European Economic Community
    (EEC), 12, 25, 27, 32, 35, 37-43,
    122, 248, 250, 251, 254
Exchange rate (and policies), 12, 13,
    35, 36, 41, 42, 44, 45, 52-55, 71,
    79, 103, 110, 112, 113, 114, 122,
    124, 135, 136, 142, 172, 174, 175,
    187, 192, 193, 215, 219, 236-238,
    240, 241, 245, 253, 255, 256
Exploitation (Marxian), 3, 5, 35-37,
    42, 58, 72-76, 78-81, 90-93, 116,
    121, 122, 196, 203, 212, 253
Export promotion, 175, 194, 223
External factors (in development), 8, 9,
    12, 13, 18, 31, 33, 37, 43, 46,
    52-54, 62, 105, 110, 122, 124, 135,
    140, 185, 219, 220, 233, 240, 255,
    256

Falling rate of profit (Marxian), 74,
    75, 81
Feudal, 34, 37, 38, 61, 72, 79
Feudalism, 72
Financial system, 218
Fiscal policy, 218
Fixed exchange rates, 44, 52, 55, 64,
    79, 82, 119, 120, 143, 146, 147,
    181, 205, 208, 240, 245
Food security, 16, 25, 41, 45, 49,
    51-53, 64, 67, 106, 112, 132, 137,
    142, 143, 158, 168-175, 178, 180,
    181, 188, 189, 207, 210, 212, 225
Food supply, 52, 112, 142, 172, 207
Foreign aid, 24, 25, 134-137, 161, 254
Forward linkages, 111
France, 32, 35, 42, 106, 107, 255
Frank, Gundar, 18, 19, 38, 39, 57,
    121, 122, 125

Free trade area, 250

Gambia, 52
GATT, 115, 248-251
Germany, 32, 35, 80, 106, 137, 197,
    255
Ghana, 16, 41, 44, 46, 52, 53, 192,
    221
Government spending, 7, 131, 215,
    218, 219, 221
Great Depression, 37, 39, 238, 249
Greece, 32
Greenhouse gases, 201
Gross domestic product, (GDP), 3, 63
Growth (economic), 3-13, 26-32,
    34-37, 68-72, 85-100, 103-114
Guinea, 30, 46, 209

Harris-Todaro, 121, 161, 164-166
Harrod's model, 96-98
Harrod-Domar model, 85, 86, 88, 94,
    96, 231
Hong Kong, 22, 26
Human capital, 93, 129, 140, 151,
    155, 156, 158
Human factor, 46, 55, 57, 219-221,
    231, 257
Human resources, 4, 5, 23, 28, 32, 44,
    47, 55, 94, 129, 141, 151, 155, 161,
    175, 195, 215

IBRD, 236
IMF, 24, 122, 220, 236, 254-256, 258
Imperialism, 58, 78, 83, 121, 122
Import substitution, 45, 112, 175, 191-
    194, 245
Imports, 7, 12, 13, 25, 46, 51-53, 100,
    114, 175, 189, 191-194, 235, 239,
    240, 241, 242, 244, 245, 250, 255
Income distribution, 10, 14-16, 18, 44,
    72, 79, 81, 82, 131, 185, 191, 208,
    222, 223, 224
Income tax policies, 134, 162, 175
Indebtedness in LDCs, 21, 23, 24, 31,

52, 54, 55, 135, 220, 242, 243,
253-257
India, 27, 38, 40, 54, 108, 122, 155,
192, 200, 242, 255, 257
Indonesia, 26, 40, 53, 108, 242, 243,
257
Induced investment, 91, 92, 94, 132,
133
Industrial development, 39, 41, 108,
185, 187, 190, 191
Industrial Revolution, 24, 34, 35, 37,
43, 102, 107, 137, 185
Industrial sector, 102, 106, 117, 174,
175, 184, 185, 225
Industrialization, 11, 13, 17, 35, 36,
39, 44, 45, 57, 58, 93, 105, 112-114,
115, 134, 164, 174, 175, 185-197,
213, 219, 223, 236, 243, 245; in
LDCs, 9, 124, 152, 186, 197, 211,
228
Industrialized countries, 124, 191, 196
Inequity, 16, 23, 131, 132, 215
Infant industry, 192
Inflation, 8, 46, 52, 53, 55, 86, 87,
131, 215, 216, 220, 221, 224, 228,
241, 245, 258
Informal sector, 8, 14, 31, 49, 122,
140, 158, 159, 163, 168, 216, 217
Infrastructure, 6, 11, 34, 44, 48, 57,
62, 79, 93, 94, 101, 106, 110, 113,
129, 133, 134, 135, 141, 142, 160,
164, 167, 177, 186-188, 189, 190,
194, 197, 205, 210, 211, 218,
220-222, 236, 254
Input-output matrix, 224
Interest rate, 44, 56, 61, 62, 67, 70,
88, 100, 104, 106, 110, 130, 131,
133, 136, 178, 206, 207, 215-217,
221, 230, 231, 240, 249, 250, 255,
256
Internal factors, 6, 18, 31, 37, 39, 46,
76, 101, 106, 127, 129, 130, 132,
219, 230, 251
International factors, 6, 8-10, 12, 24,
32-37, 41, 46, 50-52, 54, 55, 57, 58,
83, 92, 101, 103, 104, 108, 110,
113-116, 122-124, 131, 134, 135,

136, 161, 169, 195, 199, 215, 219,
235-245, 247, 248, 249, 250,
253-257
International market, 12, 51, 103, 253
International Monetary Fund, 24, 55,
58, 122, 135, 236, 254
International Trade, 24, 34-37, 101,
103, 113-116, 122, 124, 169,
235-237, 238, 241-243, 245,
247-249, 253
Investment, 3, 6, 7, 13, 21, 35, 39, 40,
42-45, 48, 50, 51, 53, 62, 68, 72,
75, 77, 79, 86-100, 104, 106, 107,
109-112, 116, 118, 122, 124,
129-135, 141, 145, 149, 155, 156,
160, 172, 175, 180, 185, 204, 205,
210, 215, 216, 218, 221, 223, 227,
254, 255
Iron law of wages, 65, 66, 70
Irrigation projects, 132, 176, 181-183,
200, 212
Israel, 37
Italy, 32, 35
Ivory Coast, 53, 56, 257

Japan, 19, 22, 24, 30, 32, 34, 36, 37,
40, 51, 106, 107, 112-114, 124, 131,
140, 172, 175, 184, 197, 248

Kenya, 44, 56
Keynesian, 85, 87, 89, 90, 92-94, 99,
100, 133
Know-how (technological), 4, 36, 82,
88, 90, 129, 130, 137

Labor surplus, 103, 117, 119, 120, 125
Labor theory of value, 73, 83
Labor force, 4, 11, 13, 17, 22, 28, 44,
45, 49, 50, 57, 63, 65-69, 80, 88,
90, 93, 96, 107, 115, 130, 145, 149,
150, 158, 159, 162, 169, 170-172,
185, 187, 188, 193
Labor productivity (in agriculture), 211
Labor surplus, 103, 117, 119, 120, 125

Laissez faire, 63, 224, 245
Land reform, 216
Land tenure, 177, 210
Latin America, 18, 21, 22, 26, 31, 33, 34, 36-39, 52, 58, 101, 116, 121, 123, 134, 169, 192, 209, 235, 242, 243, 250, 251, 254, 255, 256, 257
Law of diminishing returns, 62, 64
LDCs, 6, 8-10, 12, 13, 16, 18, 112-116, 120-125, 129, 131, 133-141, 143, 145, 146, 150-152, 155-164, 166-168, 169-184, 188, 190-194, 196, 198-201, 203, 207-213, 215, 216-224, 228, 231, 235, 237, 238, 241-245, 247-249, 250, 251, 253-258
Less developed countries, 21, 25, 33, 37, 223
Liberia, 57
Linkage effects, 111, 112
Literacy, 14, 17, 19, 44
Lorenz curve, 15, 16, 19
Low Income Countries, 22

Malaysia, 22, 26, 54, 124, 242, 243, 256, 257
Malthus, Thomas R, 61
Manpower, 45, 50, 93, 159
Marginal productivity, 5, 6, 64, 73, 87, 90-92, 95, 97, 98, 118, 119, 124, 125, 140, 143, 153, 167, 168, 204
Market economy, 62, 85, 93, 195, 206, 212
Market failure, 124, 153, 224
Marketing board, 181
Marx, Karl, 61, 70-72, 74-77, 80-83, 124
Marxian model, 61, 62, 70-74, 76, 78-83
Marxist theory, 80, 81, 83
Mauritania, 52
Meiji dynasty, 36, 107
Mercantilism, 72, 244
Mercantilist, 61, 72, 79, 236, 245

Merit good, 152-154, 167
Metropolis, 36, 42, 43
Mexico, 32, 38-40, 54, 108, 207, 243, 251, 254, 255, 257
Micro policies, 94, 222, 231
Middle East, 26, 30, 31, 41, 177, 235, 242
Migration, 18, 45, 50, 72, 121, 141, 142, 146, 151, 159-166, 208
Military rule (in LDCs), 12, 26, 45, 54, 56, 80, 105, 135-137, 220, 221, 255
Minimum wage, 66, 120
Modern sector, 14, 103, 117, 119-121, 132, 174, 217
Monetarist, 99, 216
Monetary policy, 8, 24, 55, 58, 79, 81, 93, 100, 104, 122, 135, 153, 154, 216, 217, 227, 228, 236, 240, 245, 248, 250, 251, 253, 254, 257
Money supply, 7, 215-217, 220
Monocultural, 12, 13, 45
Monopoly, 140, 193
Multinational corporations, 58, 104, 122, 134, 200, 217
Multiplier, 92, 93, 99, 132, 152
Mungo Park, 58

NAFTA, 251
National income, 3-8, 17, 24, 34, 39, 44, 45, 48, 50, 56, 57, 61, 67, 71, 73, 89, 94, 107, 132, 134, 137, 156, 158, 160, 161, 171, 172, 185, 195, 201, 215, 218, 222, 223, 225, 227, 238
Natural resources, 4-6, 12, 28, 89, 90, 92, 94, 129, 130, 142, 152, 196, 198, 201, 203, 206, 207, 212
Neoclassical, 22, 24, 25, 32, 41, 73, 85, 94, 99, 101-103, 113, 114, 123, 167, 223, 236, 237, 253
Net present value, 228, 229
New Zealand, 22, 32, 37, 106, 254
Newly Industrializing Countries (NICs), 22, 26, 32, 124, 242-243, 249, 251, 255-257

Niger, 19
Nigeria, 44, 46, 53, 56, 108, 167, 192, 257
North-South, 18, 22-26, 29, 30, 32, 34, 36, 37, 39, 122, 137, 140, 141, 143, 168, 170, 195, 197, 242, 251
North Africa, 26, 242
North America, 18, 22, 29, 30, 32, 34, 36, 37, 122, 137, 140, 141, 143, 170, 195, 197, 251

OECD 26, 27, 32, 115, 123, 124
Official Development Assistance, 52, 135, 151, 240, 254, 256, 258
Oil, 25, 26, 52, 53, 106, 135, 189, 190, 195, 196, 201, 219, 220
OPEC, 26
Optimal, 73, 74, 117, 118, 144, 148, 150, 183, 203
Optimum, 3, 6, 9, 13, 22, 28, 31, 38, 44, 46, 130, 142-145, 147, 148, 150, 172, 173, 174, 188-190, 192, 198, 244
Organic composition of capital (Marxian), 77, 78
Overpopulation, 144, 145, 150, 201

Pakistan, 27, 40, 192, 257
Periphery, 38, 39, 42, 43, 101-105, 114-116, 121, 123, 124, 253
Petroleum, 24, 26, 46, 106, 190, 203, 219, 220
Planning models, 26, 44, 51, 58, 79, 80, 150-152, 158, 188, 211, 215, 222-224, 226, 227, 230, 231, 247
Pollution, 9, 196, 197, 199, 200, 207-209, 211
Population, 6, 8-15, 17, 21-23, 25, 26, 30, 32, 37, 38, 40, 43, 45, 46, 49, 50, 57, 64-70, 72, 78, 81, 82, 88-94, 96, 104-107, 118, 120, 133, 138, 141-152, 154, 155, 158, 159, 162-164, 170, 171-174, 177, 180, 185, 187-190, 193, 195, 200-202, 206, 208, 209, 211, 213, 215, 217-219, 223; growth in LDCs, 13, 21, 50, 64, 69, 70, 82, 91, 92, 94, 96, 120, 133, 138, 141, 142, 144, 146-150, 158, 159, 162, 172, 195, 201; problem in LDCs, 6, 8-15, 17, 21-23, 25, 26, 30, 32, 37, 38, 40, 43, 45, 46, 49, 50, 57, 64-70, 72, 78, 81, 82, 88-94, 96, 104-107, 118, 120, 133, 138, 141-152, 154, 155, 158, 159, 162, 163, 164, 170-174, 177, 180, 185, 187-190, 193, 195, 200, 201, 202, 206, 208, 209, 211, 213, 215, 217-219, 223
Poverty, 10, 12-14, 21, 25, 30, 32, 46, 55, 71, 72, 79, 109, 129, 134, 146, 156, 175, 178, 182, 187, 199, 212, 215, 219, 220
Preferential trade agreement, 248, 250
Present value, 121, 164, 228, 229
Primary product, 46, 103
Primary sector, 11, 25, 49, 50, 104, 106, 159, 160, 189
Production in agriculture, 4, 8, 9, 11, 13, 14, 22-24, 28, 29, 35, 41, 43, 45, 52, 54, 57, 62, 64, 66, 67, 69-73, 75, 76, 79, 81, 82, 89, 94, 95, 100, 102, 104-106, 109, 112-114, 116, 122, 125, 130, 132, 133, 138, 139, 141, 143, 145, 146, 152, 153, 168, 169-171, 174, 175, 178-183, 186, 187, 192-195, 197, 198, 200, 206-210, 224, 226, 236, 237, 243-245, 247
Production function, 4, 67, 73, 89, 94, 95
Productivity of labor, 3, 5, 18, 19, 22, 28, 32, 39, 48, 49, 62, 65, 67, 73, 86, 87, 88, 98, 100, 103-105, 109, 114, 117-119, 123, 125, 129, 142, 143, 146, 148, 149, 152, 156-159, 163, 168, 169, 170-172, 174, 177, 181-183, 210, 211, 222, 238
Profit, 53, 61-63, 66-69, 71, 73-82, 102, 117, 118, 125, 131, 133-135, 140, 153, 217, 218, 240
Profit maximization, 73, 74, 117, 118, 140
Proletariat, 72, 79-81
Public good, 152, 153
Public sector, 93, 124, 131, 133, 154,

163, 219-221, 257
Public utilities, 167, 186, 194, 218,
220
Purchasing power parity, 241

Quality of life index, 15, 17, 18

Recycling, 207
Rent, 63-65, 67, 68, 82
Research and development (R&D), 24,
32, 33, 56, 80, 88, 113, 139, 156,
160, 161, 181-183, 231
Reserve army (Marxian), 72, 76, 82
Resource utilization, 3-6, 8, 11, 23-26,
28, 29, 32, 36, 53, 56, 57, 79,
89-93, 111, 133, 141, 143, 145,
149-152, 167, 176, 178, 188,
203-206, 208, 210, 211, 213, 215,
220-222, 231
Revolution, 24, 34, 35, 37, 43, 79, 80,
102, 107, 137, 184, 185
Ricardian theory, 64, 65, 83, 245
Ricardo, David, 61, 82, 245
Risk, 66, 107, 110, 219
Rodney, Walter, 38, 43, 58, 114, 116
Rosenstein-Rodan, 109, 110, 185
Rostow, W. W., 105-109, 124, 189,
190, 194
Rural labor force, 11, 14, 15, 17, 18,
21, 23, 31, 45, 47-50, 117, 120, 121,
122, 125, 141, 158-161, 163-171,
181-183, 187, 188, 192, 208, 211,
217, 218
Rural development, 47, 48, 159, 160,
164, 166, 167, 211
Rural sector, 11, 14, 15, 17, 18, 21,
23, 31, 45, 47-50, 117, 120-122,
125, 141, 158-161, 163-171,
181-183, 187, 188, 192, 208, 211,
217, 218
Rural-urban, 18, 45, 50, 120, 121,
159-161, 163-166, 208; migration,
18, 45, 50, 121, 159-161, 163-166,
208
Russia, 24, 25, 34, 36, 107, 113

Rwanda, 57

Safety nets, 222
Satellite, 36, 39, 43
Savings rate, 13, 35, 42, 43, 62, 63,
86-88, 94-97, 106, 109, 116,
129-131, 132, 135, 142, 152, 161,
172, 187, 193, 216, 221, 245
Scandinavian, 35
Scarce resources, 11, 50, 64, 119, 138,
160, 172, 187, 191, 193, 196, 205,
215, 216, 224, 230
Secondary education, 156
Secondary sector, 11, 50, 159, 160
Secular stagnation, 85, 89, 91, 93, 100
Selective tariff, 115
Singapore, 22, 26, 124, 157, 242
Social factors, 9, 10
Socialism, 71, 80
Socialist, 21, 22, 26, 44, 70-72, 195
Solow growth model, 85, 94, 231
Somalia, 57, 209
South, 22-32, 34, 37-40, 42, 48, 51,
52, 54, 106, 124, 170, 177, 209,
210, 242, 243, 248, 250, 255-257
South Africa, 32, 37, 42, 106, 243
South Asia, 22, 27, 29-31, 34, 40, 48,
51, 52, 170, 177, 209, 210, 257
South Korea, 22, 26, 30, 54, 124, 242,
255-257
Southern hemisphere, 22, 24, 25, 32,
42, 114, 116, 250, 257
Soviet Union, 21, 22, 25, 32, 44, 69,
80, 81, 175, 184, 195
Specialization, 104, 113, 237, 247
Sri Lanka, 52, 57
Stability, 3, 8, 10-12, 26, 40, 56, 62,
69, 87, 120, 134, 136, 172, 175,
187, 227, 238, 245
Stage theory, 124, 194
Stationary state, 62, 67-70, 245
Structural adjustment, 46, 52, 55, 58,
135, 220, 221, 254, 256, 257
Structural change, 3
Structuralism, 101-103, 123
Structuralist, 101-105, 113, 121, 123,

235, 237, 239, 253

Sub-Saharan Africa, 7-31, 33, 34, 41, 54, 56, 231, 242, 243, 255, 257

Subsidy program, 254

Subsistence sector, 14, 47, 103, 117, 119, 121, 123, 132, 171

Substitution, 45, 82, 112, 175, 191-194, 217, 245

Surplus, 43, 52, 53, 67, 73-79, 81, 103, 117-121, 125, 132, 146, 157, 171, 175, 184, 237, 240, 245

Surplus value, 74-79, 81

Sustainable, 22, 25, 26, 32, 34, 38, 46, 173, 202-205, 207

Taiwan, 22, 26, 242, 257

Takeoff, 18, 24, 35, 40, 46, 105-108, 124, 190

Tanzania, 44, 52

Tariff, 44, 115, 191, 193, 194, 244, 249, 250

Tariff wall, 115, 192, 218, 228, 244, 249

Taxation policies, 43, 82, 124, 132, 175, 204, 215, 216, 218, 219

Technical, 6, 9, 10, 81, 130, 152, 179, 190, 192, 193, 226

Technique, 223, 227; of production, 238, 243, 244, 247, 249

Technological, 3, 4, 6, 8, 32, 35, 36, 41, 45, 62, 64, 69, 72, 76, 78, 82, 88, 89, 90, 93, 94, 103, 113, 120, 129, 130, 133, 137-139, 141, 143, 147-150, 152, 181-183, 201, 236; change, 32, 82, 94, 181, 182, 201; progress, 8, 62, 64, 69, 76, 89, 90, 94, 103, 113, 133, 137-139, 147-150, 152, 182

Technology (in production), 14, 36, 49, 56, 71, 72, 82, 86-88, 90, 93, 96, 102, 103, 105, 107, 110, 113, 137-139, 143-145, 149, 150, 158, 159, 163, 171, 177, 181-183, 187, 231, 236

Terms of trade, 3, 4, 7, 9, 29-31, 33, 49, 50, 103, 110, 112, 114, 115, 122, 123, 132, 142, 147, 148, 155, 158, 159, 174, 189, 192, 224, 225-228, 237, 239, 241, 242, 244, 245, 247, 253

Tertiary sector, 11, 186

Thailand, 22, 26, 124, 242, 243, 257

Togo, 52

Tokugawa, 36

Trade (as engine of growth), 24, 34, 36, 236, 242; embargo, 243; tariff, 244

Traditional sector, 14, 117, 140, 218

Transfer, 23, 25, 36, 42, 113, 116, 117, 136, 139, 175, 183, 236

Tropical, 41, 176, 177, 209, 210

Two-sector, 105, 116, 119, 121, 164; model, 18, 25, 33, 34, 105, 121, 192, 211

Uganda, 44, 46, 52, 56

Unbalanced growth theory, 105, 109-112, 185, 194

Underdeveloped countries, 12, 13, 18, 19, 21, 22, 33, 38, 40, 47, 48, 50, 57, 58, 69, 101, 105, 116, 121, 156, 170, 209, 219, 235, 257

Underemployment, 48-50, 155, 159, 161, 163, 168, 170

Underpopulation, 144, 145

Unemployment, 18, 25, 41, 46, 48, 50, 52, 55, 71, 72, 74, 77, 78, 83, 86, 87, 117, 119-121, 124, 125, 132, 134, 137, 143, 155, 156, 159, 161-166, 168, 170, 175, 210, 215, 223, 224, 254

United Kingdom, 30, 32

United Nations, 8, 19, 101, 134, 162, 176, 236

United States, 13, 22, 24, 30, 32, 36, 42, 56, 100, 106-108, 137, 157, 161, 162, 248, 251, 254, 255

Urban sector, 11, 17, 18, 21, 23, 31, 37, 45, 47-50, 52, 53, 106, 117, 120, 121, 134, 141, 158-161, 163-166,

170, 187, 192-194, 201, 207, 208, 211
Urbanization, 40, 187, 201, 209
Utilities, 11, 48, 53, 130, 140, 141, 160, 164, 167, 186, 194, 218, 220
Utopia, 71, 72, 79, 81

Value added, 13, 109, 115, 129, 146, 178, 186, 187
Variable capital, 75, 76, 78, 82
Vietnam, 30, 40, 52, 57

Wage fund theory, 65, 66, 68
Water resources, 196
Welfare maximization, 6, 9, 10, 74, 81, 108, 124, 141, 153, 195, 203, 204, 207, 222, 227, 236, 247
West Africa, 19, 36, 58
Will to save, 63, 66, 67
World Bank, 22, 32, 54, 58, 122, 157, 183, 220, 236, 239, 242, 243, 254, 255, 256
World Development Report, 25, 26, 45, 157, 161, 183

Zaire, 53, 221, 257
Zambia, 44, 46, 52, 53, 257

About the Author

FIDELIS EZEALA-HARRISON is Associate Professor of Economics at the University of New Brunswick. Dr. Ezeala-Harrison is the author of many journal articles on economic development and is co-editor of *Perspectives on Economic Development in Africa* (Praeger, 1994).

ISBN 0-275-95479-X

EAN

9 780275 954796

HARDCOVER BAR CODE